ALTERNATE STATES OF CONSCIOUSNESS

ALTERNATE STATES OF CONSCIOUSNESS

Edited by
Norman E. Zinberg

THE FREE PRESS
A Division of Macmillan Publishing Co., Inc.
NEW YORK

Collier Macmillan Publishers
LONDON

The Free Press
A Division of Macmillan Publishing Co., Inc.
866 Third Avenue, New York, N.Y. 10022

Collier Macmillan Canada, Ltd.

Library of Congress Catalog Card Number: 76–46722

Printed in the United States of America

printing number

1   2   3   4   5   6   7   8   9   10

Library of Congress Cataloging in Publication Data
Main entry under title:

Alternate states of consciousness.

Bibliography: p.
Includes index.
1. Consciousness.   I.   Zinberg, Norman Earl,

BF311.A52   154   76-46722
ISBN 0-02-935770-5

Contents

Foreword

Thomas E. Bryant
President, Drug Abuse Council, Inc.

DURING THE PAST SEVERAL YEARS, large numbers of people have become interested in the subject of consciousness change, the process of achieving mental states and perceptions significantly different from those traditionally experienced. But while the subject has grown in popularity, the issues involved in consciousness change and their ramifications have only rarely been examined in a systematic and scientific fashion.

The Drug Abuse Council of Washington, D.C., a private nonprofit foundation established in February, 1972, to serve on a national level as an independent source of research, public-policy evaluation, and program guidance in the areas of drug use and misuse, is pleased to have been involved in two of these efforts.

The first was a February, 1973, conference on consciousness change which the Drug Abuse Council sponsored with the Smithsonian Institution in order to demonstrate the extent to which both the general public and the scientific community were interested in this subject. Ten experts from several disciplines were invited to address an audience whose members ranged from Nobel prizewinners to high school students. The general topic was consciousness change, but the specific focus of each contributor was the perspective of his or her individual discipline, area of interest, or expertise. The conference proved to be highly successful, and some of the material developed for the conference or stimulated by it was published by the Drug Abuse Council in its monograph series as *High States* and in a small book entitled *Altered States of Consciousness: Current Views and Research Problems.*

The second occasion, and the subject of this volume, was a follow-up conference sponsored by the Drug Abuse Council in April, 1975, so that experts could take a broader and more inclusive view of the subject than they had done at the first conference. As Norman E. Zinberg, M.D., the conference organizer and chairman, said in his letter of invitation, the participants in the first conference "were charged only with presenting points of view representative of their particular disciplines." Participants at the second conference were urged to make a "consistent attempt to think through the limits and dilemmas of the field of consciousness and its changes, taken as a whole" and to present papers that examined the most important problems and issues in the entire field. The second conference differed from the first conference in another important respect. Only ten people were invited to participate, and their meetings were not open to the public. This type of format, it was felt, would be more conducive to the full exchange and synthesis of views than a large public meeting.

Special acknowledgment and thanks are owed several people who participated in planning and organizing the second conference. They include, in addition to Dr. Zinberg, Jack Skuce, Hillary Mayell, Jean Johnson, and Frances Verrinder, all of the Drug Abuse Council, and Caryl Marsh, who has been a Council consultant on this subject. James V. DeLong, who left his position as Program Director of the Drug Abuse Council before the second conference took place, also devoted his efforts to see that the study of consciousness change was accepted as a valid scientific endeavor.

About the Contributors

ARTHUR DEIKMAN is currently Supervising Physician Specialist at the Bureau of Alcoholism, San Francisco Community Mental Health Services, and Associate Clinical Professor of Psychiatry at the University of California Medical School in San Francisco.

JOEL ELKES is Distinguished Service Professor at The Johns Hopkins University.

PETER T. FURST is Professor and Chairman of the Anthropology Department at the State University of New York in Albany and Research Associate at the Harvard Botanical Museum. His books include *Flesh of the Gods: Ritual Uses of Hallucinogens* and *Hallucinogens and Culture*.

CARYL MARSH is a consultant to the Drug Abuse Council and a Ph.D. candidate in Social Psychology at George Washington University.

KARL H. PRIBRAM is Professor of Psychology and of Psychiatry and Behavioral Sciences at Stanford University and Head of Stanford's Neuropsychology Laboratories.

DAVID SHAPIRO is Professor of Psychiatry at the University of California, Los Angeles, and President of the Society for Psychophysiological Research. His most recent book is *Consciousness and Self-Regulation: Advances in Research* (with G. E. Schwartz).

JEROME L. SINGER is Professor of Psychology and Director of the Clinical Training Program at Yale University. His most recent book is *Imagery and Daydream Methods in Psychotherapy and Behavior Modification.*

CHARLES T. TART is Professor of Psychology at the University of California, Davis, and a member of the Board of Directors of the Institute for the Study of Human Consciousness. His most recent books are *Studies of Extrasensory Perception, Studies of States of Consciousness, States of Consciousness,* and *Learning to Use Extrasensory Perception.*

ANDREW T. WEIL is Research Associate in Ethnopharmacology at the Harvard Botanical Museum. His best-known book is *The Natural Mind: A New Way of Looking at Drugs and the Higher Consciousness.*

NORMAN E. ZINBERG is Clinical Professor of Psychiatry at the Harvard Medical School, Senior Psychiatrist at the Cambridge (Massachusetts) Hospital, Psychiatrist-in-Chief at the Washingtonian Center for Addictions, and a consultant to the Drug Abuse Council. His most recent books are *Clinical Interviewing and Counseling* (with J. Edinburgh) and *Teaching Social Change* (with H. and M. Boris).

1

The Study of Consciousness States: Problems and Progress

Norman E. Zinberg

BETWEEN APRIL 16 AND 19, 1975, the ten participants whose papers appear in this volume, along with two observers from the Drug Abuse Council, gathered at Belmont, a beautiful, remote estate in Maryland run by the Smithsonian Institution as a conference center—to discuss alternate states of consciousness.[1] Our purpose was to investigate the extent to which the study of such states was or could become a coherent scientific discipline. Because all the participants except Joel Elkes [2] and myself (as moderator) had submitted papers in advance, which had been circulated among the participants, the conference could be devoted solely to discussion, both at scheduled meeting times and through informal interaction. That bane of conferences, the paper droned to a passive audience, was thus avoided, and the wide-ranging viewpoints and interests of the participants were given an opportunity to be aired and perhaps to coalesce.

[1] The use of this term rather than the usual term, *altered states,* stemmed from a conference sponsored by the Drug Abuse Council and the Smithsonian Institution and held on February 16 and 17, 1973, in Washington, D.C. At that conference I objected to the word *altered* because it suggests that these states represent a deviation from the way consciousness should be. I prefer the word *alternate,* which makes it clear that different states of consciousness prevail at different times for different reasons and that no one state is considered standard. *Alternate states of consciousness* is a plural, all-inclusive term, unlike *usual state of consciousness,* which is merely one specific state of ASC.

[2] Elkes' contribution to this volume is a lecture he gave some years ago.

The subject specialties of the participants may be arranged along the following rough continuum: neurophysiology and neuroanatomy (Pribram), biochemistry and psychopharmacology (Elkes), biofeedback and experimental psychology (Shapiro), cognitive psychology (Marsh), psychology and psychoanalysis (Singer), anthropology (Furst), psychology of consciousness (Tart), herbal medicine and shamanism (Weil), and psychiatry and meditation (Deikman). I myself represented psychoanalysis. At one end of this continuum is the work of Pribram and Elkes, which has been done in a traditional laboratory setting, using quantitative methods and meticulously controlled experiments. At the other end is that of Weil and Deikman, work based on the investigators' own sensations. Between these two extremes lies the work of the other participants, positioned according to the extent of their reliance on independent objective verification. Yet, despite their vast differences in professional background, approach, and technique, all the participants have done significant work on consciousness and consciousness change and are alike in their eagerness to explicate its tenuous, slippery concepts.

The subject matter of the conference proved difficult to clarify, and the achievement of mutual understanding required patience and a wide background of knowledge. Because the conference tapes are long and repetitious, I shall not attempt to summarize them in this introduction. Instead, I shall turn to some of the important ideas discussed during the conference and in the papers. They will be considered in connection with the following topics: first, the reasons for believing that work in the field of consciousness change is scientific and that the workers in this field are scientists; second, unresolved issues in this field; and, third, the areas of agreement among the participants. In closing I shall deal also with some misconceptions about psychoanalytic theory that were expressed during the conference and will point out the concepts that theory holds in common with meditation and other methods of studying the mind.

I

Almost every contribution in this volume refers to its author's efforts to approach the matter of consciousness change scientifically. Even in "The Missing Center," by Deikman, where no such claim is made, the attempt to re-create systematically the universe of the developing child suggests the scientific method. It is my impression that in speaking of science the authors had in mind the second definition in Webster's *Second International* (1936): "systematized knowledge derived from observation, study and experimentation carried on in order to determine the nature or principles of what is being studied" (p. 931). This definition could be considered to include internal, or subjective, observation as well as external, or objective, observation. It is the first definition in Webster, however—"original state or fact of knowing as opposed to intuition or belief"—that calls into question the scientific nature of the study of alternate states of consciousness. For no one can observe consciousness change objectively. We must rely either on our own experience or on the subjective reports of others' experiences, on intuition or belief rather than objective fact.

Medewar (1967) has argued that in principle science can solve only those problems relating to the world of nature and that problems involving social values, esthetic judgments, or, by implication, unverifiable subjective states have no objectively correct solutions except insofar as they conform to history or to legal, social, or psychological conventions. Unfortunately, that well-known and well-supported position would sharply limit the kinds of problems that scientists can tackle.

Many other scientists are less certain about the boundaries of science. There are those who believe that it has become so politicized, so concerned with its entrenched economic interests, and so influenced by the values of the surrounding community that alleged scientific objectivity is a myth. (Marcuse, 1955; Roszak, 1973). This possibility seriously concerned the conference participants. Alternate states of consciousness do have political implications, and a scientific discipline studying these states would tend to legitimize them. The use of consciousness-changing drugs breaks some of the most punishing laws ever passed in this country— laws which, if marijuana is excepted, claim the support of a large majority of the populace and are accepted by the culture as having a firm moral basis. The changed states that do not involve drugs do not break laws but they do challenge the reigning cultural values. Thus, they have been seen as a threat to the psychological well-being of citizens, particularly to youth but also to the population as a whole, because of our preoccupation with material growth and technological achievement (*Marihuana-Hashish Epidemic*, 1974; Nahas, 1973). This particular problem of alternate states of consciousness in relation to science may well stem from semantic difficulties. Nevertheless, all the participants were aware that most uninformed people find the subject of alternate states of consciousness frightening. The public sees this area not only as unscientific (using that word as a pejorative) but as alien and menacing:

alien in its connection to Eastern thought, menacing in its potential for socially disruptive withdrawal.

But popular belief is not science. Recently, Davis (1975) attempted to clarify the meaning of the word *science*. He declares science to be, first, a "methodology that aims at maximal objectivity by relying on verifiable observations, on logical inferences, and on predictions that can be tested against the external world; and by employing extensive communications in a disciplined community to check the observations and initially assess the inferences" (p. 1). Second, he calls science "the coherent growing *body of public knowledge* [his italics] that has resulted from the cumulative application of that methodology" (p. 1). So far, Davis' definitions of science are broader than most definitions but lie within the usual boundaries. He goes on, however, to discuss a third sense of the word, as referring to a set of *human activities*. This sense includes the psychology of those who are employing the methods of the sciences to advance knowledge, as well as the sociology of the scientific community, both within itself and in interaction with the surrounding society.

The third sense of science given by Davis applies particularly to the alternate states of consciousness conference. Most investigators of alternate states of consciousness have known that the study affects them and is affected by them and that therefore their own psychology is a legitimate and vital aspect of their endeavors. Moreover, they are aware that studying alternate states of consciousness can easily place them in a marginal position in the scientific community. The investigator must either accept what in the past has amounted almost to banishment from that community or convince its members of the legitimacy of his work. This is quite a different matter from the relatively simple task of demonstrating the merit of a new approach in an accepted field. Marginality to this extent within the scientific community amounts to virtual deviancy. Being deviant obviously affects the psychology of the individual (Zinberg, 1975a). His embitterment, discontent, and growing hostility to entrenched positions, besides the personal effect, often act on the institutions and scientific community as a goad and a burr. At least in the short run, the community may react by becoming even more entrenched and less open. Thus, as a result of both the psychological interaction between the subject and the investigator and the sociological interactions within the scientific community, the study of alternate states of consciousness has been considered beyond the pale of legitimate scientific endeavor, and investigators in this area have felt increasingly alienated.

In writing his article, Davis was concerned chiefly about the social responsibility of science. Although the study of alternate states of consciousness has not been recognized as involving social responsibility in the same sense that arms control, nuclear proliferation, or genetic experimentation does, the sponsorship of two conferences on alternate states of consciousness by the Drug Abuse Council is evidence of the field's fundamental social importance. Millions of people in this country are experiencing consciousness change and are interested in the ramifications of this change. To the surprise of many publishers, a remarkably poor book on transcendental meditation rapidly became a best seller. And illicit drug use with consciousness-changing drugs grows apace (National Commission on Marihuana and Drug Abuse, 1973; Yankelovich, 1975). Knowledge about these remarkably convincing subjective experiences needs to be codified and channeled. The public needs to be told which efforts at consciousness change are useful and which ones are not, which of the publicized approaches are legitimate efforts and which ones are rip-offs. Millions of people need help in finding valid ways to integrate such experiences both individually and culturally in order to obviate the popular fear of personal and social withdrawal and disruption (Zinberg, Boris, & Boris, 1976).

Obviously, to include psychological and sociological interactions as part of a scientific endeavor means to accept the view that science works within cultural values and is therefore limited by them. Although this situation may seem startling to those who think of science as purely objective and quantifiable, it has always existed. The advancement of science has always been dependent upon the prevailing social and intellectual climate in that scientists are obliged to find support for an area of research before they can enter it (Kuhn, 1962). On a deeper level, the very methodology of science contains nonobjective and somewhat culturally determined elements. The processes of constructing hypotheses and developing concepts are subjective and creative; they are acts of the imagination, which is limited by the capacity to perceive, which, in turn, is to a great extent culturally determined (Bateson, 1972).

Moreover, as Davis (1975) has pointed out, though science depends on the objective part of its methodology—observation, critical analysis, and responsibility—to screen results in order to determine their objectivity before they are accepted as solid contributions to knowledge, this final validation rests on an assumption, a value judgment, about the existence of a real universe and about consensual experience as a source of knowledge. Davis has dismissed this issue as residing at a different metaphysical level. But the assumption about consensual reality deeply concerned the conference participants, who, because of the nature of their subject, could not readily accept the value judgment of reality; they felt that they must question the general acceptance of the usual state of consciousness as a reality equivalent.

My attempt to place the thrust of the alternate states of consciousness conference within the mainstream of scientific thought is not intended merely to legitimize this study. Rather, I hope to construct a framework that will contain the contributions of nine scientists (excluding myself) who have very different backgrounds and very different personal views of alternate states of consciousness. When C. P. Snow (1959) said that scientists believe they have the future in their bones, he was calling attention to the basic purpose of science. No matter how privatistic a frequenter of alternate states of consciousness may need to be in order to achieve the full meaning of some of the changed states of consciousness, particularly those that are religiously oriented, each time he attends a conference on this area or reads a book about alternate states, he is showing his interest in learning more about them. Therefore the future of the study of alternate states of consciousness deserves the coherence and the dedicated attempts at validation that lie only in the bones of a disciplined group, which in this culture means scientists.

I believe that our group was made up of scientists. None of us would have slanted the truth simply because he believed in his heart that he was right, nor would he have used any tactic to convince others of his rightness. All of us knew that we were faced with an unusual problem, tormenting in its complexity, but worthy of our fullest intellectual and emotional energies. We strove for ways to present our material, no matter how subjective that material may have been, as reasonably, lucidly, and objectively as possible. And we all accepted as a goal the advancement of human knowledge.

In important ways, however, the group of scientists at the alternate states of consciousness conference differed from the usual scientific gathering. Three quite distinct concepts of methodology were represented, ranging from the laboratory orientation of Elkes, Pribram, and Shapiro through the literature-searching survey, questionnaire, and interviewing psychological research strategies of Singer, Tart, Marsh, and, to a certain extent, Furst, to the evocative, subjective use of self-experience by Weil and Deikman. Despite the agreement that all three methodologies were needed to attack the problem of demonstrating objective correlates of subjective effects, these differences led to constant questions as to what could be accepted as data or evidence.

Even more difficult than the methodological differences were the attitudinal problems. With the possible exception of Pribram, the group worried constantly about the worthwhileness of a scientific investigation of alternate states of consciousness: Were we dealing with essentially personal concerns? Were we faced with an area so private that communication was impossible? Were individual reactions and differences so intense that generalizations would be hard to reach or would be faulty? A pessimism and defensiveness about the subject matter, unusual among scientists, was manifest. For when Snow referred to scientists' having the future in their bones, he was pointing not only to the purpose of science but also to the perennial optimism of scientists. Unlike Snow, who was speaking as a novelist and observer, Ann Roe was speaking as a professional psychologist when she commented that the one thing all scientists have in common is an unreasonable amount of optimism concerning the ultimately successful outcome of their research (cited in Holton, 1975). Moreover, Holton (1975) has documented the fact that the members of the scientific community, whatever their points of view about their personal lives, demonstrate an unflagging belief that the most glorious period in intellectual history is about to dawn. Referring to Einstein's brilliant address in honor of Max Planck, Holton reasoned that scientists' commitment to "the bright world of solvable problems" is in actuality a successful flight "from the dark world of anguished compromises and makeshift improvisations that commonly characterize the human situation" (p. 17). Planck, for example, called his drive into quantum theory "the physics of despair"; Neils Bohr, too, referred to his scientific search as "the truth in the abyss." Unlike Einstein's "narrow confines of swirling personal experiences," which are unrequited by their very nature, "scientific data yield eventually to reductionistic subdivisions into simplified, lucid, manageable reconstructions."

While it is true, as Holton has acknowledged, that in the 1970s many scientists are less optimistic about the use of their work, they remain buoyant about the potential in the work itself for the growth of knowledge and manage to separate their professional zest from their personal gloom. When working with alternate states of consciousness, however, this separation of personal and professional life is well-nigh impossible. Weil and Deikman have almost negated the distinction, but even the other contributors, who are more objectively oriented, cannot manage a sufficient separation. Singer made this clear when describing his study of his dreams, both night dreams and daydreams. Furst did so when he participated in tribal rituals. An entire day of the conference was given over to the discussion of sleep, dreams, love, sexual feeling, physical experience, magical ideas, sense of self, personal awareness, memories, contemplation, and meditation. In none of these areas of study could a definite separation be made between the personal and the objective or scientific.

In addition to the psychological reason for pessimism among scientists studying alternate states of consciousness, there is a social factor. Besides the questioning of the respectability of research on alternate states by both the public and the granting agencies, the unrequited, unsolvable conflicts of living, clouded by that constant of social existence, the human portion of ambivalence, seeps into work in this area. Was this not one reason for holding the conference? All too often investigating areas considered to be deviant can become troublesome for the investigator. At scientific meetings, "Is so-and-so a druggie?" is frequently asked about serious investigators, and the only reason for asking this question is the clarity of a presentation about drugs. The weight of public disapproval not only can make the investigator suspect but also, as he learns through his work to mistrust cultural simplifications, can force him into an adversary position. Simply by the researcher's trying to pierce through myth and misconception, his explication of the truth makes him seem to all too many people to favor alternate states of consciousness or drugs. And perhaps a greater danger—as James Thurber (1940/1952) put it, "You might as well fall flat on your face as lean over too far backward" (p. 74)—arises when investigators attempting to avoid becoming personally involved with the area of study or being seen as an advocate become so limited in their investigations that they cannot pass the "so what?" test and withstand the intellectual scrutiny of other workers in the field.

Putting this work and its workers within the framework of science and scientists is a beginning, but many problems remain. Do we have here a coherent field, a scientific discipline? If so, what are its boundaries, measures, data, evidence? What are the individual perceptions of usual and alternate states of consciousness? What makes up a gestalt, and how are these perceptions changed? What are objective correlates of subjective experience and how can they be defined and communicated? These are a few of the questions with which the conference began.

II

Definitions of consciousness abound in this collection. Caryl Marsh devotes an entire section to different ways of defining consciousness;

David Shapiro's precise conception on page 152 would be acceptable to almost everyone. But even though one basic definition of consciousness may be accepted, it is not so easy to define the usual state of consciousness in contradistinction to a changed state of consciousness. At the same time, certain changed states are so marked and so easily observable or are so much a part of everyone's experience that, even if their essence cannot be effectively articulated, they can easily be accepted as alternate states. Sleep and dream states or intense intoxication are clear-cut cases. Some drug states, such as those induced by psychedelics, usually are accepted as alternate states of consciousness; yet, because the user can discourse more or less rationally and can control his body functions, the exact relationship of these states to the usual state becomes more equivocal.

The boundaries between alternate states become even more tentative when meditative states are at issue. Are alternate states of consciousness discrete states, to use Tart's word, or are the differences among alternate states of consciousness merely differences of degree, as Singer insists? Just where does deep contemplation in a usual state of consciousness become a meditative alternate state? Is losing oneself in a vivid daydream in the usual state (though on the edge of it) comparable to the extreme loss of self-consciousness experienced in giving oneself up to a line of speculative thought while on a "trip"? Obviously, there must be connections; it is, after all, the same mind, brain, body, persona in operation in both the usual and the changed states of consciousness.

As one considers what these changed states of consciousness are, however, the problem of finding a distinction multiplies. An overwhelming orgasm was referred to at the conference as a changed state, but how can one tell what is overwhelming? Is an overheated sauna in a New York health club as likely to produce an alternate state as an Indian sweat lodge? Even hypnosis, which passes the test of observable difference, is thought by many practitioners (Orne, 1972) to be simply an increased state of suggestion in the usual state of consciousness.

It was during this most basic of discussions that a sharp difference emerged within the group. (Fortunately, while sharp differences could almost always be found, alliances shifted from one issue to another according to the laws of group dynamics; therefore, permanent factions did not form.) Those who felt that they had experienced alternate states with drugs or, after arduous training, in meditative states were convinced that the feeling of reality associated with the changed state made it distinctly separate; whereas those who considered consciousness to be an entity championed the concept of a continuum and asked again and again how the changed state differed from the usual state of consciousness.

A good part of the first day was spent thinking about such transitions, for all assumed that knowledge as to how one goes from one state to another would illuminate the difference between states. All agreed with Pribram that since the brain is always spontaneously active and organizing, the messages in transition states are distributed through the neural and perceptual systems and that the efferent areas of the brain work on the sensory receptors as well as on the musculature. Nevertheless, it seems impossible for the human system to hold on to transitions. For example, a goal of one Buddhist sect, unattained as far as anyone knew, was to grasp the instant that waking turned to sleeping. And when Tart, who was doing large-scale marijuana research, had specifically asked about the transition state, he was told repeatedly that as soon as anyone asked, "Am I stoned?" he *was* stoned. The participants found themselves using words like *measureless* and *dimensionless* to describe transitions because concepts of time, quantity of response, and quality of consciousness could not be adduced.

The problem of grasping transitions cast light on other problems raised in the discussion. For some it indicated that consciousness states were discrete rather than continuous. Deikman, in particular, saw in this problem his "missing center"; that is, the state in which there is no sense of self or self-awareness with which to observe or to be self-conscious. The bulk of the discussion, however, turned to the question of cultural disparity in accepting and using alternate states of consciousness. It was generally agreed that interest in one's state of mind cannot be viewed in terms of a simplistic dichotomy between East and West. Rather, interest in such self-consciousness has always been a part of the human condition. At the same time, however, an obvious divergence has occurred between Eastern and Western cultures: Eastern religious and philosophical thought has retained direct contact with spiritualism, mysticism, and self-directed changes in consciousness; the philosophical and religious interests of the West have been influenced by technology and by an objective scientific model. In this model, transitions of any sort that are uncontrollable and unknowable are threatening. If possible, they are avoided and if not, they are ignored or downplayed. Singer repeatedly (and correctly) pointed out how little tolerance many people in the United States have for the rich fantasy life that lies on the fringes of the mind, much less for alternate states of consciousness.

Historically, the United States has been foremost among the Western nations in questioning the legitimacy of alternate states of consciousness. Speaking to this point, P. T. Furst (1976b) argued that although in modern times the Old World's attitude toward alternate states has been influenced by the New World's, the prehistoric inhabitants of the American continent showed great interest in consciousness alteration. The radiocarbon laboratory has confirmed the well-integrated, cultural use of the hallucinogenic mescal bean by Paleo-Indians toward the end of the late Pleistocene big-game-hunting period, 10,000–11,000 years ago, shortly after the last overland migrations from Asia. According to La Barre (1938/1974), the Paleo-Indians brought this interest from their Asian homeland; thus, at one time there was no divergence between East and West in attitudes toward alternate states of consciousness. Furthermore, for centuries the people on the American continent retained their interest in hallucinogenic drug rituals and other non-drug rituals that were specifically intended, as Furst explains in Chapter 3, to change consciousness as part of a symbolic religious quest. In addition, before European colonization the New World did not know the fanaticism that was to become the hallmark of Old World religion. When one indigenous American group conquered another, it was likely that both groups already had some religious practices in common, and if some other practices differed, they were accreted rather than suppressed.

A drastic change took place after the European colonists arrived. A period of fanatical idol smashing occurred, but it was relatively brief, and the religious beliefs and practices of the Indians were systematically eradicated—at least on the surface. Thus America, untainted by the European tradition of religious wars, which had impeded the development of rationality, became fertile soil for a new, cool, objective approach to nature, to symbolic rituals, and to the development of psyche and spirit. According to this argument of Furst's, the increasing preoccupation with totally rational thought led, first in America and then in the rest of the Western world, to the suppression of interest in drug-induced and non-drug-induced experiences and to the divergence of Eastern and Western thought. At the conference, many examples were offered of the contemporary Western phobic reaction to alternate states of consciousness. Weil, for instance, discussed mycophobia and showed how widespread is the exaggerated fear of mushrooms as poisonous.

Although Furst's line of reasoning establishes the existence of an old tradition of experience with alternate states of consciousness in the West, it does not help to bridge the cultural gap that now exists between East and West. Those at the conference interested in Eastern thought wished that some aspects of Eastern culture could be directly translated or imported into this culture. The others argued that becoming a Zen adept in Kalamazoo is far different from thus disciplining oneself in

Tibet. The very act of becoming a devotee in this culture was seen by some as taking the principles of alternate states of consciousness out of context, thereby making a study of the changed states difficult and objectivity about them impossible.

Included within this issue of cultural disparity was the question of mysticism, spirituality, and its close cousin morality, which led to conflict at the conference. Those who wished to translate Eastern thought and its view of consciousness change directly into their own and others' contemporary experiences did not view this question lightly. It had many facets, the first being the idea that a "higher consciousness" exists at a special level of alternate states of consciousness. Although mighty efforts were made to keep the expression of such ideas to a minimum, a few statements by both sides implied that some states were "better" than others. To one side, the usual state of consciousness supplied the necessary rationality and steadiness for scientific investigation. "Why try so hard to tamper with it," they asked, "since the other states are 'soft' and 'woolly'?" By contrast the other side proclaimed that oneness with oneself, with nature, or with pure thought needed first to be achieved in order for its inherent superiority to be recognized. Not to achieve or to seek these higher states was identified as the equivalent of agreeing not to use a basic human sense. The word *enlightenment* crept into our discussions, implying that those who choose "unenlightenment" are willing to accept a lower alternate state of consciousness.

The subject of spiritual, mystical religions generated the same kind of controversy. Were they woolly, undefinable, uncommunicable concepts, or were they openings to neglected areas of the human psyche, where peace and contentment dwell? It is hard to read in Deikman's "The Missing Center" that "the spiritual schools teach the letting go of self—but not to babies . . . or psychic cripples, deformed beyond belief" (p. 240) without getting the message that letting go of self is a "good," enlightening thing to do. And conversely, by stating that "the seeming distraction . . . and trancelike behavior of the creative scientist or artist may represent not so much a shift to an 'altered state of consciousness' as a well-trained capacity for assigning a high priority to attending in concentrated fashion to the private, ongoing stream of thought when, after all, so much of our external environmental information is redundant," Singer (p. 117) leaves little doubt as to which state of consciousness he thinks is superior. Constant implications seemed to me to hint at a desire for perfectionism. Man should be purified and made more rational or more spiritual. Our culture is squeezing the juice (spirit) out of its inhabitants by means of television, frozen foods, big cars, and other symbols of materialism; whereas it is inner space that offers salvation. During such discussions I was reminded again and again of Oakeshott's (1968) comment, "To attempt something inherently impossible is a denigrating task." Imagine a world of contemplative saints seeking only virtue, with no greed, sloth, gluttony, jealousy, or other such attributes that make us human!

Since every participant had come to the conference to advance knowledge about alternate states of consciousness rather than establish moral hegemony, the problem was not ill will; rather, it was the borrowing from Eastern culture (Eliade, 1969; Merton, 1969; Norada, 1968). The attempt to develop ideas relative to Eastern thought, which has a frank goal orientation and a clear idea of what is best, collided with the objective study of process and with a nonjudging cultural relativism. Buddhist goals, for example, include "clear perception of the object as it really is," "altruistic joy," "abandonment of evil deeds and thoughts," and the instruction "to experience only healthy states." Those participants who were deeply interested in such efforts found themselves, perhaps unconsciously, justifying their interests and idealizing or espousing Eastern goals. Thus, the stage was set for conflict with those who were committed to external research, who believed that whatever could be collected by survey, questionnaire, or laboratory research should be assessed with judgment as to better or worse and certainly without reference to God or spirit. Despite the intransigence of this problem, and fortunately for the conference, the splits within the group shifted. For example, both the neurophysiologists and the psychologists questioned the introspectivists' ideas about higher or cosmic consciousness. But when the group turned to the issue of a goal orientation versus a process orientation, the scientists joined the introspectionists in opposing what they felt to be the laissez-faire relativism of those who were process oriented.

Another example of goal orientation versus process orientation was the discussion of "teaching" people to have more awareness—that is, to be more aware—of the active images at the periphery of thought. This goal was deemed worthwhile: All agreed that one cultural problem in the West is the tendency to reduce human consciousness to straight, moral rationality; whereas being more aware of what it really means to be human might make life more satisfying. For instance, when an ambulance siren wails nearby, if one could stop the screen of consciousness, one would become aware of the primitive imagery of crushed bodies, blood and guts, or whatever personal depth had been plumbed by the sound. Also, there was fair agreement that one could have a teacher, a guru, to help in the search for meaning, greater awareness, or alternate states of consciousness. But how far can this goal of "teaching" extend? As soon as one begins to learn how to recognize one's imagery, will not the resultant imagery be more oriented to rational, disciplined, and objective modes of consciousness? The flash resulting from the ambulance siren plumbs the depths spontaneously, contains affect, and is a fresh experience for the person. If one were to follow the rules of the teacher to reach the goal, would one come to the same place? Or, would the process of reaching the "goal" change the end, even if in one sense the person got to where he wanted to be and became aware of more images? (Here too, it was evident that the fresh, spontaneous image was considered better.) Teaching the Eastern disciplines avoids this problem by choosing ambiguity—for example, studying the sound of one hand clapping. But much doubt was expressed as to whether that teaching, if translated to the West, could resist organization and objectification.

The insertion of ideas of knowing what was better touched off other controversies. Was a non-drug-induced state better or more profound than a drug-induced one? Here the lines of disagreement differed from those on other issues. The participants who had had no drug experience tended to agree with the introspectionists that drugs should not be necessary. Again, because it was so hard to describe what the changed states are like, it was difficult to keep the discussion focused solely on what makes one state different from another.

A similar problem had to be left open: the degree of emotional difficulty attributed to consciousness changes with or without drugs. There was agreement about the far end of the continuum: that people in serious trouble are attracted to this area and that heavy drug use can compound their difficulties. However, beyond that admission, disagreement was great. Singer's contention that the drug users he had studied were more passive and less imaginative than non-users raised the question of whether his sample was drawn from that farthest end of the continuum, or whether his measurements were so culturally biased as to confuse interest in inner states with passivity, or whether, indeed, he could correlate severe emotional restriction with drug use for consciousness change.

But what about spontaneously changed states? Are visions, mystical experiences, hypnogogic states, and flashbacks the expressions of a breakdown in mental functioning or are they universal human experiences that some people manage to inhibit or ignore? To put it more exactly, are such things as dream states and hypnogogic states universal, and such things as hallucinations or psychoses peculiar to some individuals?

And how can one sort of state be distinguished from the other? As for drug states, does one person's LSD experience represent pleasure, insight, and greater emotional freedom, and another's darker visions represent a breakthrough of preexisting emotional disturbances.

Not being able to resolve such questions did not mean that there was no discussion of them. In expressing their individual points of view, the participants again found themselves alternately agreeing and disagreeing with the same people. It was hard to tell whether such differences were the result of actual disagreements or simply different expressions of the same principle. The human processing capacity, which has a limited range of emotional responses, yields an infinite number of individual variations. Often people become more intense and tendentious over these tiny variations than over the larger issues: what Freud (1914/1957) called "the narcissism of small differences" (p. 69).

More important than this problem was the ambivalence felt by all the participants toward the subject of alternate states. We were clearly interested in it, but at the same time we shared the popular discomfort over it. Probably part of the ambivalence stemmed from the anxiety engendered by moving away, even symbolically, from the usual state of consciousness. This showed itself in narrowness of vision: "My particular alternate state of consciousness is fine with me, but if you vary it by a millimeter I am against it." The desire for some firm moral hegemony, whether by being "for" objective research or "for" greater experience, was part of that same anxiety. For example: "Meditation is boring." "Drugs are too frightening." "Research is a waste of time; just experience is needed."

Ambivalence was apparent also in the intolerance shown toward ambivalence itself. To struggle with concepts as fragile as those related to alternate states of consciousness would seem to require considerable tolerance for ambiguity and mixed feelings. But this was not the case; there was great pressure to take a position, to hold it, and, if possible, to convince others of it. And some views of some aspects of alternate states seemed to be so ambivalently taken that the only way one could have a clear position was to project an attitude of certainty by holding the mixed feelings in abeyance.

Ambivalence showed most clearly in the participants' preoccupation with dualism and bimodal expressions. Much of this part of the discussion, as this volume shows, was a genuine attempt to define the inherent nature of consciousness and its manifestations. But so many bimodal expressions were used—mind/brain, right hemisphere/left hemisphere, solar/lunar, conscious/unconscious, active/passive, mental/physiological,

continuous interblending/discrete, self-conscious/self-aware, nagual/
tonal, yin/yang, good/bad, higher/lower—that I could not help feeling
that the participants were working with two sides of their own feelings
about the subject matter. (If this had not been the case, it would not
have been necessary to use so many phrases to express the same or very
similar distinctions.) At times the participants had difficulty in accepting
anything, even if it agreed with what they had just said, without bringing up a contravening argument. And it was easy to use the various
dualisms to show "the other side" of whatever was being discussed.

At some points in the discussion it was difficult to know whether an
opposing argument was just a new phrase for the same distinction or
another representation of personal ambivalence toward the subject or an
important aspect of the study of alternate states of consciousness. Take,
for example, the difference between primary and secondary streams of
thought. Originally this distinction was used to show that usual and
alternate states of consciousness are continuous rather than discrete
states because the usual state contains much that is hardly recognized by
individuals or by the culture. Then it became clear that in order to
discuss secondary streams a vantage point was needed: the vantage point
of self-conscious awareness. But for that, a sense of self had to be
postulated, and it seemed impossible to define what a sense of self is and
what it would be like not to have one. How do the Eskimos, for example, make out without a word for "I"?

The problem of the insufficiency of words to communicate such
ideas was always present. What does it mean to say, "The mystical state
is the experience of unified connectedness as opposed to separation and
individuation"? Tart described punctiliously his efforts to learn Aikido
and to explain his learning of this discipline through efforts to connect
his bodily awareness to his intellect. He found that eventually his body
did learn by practice how to make this connection but not until he
stopped self-consciously trying to intellectualize the process. And now
that his body can do it, he still cannot put into words how it learned!
There could be general agreement about such an experience—all had
had similar ones—and that agreement could be elaborated upon in a discussion of how time and concepts of object awareness change with
consciousness change. But then the question of the boundaries of these
experiences would come up. Are there limits in such changes and, if so,
what are they? Where are the boundaries of self and self-awareness, and
how ambiguous can they be before this ambiguity becomes an "emotional problem"? And what about the concept of the inner "observer"?
Is that the self? Does the feeling of realness about self represent sub-

stantiation? If so, then does not the feeling of realness described in all mystical experience, as James (1902/1929) stated, also represent substantiation?

The question could and did become even more confusing. What about reality itself? Castenada's (1968) or don Juan's insistence that consensual reality is simply a construct, and a rather insubstantial one at that, got an airing. Always it seemed next to impossible to find a way, with or without words, to convey one's own experiences of oneself, of reality, of consciousness, of consciousness change. Perhaps the best statement of personal difficulty in coming to grips with this problem was made by Frances Verrinder, a Drug Abuse Council Fellow who attended the conference as an observer. She wrote later to me:

> Throughout the conference I was struck by the consistent assumption that the intellectual, thinking, rational, logical, deductive ego state is the normal state of consciousness and that other non-ego states (fantasy, dreams, physical sensation, emotional feeling, intuitive knowledge, drug-induced highs, etc.) are all aberrations from the ego norm, worthy of scientific exploration. In itself this is a highly egocentric notion!
>
> The more I reread the papers and reflect on the subject the more I feel that non-ego states are not accessible to the inquiries of the ego. I certainly do not feel that they are an area for scientific study.
>
> The fantasy that the ego state is either the only permissible state or at very least the most important state of mind which of itself constitutes reality seems to be inherent in Western culture. However, thanks to Freud, we have realized anew that the ego is only part of the whole organism. It seems to me that it is an illusion of the ego to think that it can chart, measure, limit, quantify, control, and replicate scientifically the non-ego parts of ourselves. It can't even chart, control, or measure accurately its own creations—time, past, future—or the pain that arises from the perception of these uncontrollable and unknowable ideas. (Incidentally, it occurs to me that this is what the motif of the suffering servant in the Old Testament must illustrate—the pain of *deifying* the ego, which is essentially what Judaism did.)
>
> If one views the ego as part of the whole, then one can use it to catch occasional, fascinating glimpses of what's going on in the non-ego. But even then it can only *speculate* on how much or what it knows and doesn't know. I feel that there is absolutely no point in trying to ascribe meaning to the non-ego since the very idea of meaning is in itself a product of the ego. The non-ego has no meaning; it simply *is* whatever it is. So it's not necessary (though often fun) to analyze one's dreams or fantasies; it's simply enough to dream or fantasize them since the measureless, untouchable, undifferentiated process of which they are a part is by definition be-

yond conscious control or knowledge. Or as Lao Tse would put it: Do nothing through acting, do everything through being.

It also occurs to me that the main reason for the degrees of interest in altered states of consciousness is because we all want to experience more of our non-ego states—I certainly do. But the paradox is that thinking about them and intellectually exploring them precludes experiencing them.

Most of the participants knew how Ms. Verrinder felt but doubted that careful intellectual exploration of these states precluded experiencing them. In attempting to solve this dilemma, we went round the table, and each one gave a personal anecdote of what he considered to be a changed state. Through this device we got to know one another better, but the problem of making these tenuous experiential concepts explicit remained. At one point someone recalled the suggestion Ellis made at the end of *Mescal: A Study of a Divine Plant* (1902). He advised the next worldwide medical congress to divide in two so that one-half could take mescaline and the other half could observe the experience. Our conference discussions were hard, frustrating work, but at least everyone kept on trying.

III

As the group was discussing a perennial question, "What form of science is appropriate to the study of alternate states of consciousness?" Elkes broke in to argue that the form might make little difference. He noted that the function of science is to arrive at a consensual validation regardless of form or method. As a common language and some kind of symbolic system are gradually developed to describe alternate states, a source of intuitive knowledge will appear that has its own kind of reality. Elkes described the process by which theoretical physics, which also deals primarily with abstraction, had developed, for he believed there might be parallels between the two fields. Although such an idea may appear grandiose, it did bypass a struggle over a particular method or a particular perspective, and it provided a framework for the many agreements, outlined in this section, reached by the participants in spite of their diverse backgrounds.

In the first place, all the participants believed that the usual state of consciousness is far more complex than it is generally assumed to be. The process of thinking, image formation, daydreaming, streams of thought, and discharge of affect has been insufficiently studied because of the difficulty of concretizing the process.

The problems of any research that would directly correlate the functioning nervous system with the subjective experience of consciousness are enormous. After all, the nervous system is composed of millions of nerve cells (neurons) that vary enormously in size and structure. The parts of the nervous system can be categorized in several ways for different purposes. One basic division is between the central nervous system, consisting of the brain and spinal cord, and the peripheral nervous system (everything else). Psychoactive drugs act on the central nervous system and we can assume that most of the processes underlying alternate states of consciousness essentially involve only the central nervous system.

Another way to divide the nervous system is by function. The *somatic* system includes both the central and peripheral neurons that convey impulses from the sense organs, organize them in the brain, and deliver motor impulses to the skeletal muscles. The *autonomic* system governs the smooth muscles of the intestines, urogenital tract, and blood vessels; the heart muscles; and the endocrine glands. Western science usually has categorized this division as follows: The somatic system governs the body's response to the external environment and is more or less under the conscious control of the individual; the autonomic system governs the internal environment, which is regulated automatically and unconsciously through glandular and nervous system responses. Even this basic division is the subject of increasing controversy because various proponents of Eastern philosophies insist that they can bring parts of the autonomic system under conscious control, and an increasing number of scientific experiments are verifying this assertion.

The central nervous system is a hive of specialization. Some parts have specific and identifiable functions although, as far as anyone can tell at present, most, if not all, activities involve more than one central nervous system center. It is easier to study direct motor or sensory functions where central nervous system activity can be correlated with output (that is, if you stick a pin in someone he yells "ouch" and his arm jerks) than to study purely cognitive functions. A person asked what he is thinking or feeling will give a variable, subjective, noncorrelative response.

Since basic research on drugs and the central nervous system has been going on for decades, why is it that little is known and little can be expected from this work for a very long time? Consider this list of formidable obstacles to doing such work (Zinberg and DeLong, 1974,

p. 74): (a) Neural reactions occur in milliseconds and are hard to find and to measure. (b) We can study the biochemical processes involved in the peripheral nervous system in test tubes because we can slice this tissue and watch it react to stimuli. We cannot similarly study the brain. When the brain neurons are in a test tube, they are in a resting state, disconnected from the stimuli that ordinarily determine their activities. We can supply artificial stimulation but we have no way of knowing whether this process corresponds to what happens in the body. Obviously, this difficulty particularly complicates the study of brain tissue reactions that relate to the complex functions of thought or emotion. (c) We have derived most of what we do know about neural functioning from studies of the peripheral nervous system. In this system, generally speaking, because only one connection between neurons exists at a particular point, one message gets sent to one receiver as a result of the stimulus. In the densely packed central nervous system, however, we suspect that even cells other than neurons may perform neural functions. No one knows how many messages are sent to how many receivers simultaneously. (d) Because the different units of the central nervous system have different functions and anatomies, the biochemical reactions of any particular part probably are not the same as those of any other part. We have little idea of what these differences are. (e) A unique barrier exists between the blood and the brain. Less gets through the blood vessels in the brain, but we do not know whether this process is selective: Are some things let through but not others? (f) Many brain structures are not accessible in a live subject because they are surrounded by other vital structures. Since it is pointless to study these structures in the test tube, and we cannot study them in the living subject, how do we study them at all? (g) When experiments are carried out in a live animal subject, it is often necessary to stop a chemical reaction quickly to preserve the tissue at a particular point in the process. Usually this is done by rapid excision and immersion in a low-temperature liquid. Since the entire central nervous system is surrounded by bone, this operation cannot be performed quickly enough to find out the chemicals present in various phases of the reaction. They are destroyed too fast. Nor is this experimental procedure recommended for human subjects (DeLong, 1972).

Despite these obstacles to investigation, much elegant research has delved into the central nervous system and its mechanisms, and a number of interesting theories have been developed. For example, chemicals called neurotransmitters vitally affect the transmission of neural impulses. Congruently, an important theory about the psychoactive drugs is based on the idea that they affect the production, destruction, or re-uptake of these transmitters, thus changing the patterns of neural impulses. Immense effort is going into the study of these neurotransmitters. Another significant theory concerns the basic interaction of drug molecules with central nervous system cells. It proposes that the interaction depends on a specific three-dimensional geometric shape of the molecule that is compatible with a corresponding receptor site on the cell surface.

Despite their importance and ingenuity, such theories can solve only questions concerning the site and the nature of the initial interaction between drug and cell. They do not purport to explain further biochemical events nor the ultimate relationship between these events and conscious states (Zinberg & DeLong, 1974).

Thus, the study of alternate states of consciousness is sharply hindered by the lack of a clear base of knowledge obtained from central nervous system research, as well as lack of knowledge about the usual state of consciousness. To describe the search for knowledge about alternate states of consciousness, Shapiro (p. 150) cites Brener's (1974) "analogy of a deaf person learning to talk by calibrating the responses of his own muscular vocal apparatus against the vibratory sensations talking can produce in the fingers." In order to attempt speech in this way the deaf person must first become aware of the particular muscular responses that are speech equivalents. Researchers of alternate states of consciousness are in a similar position. Because little is known about the extremely complex usual state of consciousness, the student of alternate states of consciousness does not know where to put his fingers—symbolically speaking—in order to approximate other states.

In spite of this difficulty, we were able to agree, in the second place, that consciousness, the usual state of consciousness, is, as Tart puts it (p. 160), not a natural given but a construction and that the elements making up consciousness are susceptible to other constructions. Of course, this overall agreement masked the unresolved issue of discrete alternate states versus a continuum of consciousness. But once there was agreement that sharply different states do exist (aside from the usually experienced ones such as dreams) and that potentially these states are available to everyone, three further areas of agreement became clear: that alternate states of consciousness must have physiological correlates; that they must have a flow of their own; and that they must be achieved via a change, a disruption, in the usual state.

Concerning the third area of agreement, psychobiological and neurophysiological equivalents of the subjective experience of alternate states of consciousness have not been specified as yet, but various suggestions as to possibilities made sense to the participants. For example, evidence was presented that suggested the existence in the central nervous system of key chemical compounds capable of powerfully affecting selective mechanisms that subserve basic consciousness states. The effect of this evidence on some members of the group unaccustomed to thinking in bodily terms is reflected by comments in their contributions to this volume (see Singer's remarks on p. 118, for instance). The view that alternate states may be due to alternate control processes exercised by the brain on sensory and physiological stimulus invariants and on the memory store also was discussed and accepted. Particular attention was given to biofeedback as a means of eliciting precisely defined patterns of physiological responses. The use of electroencephalograms, evoked potential, contingent negative variations, heart rate, digital skin temperature, blood pressure, respiration, electrodermal activity, eye movements, and other such procedures appealed because they are noninvasive and because the possibility for cerebral specialization has become more exact.

Next the participants began to consider the fourth area, the idea of *flow*, a term suggested by Caryl Marsh (p. 128) to indicate that each state of consciousness has noticeable characteristics that move along and vary from moment to moment—to avoid quoting William James directly. Within each state, however, the ceaseless change and variability fall within different ranges of tempo, imagery, and intensity. The basic elements of one state are present in another but the changes of quantity and quality in the way these elements are presented are sufficient to insure an awareness that the state is different. In a night dream, for instance, a figure may emerge that is so startlingly lifelike that the dreamer feels he can almost reach out and touch it or speak to it; yet the rest of the dream situation may be bizarre and unreal. The "realistic" element acquires the full dream quality not from the single realistic figure but from the overall state. Just as Tart's audience (p. 158) knows the lecture is not a dream, so the dreamer knows the dream for what it is. Someone who has taken LSD and experienced a "trip"—that is, one who follows a line of fantasy in the single-minded way characteristic of a psychedelic experience (Huxley, 1952; Zinberg, 1975b)—does not confuse that elongated experience in a reduced perceptual field with a daydream. Even the most intense daydream takes place in a context of potential awareness of external and internal reality in usual state of consciousness terms. Similarly, the process of shifting from a particular trip leaves the drug ingestor still in a realm of sharpened color, altered perceptual thresholds, and differed sensibility. The flow of the experience, whether in the usual or in a changed state, has a logic of its own, an inherent consistency that may or may not derive from the rules of cause and effect.

As it became clear that different states have particular characteristics, a particular mode of expression of these characteristics, and a flow of their own, but that the transition between states is difficult if not impossible to fathom, the participants, to their own surprise, found a high level of agreement on the fifth area: What is needed to get from one state to another? Tart's discussion of this phenomenon (p. 197) is by far the most comprehensive. I will recapitulate it only enough to show how close the participants' conceptualizations were.

Tart postulates that the mind from which consciousness arises consists of a limited number of relatively stable psychological structures. In different combinations, these structures lead to a wide variety of potential behaviors and experiences, depending on the particular body and nervous system and the particular culture at a given time. In a given culture the system built from these structures (an enormously complex process) produces the "normal" state, the usual state of consciousness. Obviously this particular organization of structures, which is powerfully and constantly reinforced by every element of the individual's interactions with family, friends, teachers, and other representatives of the culture, is firmly based. Although Tart does not mention this, his schema offers an explanation for the great emotional importance of early experience, which becomes part of the bedrock of the developing system of awareness/attention, or consciousness.

A changed state of consciousness would share psychological structures with the usual state of consciousness, but in an altered state some structures latent or unimportant in the usual state would become manifest and important, and vice versa. There would be a reordering, achieved through a disruption strong enough to upset the stability of the usual state's structural organization. For to move from the usual to a changed state would mean crossing a forbidden zone in which there were few reliable, well-arranged conscious structures. The need to pass through such a zone of disruption may explain why it is difficult to become aware of transitions. As Tart puts it, once organized into an alternate state, "this condition of my mind feels *radically different* from some other condition rather than just an extension of it"; he goes on to delineate those conditions necessary for the disruption to result in a successfully reorganized changed state.

Singer (pp. 97–101) presents certain parallel ideas: The limited mental "channels" available to each individual for processing internal or external stimuli appear to be roughly similar to Tart's structures. In Singer's view there are probably basic structures underlying the channels, but this postulate would not be contradictory to Tart's formulation. Also, Singer indicates the continuity and fixedness of these channels by showing how earlier, basic, long-term memories are triggered by later stimuli within a specific channel. This is another way of pointing out how crucial the early organization of the processing of stimuli within the mind is. Within usual experience some channels may be more active than others, but for a changed state to occur, a "discrepancy" must take place. Singer focuses on night dreams to describe the effectiveness of this discrepancy in making channels available that are not usually available, and vice versa. This conceptualization is very similar to Tart's: Both concern responses of surprise, strangeness, and increased or different affect.

Weil also sees the necessity of a discrepancy or disruption—whether by eclipse, sweat lodge, or mushrooms—in order to move an individual from one state of consciousness, the solar, to another, the lunar. He, too, documents the power of the reigning cultural outlook to interfere with the emergence of the changed consciousness and indicates that for lunar consciousness to achieve a stable position in thinking, rearrangements of psychological structures are necessary. Deikman's concept of "unlearning" follows an almost identical course. The selves and decoy selves that he sees as intended to inhibit being and fulfillment, and whose development he traces, could also be thought of as psychological structures. And, true to Tart's system concept, they must be unlearned or disrupted if some other state of consciousness is to emerge.

I was struck by the similarity between these discussions of the necessity to disrupt consciousness in order to achieve change, which particularly in Deikman's usage implied a better state, and Laing's (1965, 1968) work. Laing's continued insistence that one must be driven "out of one's wretched mind" in order to find a new order of sanity fits many of the notions expressed about the destabilization of existing psychological structures. Clinging to the usual state of consciousness out of fear of change apparently is to Laing as profound a form of mental disorder as schizophrenia, and to the extent that the schizophrenic has tolerated the disruption he is saner than the frightened conformer.

Marsh, in considering the focus of attention as part of her framework for describing the contents of consciousness, presents a similar view of the shift from one state of consciousness to another. She uses as analogies a tuning system and a spotlight; segments of stimuli can be tuned in or out, and different bands or channels can put together different gestalts of psychological elements.

This view of consciousness as a stable structure susceptible to disruption and reorganization was not limited to the psychologists or the introspectionists. Pribram specifically declares that the distinctive quality of states of consciousness "depends on overall organization, not an elements of content" (p. 222). He goes on to point out that input to the organism is influenced by its own previous output. Thus, the same stabilizing and reinforcing factors of cultural interaction result in a particular organization. This organization is maintained not by a memory store per se but by programs that are responsible for retrieval. To change states, then, a disruption of existing programs must occur and alternate control processes be developed. Pribram suggests that loss of self-awareness may occur when the brain is disrupting one program and "remembering" another. Pribram, writing with Gill (1976), has gone even further. They advocate abandoning completely the concept of discharge of affects or other energies from the system. Instead, they suggest that a system of homeostasis within the individual allows for changes within the system that activate the continued production of an equilibrium, albeit with a different makeup of system components. This process "readies" the organism to cope, or, in the terms I have been using, to stabilize in a different state. Pribram and Gill (1976) have supplied a framework for thinking through the process by which the energies of the mind operate in the change from the usual to an alternate state of consciousness.

All of these views about consciousness change, which to me seem congruent with some classical psychoanalytic concepts of ego psychology, permitted wide agreement on the sixth important point: Research is possible. A number of strategies were proposed. Shapiro spoke for the more objectively oriented of the participants when, after acknowledging the difficulties inherent in definition, objectification, and quantification, he insisted that research in alternate states of consciousness need be no different in essence from the study of other properties of biological systems. On pages 154–57 he makes specific suggestions on biofeedback research, which, because the patterns of physiological activity can be regulated by the individual, seems particularly suitable for studying alternate states. His ideas of studying changed states in the laboratory entail the conscious cooperation of the subjects, whose verbal reports could be correlated with physiological patterns.

Elkes and Pribram contended that sufficient progress has been made in delineating the specific physiological response patterns associated with different kinds of human behavior and cognition to allow some correlations, and that the greatest lack is in basic research. By that they mean the study of the brain substances and sites crucial to the regulation and flow of information within the central nervous system. The continuously and spontaneously active brain contains structures that work equally on muscles and on sensory receptors and whose distribution must be mapped for a more exact understanding of responses in different states.

Elsewhere Tart (1972) has delineated his ideas about a state-specific science, in which experimenters participating in the changed state would make an attempt to carry out observations and experiments. His ideas follow and develop even further much of the current thinking on state-dependent learning. Tart contends that what we have now is a state-specific psychological science in which what we know is relevant in this state of consciousness but may not be so in another. The different perspective of another state not only may contribute knowledge applicable within that state but also may open up new avenues of conjecture and experimentation within the usual state. During the conference it was interesting to observe the growing agreement between Tart and Singer, two academic psychologists who approached the problem of alternate states of consciousness from opposite positions. For just as Tart complained about how little effort has been made to study work done in an alternate state, so Singer complained that little has been done to study the usual state. Singer's research ideas, of course, follow that complaint. He noted that a number of observed phenomena, one of which is the peaking of daydreams at ninety-minute intervals, have not been investigated sufficiently. Large-scale questionnaires and surveys of imagery and daydreams have not been used enough to present a good picture of what the usual state is. Without giving up this position, Singer, by the end of the conference, as pages 118–20 of the published version of his paper show, now urges that similar comparison studies be done with people who have experienced alternate states of consciousness.

Marsh, Furst, Weil, and I, although in full agreement regarding the importance of the research work that has already been suggested, are more directly concerned with phenomenological observations, both objective and subjective. We believe that direct observations of the experience of alternate states within the cultural context or in some instances within differing cultural contexts represent a bedrock necessity for further studies. Before attempting to experiment outside or within alternate states of consciousness, it seems to us important to nail down the actual properties of these maddeningly amorphous states. For the fundamental question, which is asked too infrequently about both drug and non-drug alternate states, is, "What is the person experiencing that is worth the trouble?"

This method of research—nailing down the properties of alternate states of consciousness—appealed to our group sufficiently for us to attempt a rough outline of such an approach, based on each individual's personal experience of a changed state. After the properties of these states had been decided upon, the participants rated their experiences on a one to nine scale. This procedure became complicated, but it was not impossible to pursue. Vividness, for example, had to be broken down into such modalities as visual, auditory, kinesthetic, tactile, gustatory, and olfactory. In rating the reality of usual against alternate states, "absolutely convinced of the usual state of consciousness" was rated one; "absolute conviction of alternate states of consciousness was rated nine. A somewhat different item, "connectedness to ordinary feelings," also could be rated on a straight progression of one to nine. Generalized affective reactions, too—joy, rage, lability of affect, surprise, interest, and sadness—could be treated on a straight-line basis; however, self-awareness had to use the median number five as a base because one can be less self-aware as well as more self-aware. "Self-control" versus "events passing by" also needed a base, as did self/object differentiation. The story line—that is, the relationship to inner fantasy life—needed to be graded from easy continuity to a kaleidoscopic response. Other items, such as body awareness, new sensations, differentiation between external and internal experiences, organization of thought (fluidity, clarity), and motivational structures (nurturance, sex, affiliation, aggression, self versus other, power), also were handled either on a progression of one to nine or on a base of five.

This exercise occupied one morning of the conference and, to the surprise of several of the participants, promised more potential descriptive material of different states than had been thought possible. Clearly, different responses ensued from a drug experience, a fever-induced delirium, and a deep meditative state. Equally clearly, the individual's personality, his previous experiences, and the feelings with which he entered the experience constituted a second crucial variable. Both of these critical variables—the type of experience and the individual's personality—could be noted down and made a part of the descriptive process. It would be important, for example, to comment on the personality and attitude of an individual who was taking nitrous oxide for the first time. It could be noted, for instance, that the individual had never before used a psychoaffective drug other than alcohol or tobacco; that he had been quite anxious beforehand but had confidence in the group with which he was to share the experience; and that he was a rigorous, self-controlled person with considerable ability to compartmentalize feelings and intellectualize affects. If more personality factors were needed, they could be gained through a personal interview.

The setting, the physical and social environment in which the experience occurred, made up the third basic variable. The physical setting, which to a certain extent can be controlled, could be described vividly in order to allow a phenomenological picture to emerge, but the larger social setting, which cannot be controlled, also was identified as a basic part of the experience. Thus, it would be necessary to monitor changing attitudes in the social setting if one were to understand the subject's internal reaction. In 1953, for example, the "experimental subjects" who were without their knowledge given LSD by the army must have been overwhelmed by the experience. Never having heard of a psychedelic drug reaction, they could have had no idea what was happening to them and must have believed that they had lost their minds. Even ten to fourteen years later, at the high point of the "Tune In, Turn On, and Drop Out" revolution, psychoses by the thousands were precipitated by drug experiences. But today, despite the fact that more people continue to try psychedelic drugs than ever before, psychoses and other dangerous responses have dropped to almost zero. Through a process of social learning, the response to drugs has changed (Zinberg, 1975b). Even a first-time user who may not know exactly what to expect has been preconditioned. When he sees colors somewhere inside, he says, "Aha, those are the psychedelic colors I have been hearing about for a decade," not "God help me, my eyes and brain are changing!"

Young people in Thailand whose families insisted that they practice meditation and spend a year in a monastery have reported that although they were proficient meditators—and would, therefore, show the reductions in electrodermal activity, oxygen consumption, respiratory rate, and blood lactate noted by Wallace, Benson, and Wilson (1971)—they found the whole business boring. The young Thais felt none of the hope for fulfillment, the self-realization, or relaxation that characterize those choosing meditation in the United States. Once meditation becomes commonplace in this culture, will some of the positive sequelae now reported vanish as the negative sequelae of LSD have? It is clear that an incipient process of social learning that reflects the changing attitudes in the social setting plays a crucial role in the way individuals metabolize experiences (Zinberg, 1975a; Zinberg, Boris, & Boris, 1976).

Just as a disruption is essential in going from the usual to an alternate state, so one's early memories, experiences, and interactions lay down psychological structures that are rooted in the culturally avowed view of consciousness. Within the average expectable environment, adaptation demands that attention/awareness mechanisms assign priorities to the items that are culturally acceptable. Perceptual thresholds develop that allow the individual to notice most easily what he needs to notice in order to function successfully. A form of self-programming results, leading to the availability of those percepts that contribute to organized thinking. This development, in turn, leads to the kind of rigidity of thinking that all the participants at the alternate states of consciousness conference experienced when they tried to engage in a different way of looking at familiar internal experiences. But it would be a mistake to think that this inflexibility is total. The average expectable environment changes, though slowly, and an experience considered alarming in one historical era becomes commonplace in another. A study of representative high school students over the period 1967–1973 (Zinberg, Boris & Boris, 1976) showed the development of an entirely new response to marijuana and alcohol. At the beginning of the period a highly ideological position was evident: Marijuana smokers desired insight, were secretly terrified of hidden dangers (even the rebels half believed the propaganda against marijuana), practiced elaborate group rituals around getting high, were recognized by themselves and others as a delineated group, and eschewed alcohol. By the end of that short time span, the students had abandoned an ideological connection with the drug, were no longer a delineated group, had dropped or pared down most rituals surrounding getting high, had lost any awe of the drug and wanted only brief pleasure from it, and used marijuana and alcohol together or separately in order to get high. Furthermore, during this same time span teachers who had been violent and persistent critics of drugs and drug use became almost unaware of its much more widespread use.

Input into the social setting from the experiences of individuals continues to change it, and the social setting, in turn, changes these experiences. As with consciousness itself, layers of attitudes exist in the social setting that can be rearranged so that what is chosen by individuals to reach awareness, what is considered the range of reality-related ideas, and what is available and acceptable to perceive and describe become parts of a dynamic equilibrium. Social rituals are developed to legitimize new perceptions and attitudes (Harding & Zinberg, 1976; Zinberg, Harding, & Winkeller, 1976; Zinberg & Jacobson, 1976; Zinberg, Jacobson, & Harding, 1975): for example, the rituals of the early marijuana smokers that made this deviant behavior a social activity and acted as both a method of control of drug use and a form of legitimation. Such social rituals can exert both a patterning and a disruptive force—patterning for the new and disruptive for the old. Thus, although the social setting cannot be considered a part of any controlled experimental design, it can be affected, even by a conference such as this one, which may stimulate greater interest in alternate states of consciousness. And the reverberations of new ideas through the social setting can be treated as one more subjective, changing element when a new experiment is being planned.

This theory of the importance of social learning in the development of individual and social attitudes—the seventh area of agreement among the participants—rests heavily on psychoanalytic thought. During the conference most of the participants agreed—and this was the eighth and final area of agreement—that psychoanalytic theory is the necessary point of departure for the study of alternate states of consciousness, but they did not think it explains adequately the variety of phenomena under consideration. In my view, psychoanalytic theory is in almost complete harmony with the thrust of alternate states of consciousness investigation. It seems to me, indeed, that it was not the theory itself but the misconceptions about it which came to light during the conference that accounted for the participants' criticism. It would be worthwhile, therefore, to consider the most important of these misconceptions and then to indicate the ideas that psychoanalytic theory and the study of alternate states have in common.

Some years ago, when discussing a similar problem with the use of psychoanalytic theory, Mullahy (1948) pointed out how much further one could see when standing on the shoulders of a giant. And he warned the observers not to forget that the sights they were seeing would have been impossible without a boost from Freud. Like many earlier ideas, psychoanalytic notions have been integrated into everyday parlance, both professional and popular. In innumerable living rooms of the nation, certain activities a speaker disagreed with have been labeled "acting out," a term that was intended to describe activities related to the therapy itself; in innumerable articles Freud's early comments about the sexual etiology of neurosis have been presented as if they were his final position. Because Freud lived and wrote over a long period of time and often changed his mind, discrepancies and contradictions appear in his writings that understandably give rise to the kinds of misconceptions that were apparent at the conference.

Many participants thought, for instance, that psychoanalysis takes a sharp, well-defined position concerning what is mature and what childlike and that this includes thinking as well as doing. Comments about

Freud's view of maturity, "to love and to work," implied that meditation would not be considered worthwhile in the psychoanalytic view. Because psychoanalysis was seen as entirely rational, intellectual, and bound to conform to cultural dictates, it was imagined that other, less culturally accepted pursuits would be considered childlike and immature. Yet when the discussion turned to ideas of "higher" consciousness, psychoanalysis was criticized for not providing room for transcending concepts. What these apparently opposing complaints have in common is unwillingness to accept the process orientation of psychoanalysis. In effect, to complain unjustifiably about what goals are put forward and then to complain about the lack of a goal represents the frustration of people who want psychoanalysis to have more specific ideas about "what is right" than the only goal it has—the mastery of self-deceit, or the achievement of self-understanding. The wish for psychoanalysis to have the "right" goals personifies, ironically, the well-known American urge for functionalism, for getting something "fixed." If psychoanalysis does not have a clear-cut goal that is accepted as right, it is felt that psychoanalysis cannot then operate to fix what is wrong. This view is similar to the common dissatisfaction with the psychoanalytic insistence that whatever material a person produces is worthy of study, but where that study takes one is the individual's business, not the psychoanalyst's or the theory's. Seeing psychoanalysis in this light entails no quarrel with any study of consciousness or alternate states of consciousness, and it certainly does not signify any equation between psychoanalytic goals and those of the reigning culture.

At the conference it seemed that psychoanalysis, usually personified by Freud, has set up the ideal straw man. In discussions about reality and dream states the line frequently was drawn between a psychoanalytic view, on the one hand, and an alternate state or Eastern religious view, on the other. For example, Weil asserts (p. 49) that psychoanalysis cannot make sense of dream yoga, and he gives as one reason for this view the idea that the dreamer can consciously manipulate his dream. In *The Interpretation of Dreams* (1900/1938), Freud devotes a section to a discussion of dreams that are produced to satisfy the analyst. Although he believes the process to be more unconscious than conscious, he makes clear his conviction that people can and do manipulate their dreams. Certainly he would agree with Weil that the lunar sphere of the mind is as real as the solar even though most of our conscious attention is given to the solar.

Moreover, the participants lacked sufficient understanding of the admittedly complex relationship in psychoanalytic theory between the

conscious and the unconscious and between primary process and secondary process. Primary-process thinking in psychoanalytic theory is considered unconscious, and only the derivations emerge into consciousness.
However, much secondary-process thinking, such as the choice of defense mechanisms or motivational structures, is unconscious also although
it can become conscious under certain circumstances, such as incipient
disorganization or intense concentration in or out of therapy. Hence,
Weil's point—that some Eastern thought encourages *conscious* manipulation of dreams—does not necessarily clash with psychoanalytic theory
even though dreams are seen as representing "the royal road to the unconscious," which is our most direct contact with primary-process thinking. The reason there is no clash between these two systems is that in our
ability to order dreams for the analyst or for our own enlightenment we
involve secondary-process motivational structures. These structures are
employed unconsciously. It is a sine qua non of psychoanalytic practice
that once a person has experienced the psychoanalytic process it is available to him, when he wants to use it, for the rest of his life, and that one
of the best ways whereby a person alerts himself to use it is through
dream messages to himself. It is in this way that dreaming partakes of
secondary-process thinking. The basic underlying symbolization in the
dream, which contains elements of the primitive underlying primary-
process concerns, may tell the dreamer something about the origin of his
current anxiety. But the secondary-process motivation to dream would
figure in the dream also.

I have (Zinberg, 1975b) demonstrated that in the intense response
to a psychedelic drug an item can change position from primary to
secondary process in the same way as that described for a dream. Those
people who used LSD early and had no significant cultural preparation,
or social learning, experienced the symbolization in their thoughts as a
breakthrough from the depths of the mind, which could be characterized
as primary-process derivatives. When personality structural elements—
that is, the ego—were prepared for the experience and, generally speaking, felt in control of it, the same ideation no longer represented a breakthrough in its meaning to the individual. Thus, the determination of
what signifies an unconscious breakthrough in psychoanalytic theory
depends on other factors. In my opinion, meditation also, even if done
successfully, may mean different things to different individuals who incorporate the experience at different psychological or historical times, as
the interviews with the young Thais showed.

Another striking misconception about the view of mental structures
taken by psychoanalytic theory is the persistent confusion of secondary-

process thinking with conscience. Remarks of the participants indicated that they saw alternate states of consciousness as a means to free them from the prescriptions and proscriptions of contemporary culture and turn them back to an elemental sense of being. It was as if they equated usual state of consciousness rationality with these prescriptions. In the most extreme presentation of the view, even self-awareness itself is a forced self-consciousness concerned principally with judging the individual. The process of selectivity in consciousness becomes a decision about what is "good" to have there and what is "bad." This seemed a part of the syndrome of using psychoanalytic theory as a straw man for the idea that all things cannot be in consciousness at the same time and that the decision about what is permitted to emerge is a functional decision, just as much a part of all Eastern theories of the mind as of psychoanalysis. Focusing attention/awareness in order to avoid distracting stimuli, either internal or external, remains a vital part of any effort to work with the mind, and the decisions about what to exclude are based on the task at hand and not on whether something is considered good or bad.

The same misunderstanding of functionalism, or what Weisman (1965) calls the "existential core of psychoanalysis," appeared in the insistence of some participants that the chief aim of psychoanalysis is to study the past and its hold, not to study how the person works in the present, what one might call his state of being. Certainly modern psychoanalysts, and probably the previous generation as well, while not minimizing the importance of the past and the pressing influence of early psychological structures, have balanced this interest with a full awareness that anyone must come to grips with his existential present, regardless of the past. The caricature of the psychoanalyst mooning with his middle-aged patient over an unloving mother gainsays the reality of the analyst who says, "O.K., so your mother didn't love you. How do you still allow that to dominate your present life?"

Once these misconceptions have been corrected, many of the statements participants made about drug and non-drug alternate states and particularly about alternate states associated with the more meditative disciplines seem very similar to various aspects of psychoanalytic theory.

Both approaches, for example, stress contemplation and introspection. Formal psychoanalysis is still "the most intensive, introspective technique ever devised" (Zinberg, 1965, p. 108). It provides the time—several hours a week for years—for systematic contemplation of one's inner life and its ramifications. The technique discourages action or pure behavior: Analysts say to patients, "We study where these feelings lead us, we don't act on them." In fact, both techniques make every effort to differentiate between two kinds of activity: behavior, or motor activity, and the activity of the mind, which psychoanalysis calls *ego activity*. Psychoanalytic technique requires the patient to lie down, the analyst unseen behind him, just as the meditative techniques aim to minimize the press of stimuli from the external environment and to maximize the awareness of one's inner state of being. In both, the consistent attempt to focus awareness on specific attentional achievements dominates the process. And, although this would not be the conventional way to look at psychoanalysis, I believe that in asking the individual to suspend the usual judging and grading of thoughts and to permit contact with what is there, both meditation and psychoanalysis encourage alternate states of consciousness. Some analysts, Reik (1948), in particular, have referred specifically to these consciousness changes and to the resulting, almost hallucinogenic, imagery.

Both techniques also stress inhibitions. As Elkes put it during the conference, "The brain, too, needs to be able to avoid things." In order to participate actively in both processes it is necessary to develop inhibitions against extraneous external stimuli. Gurus as well as analysts point out that neophytes' interest in external stimuli and their presence or activity interferes with the ability to focus on one's own internal affairs. And, in reverse, dealing with inhibitions against concentrating on oneself, on knowing what one thinks or feels, on emptying one's mind of previous, repetitive attitudes and affects, of all the baggage of everyday, incessant interactions, in order to get into oneself freshly and fully is a principal aim of both techniques. Certainly the means differ. Analyzing the resistance to dealing with the inhibition is very unlike overcoming it by way of a mantra or a series of physical or psychological exercises. Yet for both disciplines the experience of "knowledge" includes an understanding of the inhibitions against acquiring knowledge.

Furthermore, psychoanalysis explicitly develops the notion of perceptual thresholds to explain the process of selecting out stimuli so as to maintain the usual state of consciousness. For the person to come to greater awareness of alternate states of consciousness or the inner life in general, changes must occur in these thresholds, too. Both approaches to the inner life and the possibilities inherent in alternate states of consciousness agree that although all people do experience consciousness changes, such as dreams and hypnogogic states, and are capable of further ventures into alternate states, such changes are not necessarily felicitous for many people. The way to this conclusion varies. Psychoanalysis, on the one hand, is concerned about the stability of the individual and the psychological cost of interfering with the effective functioning of the perceptual and defensive apparatuses. It judges some people to have achieved as effective a fit between their capability and the demands placed on them as is useful in their particular circumstance. The Eastern point of view, on the other hand, is more directly hierarchical. It is best exemplified by that well-known Westerner don Juan, who makes it clear that to become "a man of knowledge" one must be specifically fitted and specially selected (Castaneda, 1968) although he does not specify the criteria for each.

But those who desire or who are chosen to change consciousness must find it reasonable to vary perceptual thresholds so as to experience states that are usually inhibited without losing the ability to "remember" how these thresholds operate in the usual state. Singer has cited the work of Csikzentmihalyi (1974), who identified five elements central to experiencing consciousness change:

1. The merging of action and awareness in sustained, nondistractible concentration on the task at hand;
2. The focusing of attention on a limited stimulus field, excluding intruding stimuli from awareness in a pure involvement devoid of concern with outcome;
3. Self-forgetfulness with heightened awareness of functions and body states related to the involving activity;
4. Skills adequate to meet the environmental demand;
5. Clarity regarding situational cues and appropriate response.

These five principles are basic to getting in closer touch with one's inner life through meditation, trance states, or psychoanalysis.

In psychoanalysis at least, and I suspect in other disciplines as well, there are two phases in the process of changing consciousness. First, there is the merging and focusing of attention/awareness, the self-forgetfulness, and so on, as one free associates with increasing facility and un-self-consciously bares the workings of one's mind. The second phase, which assesses and begins to make sense of the patterns that emerge, is more cognitive, self-conscious, and reintegrative. Obviously, the two phases are not entirely separate, and as one becomes more experienced and more aware, the phases become less and less separate. If focusing attention/awareness with the exclusion of distracting stimuli is the basis of all Eastern mental disciplines, and the purpose of this skill is to bring to the individual a more coherent or integrated sense of being at all times, not just when meditating, the Eastern technique is largely congruent with the two phases of psychoanalysis (Goleman, 1976). The idea that these procedures are antagonistic is seen to be incorrect, and the participants' use of at least some aspects of psychoanalytic theory in their discussions becomes understandable.

In view of this agreement on theory among the participants, as well as the other areas of agreement—the great complexity of the usual state of consciousness, the recognition of alternate states of consciousness as clearly differentiated states, the underlying physiological correlations of subjective experience, the flow of states of consciousness, the need to disrupt or destabilize the usual state of consciousness in order to achieve the alternate state, the capacity to use a variety of research techniques, and the role of social learning—an overview of the conference indicates a bright future for alternate states of consciousness as a field of study and even as a scientific discipline. But if this opinion of alternate states is to be accepted, considerable education of both the professional and the lay community will be necessary. There is no doubt about the popularity of the subject, but there is doubt about its respectability, or perhaps I can say that there *was* doubt before the publication of this and other recent works (Furst, 1976; Weil, 1972). These doubts, as I have already indicated, have arisen from the association of alternate states of consciousness with illicit drug use and with outré Eastern sects. Thus, the cloud of deviancy and disreputability that hangs over the field must be lifted by legitimate scholarly discussion and publication. One would hope, too, as Furst mentions, that some legal changes can be made that will ease experimentation with drugs.

This sort of legal change would not only assist in the accretion of knowledge of the field but also indicate that the whole issue of alternate states of consciousness is not so frightening as it seems to many people. No one at the conference underestimated the extent to which Americans cling to the usual state of consciousness. The cultural fear of de-automatization of the usual state, which is equated with loss of control or madness, correlates well with the national worship of Mom and Country that prevailed before the era of the feminist movement and Vietnam. As all the conference participants wholeheartedly agreed, however, the fear of alternate states of consciousness has been overwhelmingly exaggerated. The study of alternate states both individually and as a scientific endeavor need not be frightening, and it should be very interesting. I hope the reader will find it so.

2

The Marriage of the Sun and Moon

Andrew T. Weil

MANY WRITERS ON CONSCIOUSNESS have pointed out that states very real to those who experience them are frequently difficult to describe or document objectively. As a consequence, a great discrepancy exists between direct, experiential knowledge of alternate states of awareness and theoretical understanding of them. And because individuals in our culture do not readily discuss their experiences of this sort, even the experiential knowledge does not circulate freely.

I must emphasize at the outset my prejudice that the experience of an alternate state of consciousness is intrinsically more valuable than any amount of theorizing about it, unless the theory helps individuals to make more and better use of the states available to them.

Several years ago I published a comprehensive theory of alternate states of consciousness based primarily on personal experience and secondarily on objective experiment and observation (Weil, 1972). (It is worth remembering that the words *experience* and *experiment* come from the same root.) The main points of that theory were the following:

1. Human beings are born with a drive to experience modes of awareness other than the normal waking one; from very young ages, children experiment with techniques to change consciousness.
2. Such experiences are normal. Every person spends large amounts of time in other states, whether he or she retains awareness of them.
3. Alternate states of consciousness form a continuous spectrum

37

from ordinary waking consciousness. For example, there is no qualitative difference between watching a movie (light concentration) and being in a trance (deep concentration).

4. Although specific external triggers, such as drugs, may elicit these states, they do not cause them. Alternate states of consciousness arise from interactions among purely intrapsychic forces. External triggers provide opportunities for people to allow themselves certain experiences that may also be had without the triggers. Thus, a drug-induced state may be essentially the same as one induced by chanting or meditating.

5. It is valuable to learn to enter alternate states deliberately and consciously because such experiences are doorways to fuller use of the nervous system, to the realization of untapped human potential, and to better functioning in the ordinary mode of consciousness.

I wish to discuss the intrapsychic dynamics that lead to the experience of nonordinary consciousness, to comment further on the innate drive to change consciousness, and to speculate on the evolutionary significance of this drive. I proceed by describing and analyzing three experiences that can make people high: direct observation of total eclipses of the sun, ingestion of psychoactive mushrooms, and participation in the ritual of the Indian sweat lodge.

The Eclipse Experience

Persons in the path of a total eclipse of the sun experience dramatic alterations of consciousness if they allow themselves to view the event. Surprisingly, many people who are overtaken by eclipses do not watch them because they are afraid. In primitive societies eclipses signify bad luck of one sort or another. For example, some East African tribes think that the sun becomes sick during an eclipse and puts out evil emanations dangerous to humans and animals. They hide themselves indoors during the period of totality or look away from the sky if they are caught outdoors. In civilized societies this attitude crops up as fear of blindness, and in some medical warnings about the dangers of looking at solar eclipses there is the same idea that the sun emits certain especially dangerous radiation while it is covered by the moon. Accordingly, many eclipse watchers in our society insulate themselves from the experience by using pinhole projection devices and keeping their backs to the sun; others spend the time of totality looking through cameras or instruments instead of at the sky.

In fact, there is no danger in looking directly at the eclipsed sun with the naked eye during the period of full totality when the corona is visible. (Immediately before and after this time, the light from the remaining solar disk is blinding as usual, and protection for the eyes is necessary.) People who do look directly at total eclipses experience strong senses of de-realization as the moon's shadow approaches. Time perception changes greatly, so that the period of totality often seems much shorter than the actual elapsed clock time. In the unique light of the corona, reality becomes dreamlike, and people report unusually intense feelings of detachment. Immediately after the eclipse, euphoria is pronounced among those who have watched, and many persons continue to feel high and energetic for hours.

I have had the good fortune to see two total eclipses of the sun and have interviewed several dozen people at these events (Weil, 1973). Both from my own experiences and from the reports of those interviewed, I have no doubt that the eclipse experience is a powerful alternate state of consciousness qualitatively similar to states induced by psychedelic drugs or by hypnosis. Significantly, several respondents told me immediately after an eclipse that they could remember the period of totality only "as in a dream."

Many persons who have the eclipse experience long to have it again; some chase eclipses all over the world, year after year. The desire for the experience and the fear of it manifested by many others are typical of human ambivalence toward alternate states and the things that trigger them.

Why does a total eclipse of the sun make people high? Possibly the novel light of the corona shakes us out of our usual perceptual framework, enabling us to see our relationship to external reality in a new way. Possibly the exact alignment of earth, moon, and sun has some special and direct effect on brain function. I am afraid that any suggested explanation must be the purest guesswork. There is simply no information about the influence of eclipses on consciousness; in fact, there is no recognition in the literature on alternate states that eclipses are one pathway to them.

In the light of my eclipse experiences I find it most interesting that the esoteric traditions of both the East and the West use images of the conjunction of the sun and the moon to convey information about the potential of the mind. In European alchemy, for example, the "marriage of the sun and moon" is a symbolic description of the work to be accomplished. A similar image is the compounding of gold and silver, the metals that stand for the same principles as the two heavenly bodies. Esoteric alchemy was not merely an exercise of physical transformations of material elements but, more important, a set of coded instructions for self-development that could lead eventually to the gold of enlightenment. Yogic literature talks about electric (solar) and magnetic (lunar) nerve currents in the human body and the need for harmonizing and blending the two. These conceptualizations all point to the existence of two distinct aspects of mind that stand in relation to each other as the sun and moon in the sky. Moreover, the suggestion is clear that the psychological basis of high states is an interchange of energies between the solar and lunar compartments of the mind.

Nearly all commentators have recognized a fundamental dualism in the mind and have relegated different types of mental events to one of two opposite and complementary psychic spaces. There are many names for these two compartments (Ornstein, 1972, 64–67; Deikman, 1971), but there is also high consistency from system to system about their characteristics. That aspect of mind most active in ordinary waking consciousness, which uses intellect as the chief means of making sense of reality and manipulates verbal symbols, is often seen as masculine, right-handed (in the symbolic sense), and day oriented. Complementing it and contrasting with it is the feminine, left-handed, nighttime consciousness: the realm of dreams, intuitions, and nonverbal communication.

It is difficult to find neutral names for these two phases of human consciousness because each set is the property of one special-interest group or another. In the past I have used the terms *conscious* and *unconscious*, but these have particular meanings in psychoanalytic theory, a model I do not find useful in trying to understand alternate states of consciousness. Furthermore, I no longer believe in the aptness of the word *unconscious* to describe the night side of the mind. In the symbolism of the Tarot cards, day consciousness is represented by the Magician, a male figure standing in a gesture of active concentration; he is associated with the color yellow. His complement is the High Priestess, a blue-robed virgin, seated in a receptive pose. These symbols, in their details, are good depictions of the nature and potential of the two phases of mind, but they are part of a larger collection of symbols irrelevant to the present discussion.

Perhaps the most neutral of the symbols available to us are the primal representations of the basic dualism of reality: the sun and the moon. Not only are these heavenly bodies familiar to all of us, they have struck many thinkers as appropriate designations for the masculine and feminine aspects of human consciousness. The moon, especially, represents well the night side of the mind. Indeed, the High Priestess of the Tarot deck is nothing other than the virgin moon goddess who appears in the celestial hierarchies of so many cultures.

I propose, then, to use the terms *solar* and *lunar* to denote the two compartments of human mental activity. Although I am not suggesting any causal relationships between the sun and moon and mental events, I do believe in a tight correlation between the qualities of those bodies and the qualities of the two phases of consciousness. In particular, I would draw attention to the sun's property of overwhelming all other sources of light and radiation when it is above the horizon and the moon's cyclic waxing and waning in intensity. The sun and the moon are symbolic of the mind in the true sense of the word; that is, they not only represent the dualism of consciousness but are actually expressions of that same dualism, which is manifest in the sky as well as the mind. This is an important point: After all, the actual union of the sun and the moon during the moments of a total eclipse does, in fact, make people high.

If the psychological basis of alternate states is some sort of interchange of energies between the solar mind and the lunar mind, what, then, is the situation in ordinary waking awareness? It seems reasonable to compare ordinary consciousness to ordinary daytime. The sun shines in the sky, and the moon is invisible. Many people in our society never see much of the moon. They live in cities, where buildings and artificial light hinder observation of the night sky, and they are indoors or asleep while the moon passes through its cycle. Reasoning by analogy, we may conclude that many people in our society are also relatively unconscious of the lunar forces within themselves. Possibly, the tendency to describe the lunar mind as unconscious indicates how commonly we deny it access to the ordinarily conscious solar mind.

Presumably, two distinct kinds of changes would alter the ordinary condition of the mind. Anything that diminished or focused the intensity of the solar mind might enable it to notice and interact more with the lunar mind. Anything that stimulated the lunar mind might permit it to achieve balance and interact with the solar mind. Various methods of achieving alternate states of consciousness illustrate these complementary approaches.

Psychoactive Mushrooms

Human cultures throughout the world have linked mushrooms with the moon and with water, the feminine or lunar element, as opposed to fire, which is masculine and solar. I have written elsewhere (Weil, 1975) that mushrooms are powerful symbols of lunar forces, again meaning that they actually embody those forces and do not simply represent them. Mushrooms are associated also with death and madness (lunacy), with flights of the soul from the body, with night and magic —in short, with many manifestations of the realm of experience that is normally unconscious in most of us.

Many kinds of mushrooms are capable of triggering alternate states of consciousness. The mushroom experience resembles trips on other hallucinogens but has certain special characteristics. People who eat psychoactive mushrooms often remain very aware of the taste of the fungus throughout the intoxication. Some users feel that taste diffused throughout their bodies. Many persons report visions of mushrooms. Regular users interpret these sensory experiences as indications of the flooding of their bodies and minds with some kind of energy peculiar to mushrooms.

The pharmacology of psychoactive mushrooms is very diverse. Many species owe most of their properties to hallucinogenic indoles (psilocybin and psilocin) that are related to LSD and the tryptamines. Other species (*Amanita muscaria* and *A. pantherina*) contain unusual compounds (ibotenic acid and muscimol) whose effects are not well studied. Still other species (*Gymnopilus spectabilis*, for one) contain substances related to the active principles of kava-kava, the narcotic drink of the South Seas, prepared from the root of a pepper plant. The pharmacology of other active fungi is completely unknown: the hallucinogenic puffballs of Mexico (genus *Lycoperdon*), for example, and the intoxicating tree fungi of Alaska (genus *Fomes*). Each year new information comes to light suggesting that still other species are in use for their effects on the mind, including some varieties of mushroom usually considered poisonous by mycologists. Most mushroom books call the panther fungus (*A. pantherina*) extremely toxic or deadly, yet it is becoming a popular recreational drug in the Pacific Northwest. Interestingly enough, people who accidentally consume it while hunting food mushrooms often wind up hospitalized with severe symptoms, while those who deliberately eat it (usually in higher doses) report little or no sickness and welcome the psychophysical effects (Ott, 1976). It appears that psychoactivity is widespread in the fungal world and that powerful species are universally distributed. In the United States the deliberate use of psychoactive mushrooms to effect major alterations in consciousness is increasing steadily as people learn to recognize the active varieties and try them (Pollock, 1975).

For the past three years I have studied psychoactive mushrooms in Mexico, Colombia, and the United States and have had the opportunity to try a number of species and talk with many experienced users. The lack of any unity in the pharmacology of the mushrooms has prompted me to look elsewhere for a simple explanation of their effects. I have been drawn back to the users' contention that the mushrooms deliver doses of some special sort of energy to the system. In trying to characterize this energy I have found unexpected help in macrobiotic dietetics, which classifies edible mushrooms as "so yin" that they must be eaten with caution. In the Oriental scheme, yin is the primal, dark, receptive, feminine, lunar force that eternally complements and opposes the light, creative, masculine, solar principle of yang. Whenever classifications based on this concept are applied to foods, mushrooms come out way on the yin side.

Because mushrooms do, in fact, grow up during the night and are destroyed by sunlight, because they are intimately connected with water, and because they can cause madness, death, and ecstasy, I think they do give us high doses of yin energy. Furthermore, I think it is reasonable to propose that mushrooms stimulate the lunar sphere of the mind, causing changes in consciousness by intensifying the activity of that sphere so that it comes more into balance with the solar mind.

Here, perhaps, is an explanation of mycophobia—fear of mushrooms—which is so prevalent among human beings. Mycophobia is vastly out of proportion to the actual risk of serious mushroom poisoning. I would guess that it really reflects fear of the darker side of the human mind, that it originates in the solar sphere, and that it is a manifestation of the same uneasiness that expresses itself as fear and ambivalence about drugs, eclipses, and other external objects and events that bring about changes in consciousness by establishing new relationships between the two compartments of the mind.

The Indian Sweat Lodge

Sweat bathing is a common ritual among North American Indians. It is both a hygienic practice and a religious one. As a religious ritual it is an intense experience that produces marked alterations in consciousness.

The sweat lodge is of simple construction: an open framework of willow saplings bent and tied together to form a circular hut perhaps five feet in diameter and three or four feet high. Over this framework are draped animal hides, canvas, or blankets so that the interior is completely dark and insulated. A shallow pit is dug in the earth in the center of the lodge. Participants in the ritual, usually from four to eight depending on the size of the lodge, sit unclothed on the ground. Attendants on the outside fill the pit with red-hot rocks that have been heated in a strong bonfire. The lodge is then sealed up from outside, leaving the participants in darkness and increasing heat.

Among the Sioux, the sweat lodge is consecrated ground on which man contacts the Great Spirit of the Universe. Sprigs of sage are placed among the willow poles, and cedar incense is burned on the hot rocks as the ritual begins. The medicine man in charge of the sweat offers prayers for the efficacy of the ritual and for the well-being of the participants. He passes around the sacred pipe filled with an aromatic mixture of tobacco and red-willow bark. Each person prays with the pipe and smokes it. The leader then begins his chants. When he is finished he starts to throw water on the glowing rocks.

As the water hits the rocks, an explosive hiss seems to shake the lodge. Seconds later a wave of intense heat envelops the body. As soon as this wave passes, the leader adds more water, causing another explosion of sound in the darkness and another wave of intense sensation, stronger than the last. The process continues until no one can stand any more, at which point the shouting of a special phrase (meaning "All my relations!") signals the outside attendants to throw off the coverings of the lodge, leaving it open to the winds. As soon as the participants recover, the lodge is sealed again, and another cycle of praying, smoking, chanting, and scalding takes place. A full ceremony may include four or five cycles of increasing intensity.

When the sweat lodge is used simply to clean the body of surface dirt or to warm the bones in a cold climate, it offers a pleasant experience but one that does not transcend the ordinary. However, when a powerful medicine man conducts a solemn ritual therein, the sweat lodge can provide a life-changing experience.

I was introduced to the sweat lodge by a Sioux medicine man on the Rosebud Reservation in South Dakota. The first time I was in the lodge I could not believe how hot it got. The sensation of live steam was so strong that I thought my skin was on fire, and I quickly learned that I had to keep wiping the sweat off my skin to avoid getting burned. (Water conducts heat to the skin faster than air.) It is possible to get first- or second-degree burns in the sweat lodge, but, curiously enough, one's mental state seems to be the most important determinant of the fate of one's skin. Burning occurs only when you lose contact with the psychic energy of the group and see yourself as an isolated individual trying to defend yourself against the onslaught of heat. With trust and confidence in the medicine man and willingness to abandon yourself to the powers in the sweat lodge, you do not suffer physical damage even though the sensations are as intense as any you have ever felt and the temperature in the lodge is near 100°C for brief periods.

In the sweat lodge one meets and conquers many fears. All the terrors of darkness, noise, fire, and helplessness rise up to challenge the participants in the ritual and are defeated by the collective faith of the group. When the steam explodes from the rocks there is no time for thinking; all mental effort is focused on the wave of heat about to break. Coping with that wave, receiving it, and riding over its crest take full concentration. The reward of perseverance is a terrific high. At the end of a good sweat, people feel euphoric, lifted out of themselves, purged of anxiety and depression, healthy, and full of energy. On coming out of sweat lodges I have felt high in many of the same ways I have felt on using psychedelic drugs. The high lasts an hour or so and gradually gives way to great relaxation and a desire to rest. Increased awareness of one's own strength and a sense of well-being may persist for a long time.

The devices by which the sweat lodge brings about a high seem to me to operate on the solar compartment of the mind. The act of entering the darkness of the lodge in the first place is a symbolic withdrawal from the ordinary world of daylight. The chanting of the medicine man brings about an initial degree of concentration, the prerequisite for many kinds of alternate states. Chanting, whatever its form, is a powerful technique to change consciousness. It seems to work by occupying the ordinary mind that is usually busy thinking and paying attention to multifarious external stimuli. In a similar way the sharp noise of the steam focuses awareness on a specific auditory sensation, increasing the depth of concentration. But it is the intense waves of heat that carry this process to an unusual extreme. There is no question that the experience in the sweat lodge would be horribly painful to someone unprepared for it. Nor is there anything unusual about pain serving as the basis for alterations of consciousness. What is interesting about the sweat lodge is that set and setting encourage the participants to interpret the strong stimulation as good and healthy and that with this set and setting the sensation is one of pain that does not hurt. And what is more, this experience of pain that does not hurt leads to a powerful high in the complete absence of tissue injury.

Non-hurtful pain is well known in hypnosis and other trance states and with the administration of opiates. It is less well known in psychedelic states, but I have seen it occur there often, again leading to highs. Now, it is important to distinguish between the anesthesia of hysterical dissociation and the high experience of non-hurtful pain. A badly wounded soldier on a battlefield may perform heroically, unaware of his injuries. A mother, seeing her child pinned beneath a car, may lift the car unassisted and be unaware that she has suffered crushing fractures of her vertebrae until she learns that the child is all right. In these cases intense emotion leads to a kind of trance state in which a barrier develops between nerve impulses from the body and awareness centers in the higher brain. Real injury has occurred, but the message of it does not make it through to consciousness for some time. By contrast, in the experience of non-hurtful pain full awareness of the body persists. Sensations are perceived as strong but not noxious; no injury results; and one feels energetic and high at the end. It is tempting to invoke something like hysterical dissociation to explain this experience, but that mechanism, although it can account for anesthesia, cannot explain the absence of tissue injury despite stimulation that would certainly cause damage under other circumstances.

I had my first experience of non-hurtful pain under the influence of LSD. I found myself walking barefoot over a stretch of sharp stones near my house that I had never been able to walk on before. I was very aware of the pressure of the stones on my feet, but the sensation was simply strong and neutral. The sensation was so novel that I explored it for some time, running back and forth on the stones and jumping up and down on them. Yet at the end of this experience I had not the slightest marks on the soles of my feet. A few days later, when feeling ordinary, I tried to walk over the stones again but could not repeat my performance. Even a few steps hurt and left marks.

The Sioux sweat lodge, without psychedelics, reinforced my belief in the importance of the phenomenon of non-hurtful pain and motivated me to experiment further. Using LSD and MDA (methylene dioxyamphetamine) I found that under certain circumstances I could interact with fire or hot or sharp objects or receive strong blows on the body but suffer no injury; a high followed from the interaction. The drugs did not automatically confer this immunity from damaging pain but simply made the experience more likely; I still had to be in the right frame of mind. After a number of practice sessions I found that I could reproduce the experience without drugs, especially if I was with others who had had such experiences and we used chanting as a means of producing the necessary state of concentration. I discern the following principles at work in this process:

1. There is a psychophysical state in which powerful sensations that would normally be perceived as painful and cause bodily damage do not hurt and do cause highs.
2. Fear of the stimulus is the greatest obstacle to this experience.
3. The presence of someone who has experienced the state and is not afraid of the stimulus is the greatest facilitator of the experience.
4. A preliminary degree of concentration is necessary for the state to occur. Chanting, drugs, hypnosis, and probably many other techniques can bring about such concentration.
5. Concentration is greatly deepened by the stimulus itself. During the experience of non-hurtful pain, all attention is on the sensations coming from the body, with none on verbal thought. In other words, the activity of the solar mind is highly focused.
6. The high of this state begins during the period of intense stimulation and reaches a maximum after the stimulation ends.

I would like to offer a hypothetical mechanism to explain the experience of pain that does not hurt. A strong stimulus presents the body with a challenge of energy: thermal energy in the case of steam or fire, kinetic energy in the case of a blow. How the body deals with this energy depends on the state of the nervous system when the stimulus arrives. Under certain conditions the peripheral nervous system might be capable of receiving unusually large amounts of physical energy, transmuting them electrochemically, and conducting them away from the periphery to the central nervous system. In the central nervous system, this energy could be discharged through the head in some harmless way or experienced as a high; the peripheral tissues, meanwhile, would be spared any adverse effects.

Such receptivity of the peripheral nervous system could occur only in the absence of interference from above. A state of fear or an effort to defend oneself against the perceived threat of strong stimulation might create a condition of neuromuscular tension that would impair or prevent peripheral nervous receptivity. The energy of the stimulus would then not be able to flow into the nerves directly but would instead spill into the peripheral tissues, causing damage and pain. The experience of pain would then increase neuromuscular tension in a vicious cycle.

In this scheme the hypothesized condition of peripheral nervous receptivity would be a consequence of a particular central state. Specifically, a balanced interchange of energy between the solar and lunar compartments of the mind would permit the central nervous system to enter into the necessary relationship with the peripheral. This interchange might arise through stimulation of the lunar compartment or focusing of the solar compartment, or both.

My interest in the potential of the human nervous system to interact with unusually strong forces has led me to review the literature on fire-walking as practiced throughout much of Asia and in some Western countries, such as Greece. There is much documentation, both written and photographic, of the ability of human beings, under certain circumstances, to walk unprotected on red-hot coals or stones or through bonfires (Leavitt, 1973; Perera, 1971). There has been little scientific study of fire-walking, and generally scientists have sought materialistic explanations of the phenomenon. Some have proposed, not very imaginatively, that Asians have tougher feet than non-Asians or that fire-walkers are simply deceiving Western observers in one way or another. Others have suggested that perspiration forms a thin insulating layer that protects the skin from the heat.

My personal experiences with the sweat lodge make me less inclined to look for simple physical explanations of fire-walking. I note that the presence of experienced fire-walkers is necessary for the success of novices. Usually, participants in fire-walking rituals work themselves up to the main events by long periods of chanting and dancing. Among certain Hindu fire-walkers of Singapore whipping is used to banish fear and deepen concentration; apparently, the blows cause no pain or injury although they are delivered with great force (Babb, 1974). Certain Japanese Buddhist sects perform ritual walks over red-hot coals while chanting silently a particular sutra. I have interviewed several members of one of these sects. They confirm the suppositions that concentration is vital, that a break in concentration (in this case in the rhythm of the chant) leads to burns, and that successful completion of the fire-walk results in a powerful high, marked by euphoria, energy, and new confidence in one's abilities and strengths. All of this leads me to conclude that the true explanation of the ability to walk through fire unharmed lies in a different functioning of the nervous system brought about by a change in relationship between the solar and lunar compartments of the mind.

Research Problems

The greatest difficulty in the scientific study of consciousness today is the gulf between materialistic and nonmaterialistic views of the mind. It is unfortunately true that most neuroscientists are hard-core materialists who cannot believe in the reality of experiences without obvious physical bases. Because we are far from understanding the physical mechanisms of alternate states of consciousness, many scientists who study the brain are able to dismiss the whole field as mystical nonsense. A neurochemist investigating dopamine receptors in the limbic forebrain would have little time for the concept of a solar and a lunar mind that I have used in this chapter, even though the limbic forebrain may turn out to be an important locus of lunar consciousness.

A complementary problem exists with psychiatrists and psychologists who use abstract concepts like id and ego but resist the idea that such concepts must correlate with physiological realities. The early Freudians ostracized Wilhelm Reich chiefly because he insisted that unconscious experiences were recorded in the muscles and could be reached by manipulation of the body as well as the mind. Modern Freudians still are uncomfortable with suggestions that the unconscious is anything but an abstraction. For example, psychoanalysts regard the dream world as essentially unreal, full of symbols to be used in the analytic process but certainly not an actual place available for visiting. Psychoanalysts cannot make sense of the process of dream yoga as practiced by some Tibetan Buddhists and the Senoi people of Malaysia and as taught by don Juan to Carlos Castaneda (1972, pp. 126 ff.), in which the dreamer learns to enter the dream world consciously and eventually to manipulate it. A cornerstone of the present theory of alternate states is that the lunar sphere of the mind is as real as the solar, connected with the activity of real parts of the real brain, unconscious only because we live mostly in our solar minds and direct most of our waking attention there.

If we are to make headway, we must find areas of contact between experiential knowledge of other states and experimental knowledge of the nervous system. Of course, some such efforts are under way. In the past few years, for example, there has been much talk of differential functioning of the left and right cerebral hemispheres and some attempt to equate this anatomical division with the dualism in mind seen by most psychologists of consciousness. In providing common ground on which neuroscientists and psychologists may meet, this work has done a good service. But I am not sure it points us in the right direction.

Although a difference certainly exists between the two hemispheres, particularly in regard to language, I do not believe the two sides of consciousness can be equated with the two halves of the brain. The mistake comes of interpreting too literally the distinction between left and right. The most extreme version of this mistake I have encountered is a system of mind development recommended in certain southern California circles. It consists of binding the right arm in a cast and sling in order to develop the nondominant cerebral hemisphere and thereby the intuitive faculties. "Left" and "right" should be construed as symbolic designations of the two phases of mind. I believe we can correlate these two aspects of consciousness with different brain loci but that we are much more likely to have success in looking for a vertical split than a horizontal one. "Left" to me connotes below and within as opposed to above and without. Thus, I see the natural locus of lunar consciousness as deep brain and brainstem structures as opposed to cortical ones, and I am hopeful that one day we will be able to detect increased activity of the deep centers during experiences of alternate states.

As a physician I am acutely aware of the widespread ignorance of alternate states in my profession, a situation most unfortunate in view of the tremendous implications of these states for medicine. For years, psychiatrists in the Freudian tradition and doctors who look to them for authoritative concepts have dismissed certain common powerful experiences as "oceanic feelings" of no great significance. I am convinced that it is during such episodes that the nervous system is in the special physiological state I have described as the basis of the experience of nonhurtful pain. Very few physicians and psychiatrists know the reality of that experience or its vast significance. Not only is it a natural high of great personal worth and meaning; it also represents a condition of unity between mind and body that may be supremely valuable and logical, appearing unusual only because we have been conditioned to believe that such unity is impossible.

It is the intimate connection between the experience of being high and the dramatic change in physiological response to the environment that leads me to see great evolutionary logic in the strong tendency of human beings to search for ways of changing consciousness. I have written elsewhere about activities of young children that serve to alter consciousness (Weil, 1972, p. 20) and have suggested that these activities are universally present in human cultures, representing an innate drive arising from the structure of the human nervous system. I include such behaviors as the rhythmic rocking of infants who have just learned to sit up, the spinning and whirling of older children, and games of hyperventilation and mutual choking or chest squeezing. I continue to regard these activities as very widespread if not ubiquitous and am amazed that a number of psychiatrists, including some child psychiatrists, have stated publicly that they have never seen children engage in them. Of course, children do not perform these behaviors in the offices of psychiatrists and often keep this sort of play secret from grown-ups. Recently, a colleague of mine who is in grade school administered a questionnaire about spinning to her classmates and to other schoolchildren. A very high percentage of respondents admitted to being spinners, and some were quite eloquent as to what they liked about the activity. Here are the statements of some ten-year-olds: "It gets you dizzy and it makes you feel good." "It's like you've gone crazy." "It's like I'm flying." "I like the floating feeling." "I feel energy going around my body." "It's just fun." Clearly, these children are experiencing changes in consciousness.

I hope it will be possible to gather more statistical data on the occurrence of these behaviors and to look for correlations with other variables. Are the children who spin better daydreamers? Will they as adults be most likely to experiment with psychoactive drugs? Are they more creative than non-spinners? It would be interesting and useful to know the answers to these questions.

We live in an age favorable to the investigation of our subject. In many past ages, manifestations of lunar consciousness were regarded as nonexistent or evil. Persons who tried to draw attention to their reality and importance were shouted down or driven out of respectable intellectual circles. Today, there is increasing acceptance of the lunar side of human nature and the beginnings of willingness to try to integrate that half of consciousness with the solar. This process is not without its dangers. The lunar sphere, though it is a place of great power and the doorway to full realization of the potential of the nervous system, must not be allowed to overwhelm the solar mind. The lunar world is also the world of illusion, chaos, and madness. For just that reason, our ordinary minds prefer not to have much to do with it. Denied the modifying influence of lunar activity, our ordinary minds are sterile; without the directing and guiding function of solar consciousness, the lunar mind is productive of disorder, violence, and insanity.

When people who have lived exclusively in ordinary consciousness begin to contact the mind that is below and within, whether by drugs or meditation or the yoga of dreams or whatever, they may tend to reject rational intellect and other functions of the solar mind in favor of the visions they discover. It is important for students of consciousness, in their own lives and in their work, to demonstrate that the goal is to open the channels between the two minds and to encourage back-and-forth flow between the two without stifling either one. In this way we can become truly whole and healthy and begin to see that the distinctions we have made between mind and body, self and not-self, man and nature are merely external projections of an unnatural separation we have come to accept within ourselves.

3

"High States" in Culture-Historical Perspective

Peter T. Furst

BY WAY OF INTRODUCTION to what is intended as a cross-cultural and culture-historical contribution to the topic of alternate states of consciousness, let me briefly describe a somewhat drastic Aztec technique of attaining ritual "high states" that did not specifically require drinking, eating, or smoking one of the many botanical hallucinogens in the extensive psychedelic pharmacopoeia available to the peoples of Mesoamerica. Even so, at least one of these substances did play a part in the particular method I shall discuss.

The great sixteenth-century chronicler Fray Diego Durán left us a vivid description of a highly toxic ointment or pitch with which Aztec priests of the god Tezcatlipoca, Smoking Mirror, smeared their bodies for the purpose of triggering the proper mental state for communication with the deity and other supernaturals. Tezcatlipoca was considered to be a great transformer and sorcerer, and Durán suggested that it was the purpose of the magic ointment to transform one who used it on his own body into a "wizard" and "demon," the latter being the term usually applied by the pious Spaniards to the native deities. Known as *teotlacualli*, divine food, the magic ointment included "poisonous beasts, such as spiders, scorpions, centipedes, lizards, vipers, and others" (1971, p. 115) that were collected in large numbers by young boys and kept in the *calmecac*, the school for training Aztecs in priestly duties.

This was the divine food with which the priests, ministers of the temples, and especially those with whom we are dealing, smeared themselves in ancient times. They took all these poisonous animals and burned them in the

53

divine brazier which stood in the temple. After these had been burned, the ashes were placed within certain mortars, together with a great deal of tobacco; this herb is used by the Indians to relieve the body so as to calm the pains of toil. In this it is similar to Spanish henbane, which, when mixed with lime, loses its poisonous qualities, though it still causes faintness and is harmful to the stomach. This herb, then, was placed in the mortars together with scorpions, live spiders, and centipedes, and there they were ground, producing a diabolical, stinking, deadly ointment. After these had been crushed, a ground seed called *ololiuhqui* was added, which the natives apply to their bodies and drink to see visions. It is a drink which has inebriating effects. To all this were added hairy black worms, their hair filled with venom, injuring those who touch them. Everything was mixed with soot and was poured into bowls and gourds. Then it was placed before the god as divine food. How can one doubt that the men smeared with this pitch become wizards or demons, capable of seeing and speaking to the devil himself, since the ointment had been prepared for that purpose? (Durán, 1971, pp. 115–116)

According to Durán, the Aztec priests painted themselves with this toxic mixture so that rendered unafraid by its magic powers they could visit dark caves and "somber, fearful cliffs" (p. 116). They also employed the same mixture in shamanic divinatory curing rites, applying it to the affected parts of the patient's body to deaden pain.

The tobacco (Aztec *piciétl*) that figured in the priestly ointment was *Nicotiana rustica,* a hybrid domesticate of South American origin that enjoyed—as it still does—wide distribution and ritual use among aboriginal Americans and is several times richer in nicotine than our modern cigarette and pipe tobaccos. There is ample ethnohistorical evidence that Mexican Indian shamans made use of the tobacco's potent qualities to trigger high states comparable to those induced by other hallucinogenic species, though apparently usually alongside other psychoactive plants. In fact, so far as we know, the only Indians to employ tobacco in the manner of a hallucinogen to the exclusion of all other species are the Venezuelan Warao of the Orinoco Delta, whose shamans induce ecstatic trances by saturating themselves with the smoke of as many as two dozen two-foot-long "cigars" in the course of a single séance (Wilbert, 1972).

Ololiuhqui, also listed by Durán as an essential ingredient of *teotlacualli,* is the name the Aztecs gave to the potent psychotomimetic seeds of the white-flowered morning glory *Rivea corymbosa,* among the most sacred of the hallucinogenic plants used by the peoples of prehispanic Mesoamerica. Along with the seeds of at least one other morning glory (the violet-colored *Ipomoea violacea*), *ololuc,* as it is known today, is still ritually employed by some Mexican Indian populations, mainly by shamans or *curanderos* for the purpose of divinatory curing. In some instances only the curer takes the morning glory infusion (which, as Hofmann, the discoverer of lysergic acid diethylamide, determined in 1960, is rich in lysergic acid derivatives); in others, only the patient; occasionally, both curer and patient imbibe the hallucinogenic drink in order to discover together the supernatural cause of the illness.

At least one of the poisonous spiders in the divine ointment must have been the species the Aztecs called *tzintlatlauqui*, whose description by Durán's contemporary Fray Bernardino de Sahagún (1963, Vol. 11, p. 88), as a small, round, jet-black creature with a "chili-red" abdomen suggests that it was the black widow, *Latrodectus mactans.* This spider has a remarkable distribution, from Canada to Tierra del Fuego, and a well-deserved reputation for the potency of its neurotoxic poison, which Aztec physicians employed as a therapeutic salve for gout as well as pustules. Fortunately, the black widow is shy and rarely bites without extreme provocation—but when she does, the reaction can be severe.

A much greater public menace must have been posed—as it still is—by the venomous scorpions whose neurotoxic poison also was added to the priestly ointment. Presumably the principal species so employed was the so-called Durango variety, *Centruroides sculpturatus,* as well as its close cousin and rival in extreme toxicity, *C. gertschi.* Both species are small, slender, and rather innocent in appearance, certainly much more so than many other species that look far more dramatic but are in fact relatively harmless. If not counteracted in time, *Centruroides* poison can be fatal, especially to children, and in any event the suffering from its sting is considerable. Again, scorpion poison was utilized by Aztec physicians as an external medicine, if not always to assist in crossing the uncertain boundary between alternate states of consciousness.

In the absence of more detailed description we can only guess at the other venomous ingredients of *teotlacualli.* Several species of poisonous snakes were available, as were centipedes, caterpillars, and the large, sluggish, but very venomous beaded lizard, *Heloderma horridum,* close relative of the Gila monster *(Heloderma suspectum).* In any event, to answer Durán's question with a question, who indeed could doubt the power of such a fearsome mixture on the mind as well as the body? This is precisely why I have dwelt in such detail on Durán's "divine food" in relation to alternate states of consciousness, or high states: Covering large areas of skin for prolonged periods, containing not only venoms that would be deadly if they entered the bloodstream directly but also potent psychochemicals of botanical origin, *teotlacualli* at the very least would have caused serious skin reactions, if it were not actually absorbed to some degree into the system. In either event, it could well have had drastic effects on the body's metabolism, including some alteration in the user's state of consciousness—even if he did not actually intoxicate himself at the same time with morning glory infusions, as Aztec priests were wont to do on sacred occasions.

The point is this: Notwithstanding the great number of hallucinogenic plants known to the inhabitants of pre-conquest Mesoamerica and South America and their descendants in the colonial and modern eras, the physical assimilation of botanical intoxicants through the mouth, nostrils, or rectum (by means of enemas), though obviously ancient and widespread, was by no means the only technique for triggering high or ecstatic states or divinatory trances. Even extremely painful physical ordeals, reminiscent of Plains Indian Sun Dance rites, were practiced not merely to draw blood to offer to the gods (though that was clearly one reason for self-mutilation rituals) but also to seek visions. And in South America, some tribes had, and have, poison ordeals in which hunters pursue purification and revelatory encounters with other worldly beings by inoculating themselves with enormously powerful frog and toad venoms.

Of these other pathways to alternate states,[1] more later. For the moment I want to concentrate on the better known methods of utilizing hallucinogenic plants, whose proliferation among New World peoples, at least from Mexico south, surely bears explaining.

Twentieth-Century Perspectives

The modern study of the cultural use of hallucinogens may be traced to Hofmann's identification of LSD–25 in 1948. Almost coincident with the discovery of LSD was the discovery in rural southern Mexico that a cult of divine psychedelic mushrooms very much like cults described in sixteenth- and seventeenth-century colonial sources had survived among the Indians through the more than four centuries since the

---

[1] Although I use Zinberg's (1975b) term *alternate state of consciousness* in preference to *altered state of consciousness,* I agree with Tart (1972a) that these constitute "a qualitative alteration in the overall pattern of mental functioning, such that the experiencer feels his consciousness is radically different from the way it functions normally" (p. 1).

conquest. The rediscovery and systematic investigation of the mush-room cult, particularly by R. G. Wasson, began in the mid-1950s. By then a considerable number of native psychotropic species had been securely classified. And, in time, their chemical properties were identi-fied by Hofmann. Another milestone was the identification by Schultes (1941) of the seeds of morning glories as the sacred Aztec hallucinogen *ololiuhqui;* Hofmann, nearly twenty years later, found that the active principles of the seeds are closely related to those of lysergic acid derivatives. Still another milestone would have to be the determination by R. G. Wasson (1968), in a remarkable piece of multidisciplinary scholarship, that the mysterious plant deity Soma of the Rig Veda could have been none other than the famous "magic mushroom" of Eurasian folklore, the psychotropic fly agaric, *Amanita muscaria.*

These and other developments in ethnology, ethnobotany, and chemistry bear a functional relationship to the realization over the past several years that the most important botanical hallucinogens are struc-turally related to biologically active compounds that occur naturally in the mammalian brain. For example, psilocybin and the psychoactive alkaloids in morning glory seeds are indole-tryptamine derivatives simi-lar in chemical structure to serotonin (5-hydroxytryptamine); mes-caline is related to noradrenaline. In addition, noradrenaline in the brain has been found to correspond structurally to caffeic acid, which is de-rived from chemicals found in several plant sources, including coffee beans and potatoes. Chemical systems active in the human brain, then, are now known to be close kin to growth-promoting substances in plants, including a number that are powerfully psychoactive. This is a discovery of no mean evolutionary as well as pharmacological implica-tions.

A DIALOGUE BETWEEN TWO SCHOLARS

Of great importance to students of hallucinogen use in the New World is a "conversation across the disciplines" between an ethnobota-nist, the same Richard Evans Schultes who on a field trip in Oaxaca ended a long-standing dispute over the botanical identity of *ololiuhqui* (and, incidentally, was the first to identify some of the sacred mush-rooms used by Oaxacan Indians), and an anthropologist, Weston La Barre, a long-time student of shamanism and of religious movements born out of profound crisis situations. Their dialogue (La Barre, 1970) helped place the whole psychedelic phenomenon in a broad culture-his-torical and ideological framework.

Schultes and La Barre were hardly strangers to the problem or, for that matter, to each other. The former has long been the foremost authority on New World hallucinogens; the latter is a prominent scholar in the anthropology and psychology of religion, author of, among other works, *The Peyote Cult* (1938/1974), a classic study of the Native American Church, or "peyote religion."

It was, in fact, peyote, *Lophophora williamsii*, the spineless, bitter-tasting, hallucinogenic cactus first described as a sacred plant of Indian ritual by the sixteenth-century Spaniards and, beginning in the nine-teenth century, the sacrament of the syncretistic pan–North American Indian religion, that originally brought them together: In 1938 La Barre, a doctoral candidate in anthropology, invited Schultes, then a senior in biology, to join him in field research on the nature and culture of *Lophophora williamsii*. La Barre incorporated their findings into his doctoral thesis and *The Peyote Cult* (1938/1974); for Schultes this experience led via Mexico and his classic study of *ololiuhqui* (1941) to a lifelong commitment to ethnobotany, especially the indigenous New World hallucinogens.

In 1970, La Barre published a paper entitled "Old and New World Narcotics: A Statistical Question and an Ethnological Reply," which sought to account in terms of culture history for the astonishing pro-liferation of sacred hallucinogens among Indian tribes in the Americas. The "statistical question" had been Schultes': How, he had written, is one to explain the striking discrepancy between the great number of these plants known to the original Americans, who had discovered and utilized, sometimes in very complex pharmacological combinations, eighty to a hundred different hallucinogenic species, and the much smaller number—no more than eight or ten—known historically to have been employed in the Old World? From a strictly botanical viewpoint, said Schultes, one would have expected the reverse to be true: The Old World has a much greater land mass than the New; its flora is at least as rich and varied and contains as many potential hallucinogens; hu-manity or proto-humanity originated and has lived in the Old World for millions of years, as against at most a few tens of thousands in the Americas, and therefore had immeasurably longer to explore the en-vironment and experiment with different species. Given these circum-stances, Schultes concluded, the answer must be cultural.

Exactly, replied La Barre. American Indian interest in hallucino-genic plants, he argued, was tied directly to the survival in the New World of an essentially Paleo-Mesolithic Eurasiatic shamanism, which the big-game-hunting and food-collecting ancestors of the American Indians carried with them out of northeastern Asia.

Now, one of the cornerstones of shamanism is ecstasis and transformation—the ability of the shaman in ecstatic trances to assume other forms and to project his soul beyond his body into the company of the spirits of animals, the dead, the gods, and the other supernatural beings that, in indigenous cosmologies, populate the otherworlds as well as the natural environment. That being the case, La Barre contended, the earliest Americans, as well as their descendants, were, so to speak, "culturally programmed" for a conscious exploration of the environment in search of means by which to attain that desired state.

It was La Barre's (1970) hypothesis, then, (a) that the magico-religious use of psychoactive plants by New World Indians represents a survival from a very ancient Paleo-Mesolithic shamanistic substratum and that its linear ancestor is likely to have been an archaic form of the shamanistic Eurasiatic fly agaric cults that survived into the present century at least in Siberia; and (b) that while profound socioeconomic and religious transformations brought about the eradication of ecstatic shamanism and knowledge of intoxicating mushrooms and other psychotropic plants over most of Eurasia, a very different set of historical and cultural circumstances favored their survival and elaboration in the New World. These insights, to which R. G. Wasson's work on the sacred fly agaric of Eurasia and on the Mesoamerican mushroom cults made a fundamental contribution, have since been enlarged.

La Barre's hypothesis is so fundamental to understanding the traditional botanical hallucinogens that it will be useful to spell out his insights in somewhat greater detail, especially inasmuch as recent developments in the dating of archeological remains bear directly and decisively on his hypothesis and the related suggestions of such scholars as Wasson and Schultes.

The First Americans

American Indians are descended from small Paleo-Asiatic hunting and food-gathering bands that trickled into the then uninhabited New World in the late Upper Paleolithic and in the Mesolithic across the 1300-mile land bridge connecting present-day Siberia and Alaska. Most scholars date the oldest migrations to 40,000 or 50,000 years ago; the last major overland movements before the melting of the glaciers and the corresponding 200- or 300-foot rise in sea level that inundated the land passage, at the same time opening ice-free corridors for southward movement, are dated to 12,000 or 15,000 years ago.

There is an abundance of early radiocarbon dates from Paleo-Indian hunting and occupation sites in North and South America that lie somewhere along a continuum from ca. 10,000 to ca. 30,000 years ago. Nevertheless, some of the oldest age determinations are highly controversial. What we can say with certainty is that more than 12,000 years ago there were people virtually everywhere in the New World. We know also that these ancestors of the modern Indians sustained themselves with Pleistocene big game, such as mammoth, mastodon, giant sloth, camel, and horse, as well as with smaller animals and wild plant foods, and that their technology and general adaptations resembled by and large those of their contemporaries in comparable environments in Eurasia.

Unfortunately, ecology and adaptation tend often to be used—especially by the cultural-materialist school of American anthropology—in the narrow sense of economics and technology, in relation to the "energy potential" of a given environment. In fact, adaptation has its ideological component, just as the environment not only comprises observable or touchable phenomena such as plants, animals, and minerals but also includes manifold phenomena that for all their ordinary invisibility may nonetheless be perceived by a given society as very real. As often as not, these nonordinary phenomena and the way they are integrated into the cultural system determine particular behaviors far more precisely than material facts or physical needs. Why else would a South American Indian tribe, to cite only one example from the "primitive" world, prefer protein starvation to the killing and eating of the tapir, of which there is an abundance in the natural environment but which must not be hunted because the people consider it to be their ancestor? In other words, whatever their level of technological complexity, we can assume that the first Americans moved in, and acted reciprocally with, an ideational universe no less than the physical one, presumably with no sharper a dividing line between these two essential planes of existence than one discerns today in the few surviving hunting cultures and other still functioning traditional systems. It is probably not too much to say that some form of mysticism or religion has always been a fundamental aspect of the human condition.

But the first Americans were hardly primitive. On the contrary, what little early skeletal material we have shows them to have been thoroughly modern *Homo sapiens*, ranging in physical type from Asiatic Caucasoid (an archaic type represented, before they became mixed with the Japanese, by such peoples as the Ainu of Hokkaido, among others) to nonspecialized Mongoloid and generally resembling modern Indian populations. The direct ancestors of the American Indians, then, were not only biologically but also mentally the product of hundreds of thousands of years of human evolution in Asia to a modern type and therefore can be assumed to have shared with other Asiatic populations aspects of religion originating in and adapted to their lifeway as hunters of game and collectors of wild vegetable foods—some for the stomach, some for the mind.

Shamanism

As we know from ethnology, the symbolic systems, or religions, of hunting peoples everywhere are essentially shamanistic, sharing so many basic features over time and space as to suggest common historical and psychological origins. At the center of shamanistic religions stand the personality of the shaman and the ecstatic trance experience—the proto-typical altered state of consciousness—that is uniquely his in his crucial role as diviner, seer, magician, poet, singer, artist, prophet of game and weather, keeper of the traditions, and healer of bodily and spiritual ills. With his spirit helpers or familiars, the shaman is preeminently guardian of the physical and psychic equilibrium of his group, for whom he inter-cedes in personal confrontation with the supernatural forces of the upperworld and underworld, to whose mystical geography he became privy during his initiatory crisis, training, and ecstatic trance. An illness through which the shaman receives his call—often, though not always, in adolescence—is virtually universal; as a rule such illness is curable only when its cause has been divined and the candidate has agreed to follow the supernatural behest to become a shaman.

Often, the shaman's ecstatic dream has involved the use of some hallucinogenic plant believed to contain a supernatural transforming power over and above the life force or "soul stuff" that in animistic-shamanistic religious systems inhabits all natural phenomena, including those we would classify inanimate. As mentioned earlier, American In-dians—especially those from Mexico south—knew of and employed between eighty and a hundred different psychoactive species. Frequently, more than one of these substances figures in initiatory purification and trance. So, for example, during training, neophyte shamans of many Amazonian tribes are given repeated infusions (often through the nostrils) of *Nicotiana rustica*, having first starved themselves over many weeks to near-skeletal state. This tobacco is in itself sufficiently potent to induce a trance state. Amazonian tribes usually follow the tobacco infusion with hallucinogenic snuff made from the seeds of the *Anadanenthera peregrina* tree or the bark of *Virola* or with the powerful psychoactive drink widely known as *yajé* or *ayahuasca* (*Banisteriopsis caapi*).

There is no question that shamanism has great antiquity: Archeological evidence suggests that something very like the shamanistic beliefs of contemporary hunter-gatherers was present among Neanderthal man in Europe and central Asia more than 50,000 years ago. Moreover, the numerous correspondences between shamanistic beliefs and techniques all over the world have often been cited as evidence for common historical origins in a very ancient substratum. And even if we were to reject the historical explanation in favor of a bio-psychological one (that is, similar shamanistic beliefs and behaviors in the prescientific world can be explained by the worldwide sameness of the human psyche), we would still end up with the same sort of time depth, if not a greater one, since presumably the highest primates have been searching for ways to explain their universe and themselves in relation to it since the dawn of self-consciousness. It is at least possible, though not provable, that the practice of shamanism as an "archaic technique of ecstasy," to use Eliade's (1964) classic definition, may have involved for hundreds of thousands of years the psychedelic potential of the natural environment. This is the more likely in that the reindeer, with which man, initially as hunter and then as herder, has lived in an intimate relationship for tens of millennia, has itself a certain intriguing relationship with the hallucinogenic fly agaric mushroom, even to the point of inebriation (R. G. Wasson, 1972), a phenomenon that could hardly have failed to impress the Paleo-Eurasiatic peoples of long ago as much as it has impressed recent Siberian tribesmen. The latter have been described by travelers as deliberately tracking, killing, and eating mushroom-intoxicated reindeer not because such animals were easier to catch but because they were thought to be imbued with the kinds of transformational powers shamans assimilate by eating the sacred psychoactive fungus (cf. R. G. Wasson, 1968). One might speculate, in fact, that the reindeer's mystic function as the Siberian shaman's "celestial mount" carrying him to other worlds arose from the observed relationship between this animal and the hallucinogenic mushroom and that the reindeer disguises and antlers found on horses in the frozen tombs of Scythian nobles in Siberia also reflect this ancient connection.

I should add here that those of us who have studied the shamanistic use of hallucinogenic plants cross-culturally and historically have not been able to agree with the suggestion that the use of psychochemicals to attain the ecstatic trance may be a late development in shamanism, representing a degeneration of archaic techniques (Eliade, 1964, p. 477). On the other hand, Eliade is absolutely right that the use of psychoactive drugs was encouraged by the quest for magical inner heat (a precondition well known from Siberian shamanism) leading to trance and that intoxication was equivalent to death: "The intoxicated person left his body, acquired the condition of ghosts and spirits. Mystical ecstasy being assimilated to a temporary 'death' or to leaving the body, all intoxications that produced the same result were given a place among the techniques of ecstasy" (p. 477). Elsewhere he suggests another reason why psychoactive drugs might have become part of shamanic techniques of ecstasy: Arctic shamans, like other inhabitants of the extreme Northern Hemisphere, are subject to an illness known as "arctic hysteria," which in ordinary folk can manifest itself as mental illness but which shamans have learned to control and utilize to trigger the characteristic shamanic trance state. "In the sub-Arctic," Eliade (1964) writes, "the shaman, no longer the victim of cosmic oppression, does not spontaneously obtain real trance and is obliged to induce semi-trance with the help of narcotics or to mime the journey of the soul in dramatic form" (p. 24).

However, the subarctic was settled by Paleolithic peoples with shamanistic religions millennia before any of them could have ventured on any permanent basis into the farthest north. The best estimates are that the ancestors of arctic peoples did not move into their eventual homeland until ca. 6000 B.C., if that early; in any event, survival in the rigorous northernmost environment would have been difficult until well after the characteristically Mesolithic technology of the recent Eskimos had been developed. Thus, the channeling of arctic hysteria into shamanistic trance states was probably also a relatively late phenomenon of shamanism, other techniques of attaining the ecstatic state preceding it by many thousands of years. Also, we must not forget that arctic shamans did not have available to them the many psychoactive or intoxicating plants in which the temperate and tropic regions of the world abound; fermenting wild berries or drinking the fermented stomach centers of a freshly killed browsing polar bear (as some Eskimos are reported to do) would have been virtually the only techniques of intoxication available to them until very recently. And although, subjectively, alcohol intoxication may serve related purposes in some cultures, objectively, fermented or even distilled liquors are of a very different order from hallucinogens as a means for placing oneself in the mental state considered essential for proper shamanizing. In any event, his scholarly expertise in the field of shamanism notwithstanding, on the issue of the spontaneous versus the drug-induced ecstatic state Eliade is probably wrong.

Although they must have had ingenious means of surviving the rigors of the arctic environment, comparable to those of the more recent Eskimos and other Northern peoples, the Upper Paleolithic and Mesolithic migrants from northeastern Asia might rightly be regarded as primitive on the basis of their technology alone. But we should not fall into the common error of equating technological complexity with intellectual capacity. On the contrary, when studied in depth, the intellectual cultures of some of the materially least complex peoples—e.g., the remnants of the Bushman people of the Kalahari Desert, Australian aborigines, the traditional Eskimos, tropical forest Indian hunter-gatherers, or the pre-agricultural aboriginal peoples of California—have been found to rival in metaphysical complexity and poetic imagery some of the world's great institutionalized religions. Besides, as Schultes and others have pointed out, the most primitive of incipient cultivators or food-gatherers of South America, for example, have turned out to possess sophisticated and effective traditional systems of classifying nature, and some of them long ago discovered how to prepare complex psychopharmacological and therapeutic compounds that became available to the industrialized world only after the rise of modern biochemistry (cf. Schultes, 1967, pp. 33-57).

Old World Bases of New World Religions

It goes without saying that no system, no matter how conservative —and religion is extraordinarily so—is static, and much of what we find in the religions of Indian America was obviously elaborated in situ over a long time, in the context of ongoing adaptation to changing relationships with the environment. So I do not mean to imply that American Indian religions are Asian or that they have not undergone considerable change from their ancestral forms. Nevertheless, there are demonstrably so many similarities between the core elements of the religions of the aboriginal New World and those of Asia that at least in their foundations the symbolic systems of American Indians were probably already present in the ideational world of the original immigrants from northeastern Asia. This explanation accounts more economically for parallels between them than the hypothesis of transpacific contact and the diffusion of cultural elements from the Old World to the New in later times, although such contact, and possibly even actual Asiatic influences, cannot be ruled out.

Be that as it may, the foundation of American Indian religion, and its dependent concepts and behaviors in such important areas as the etiology of disease and curing, is unquestionably shamanistic. They include numerous concepts, recognizable even in the highly structured cosmology and rituals of hierarchic civilizations (e.g., the Aztec, among them): the separability of the soul from the body during life (e.g., by soul loss, by straying during sleep, or by rape or abduction, or the soul's deliberate projection beyond the body, as by shamans in ecstatic states); shamanic flight; the initiatory ecstatic experience, especially of shamans, and "sickness vocation" for the latter and sometimes also for other kinds of curers on the "sub-shamanic" level (e.g., midwives and bonesetters in contemporary highland Guatemala and Mexico); restitution of life or rebirth of man or animal from the individual's bones; the classification of all phenomena, including those we would classify as without life, as animate; supernatural causes and cures of illness; different levels of the universe with their respective spirit rulers and the need for feeding these on spirit food; the qualitative equivalence of different life forms; man-animal transformation (especially, but not exclusively, by religious specialists); transformation rather than creation ex nihilo to explain the origin of different life forms; animal spirit helpers, alter egos, and guardians; supernatural masters or mistresses of animals and plants; and the acquisition of supernatural or "medicine" power from an outside source. With the concept of transformation so prominent in these traditional systems, it is not difficult to see why plants capable of transforming or radically altering consciousness have come to stand at the center of religions over considerable areas.

Divergence Between New World and Old World Religions

Now, as La Barre's hypothesis was elaborated, while Asia and Europe formerly shared in a shamanistic world view, the Neolithic revolution and subsequent fundamental socioeconomic and ideological developments, often cataclysmic in nature, long ago brought about fundamental changes in the old religions or even suppressed them (although traces of shamanism can here and there still be discerned in the institutionalized churches). In the New World, by contrast, the ancestral lifeway of hunting and food-gathering and the religious beliefs and rituals adapted to this lifeway persisted in time and space to a far greater extent than in the Old. Even in the agricultural religions of the great civilizations that flourished in Mesoamerica and the Andes, the fundamental shamanic ideology was much better preserved, just as wild foods continued to play an important role in the diet of settled farming peoples.

Indeed, the two situations are really not even comparable. There are many historical reasons for this difference, but one that should be stressed is that before the European discovery and conquest the New World as a whole did not know the fanaticism that is the unfortunate hallmark of some of the major Old World religions, especially Christianity, which massively transformed the areas in which it took hold by zealously eradicating or attempting to eliminate all traces of older belief and ritual. That this effort was not always successful is evident in Mesoamerica and elsewhere in the New World, where for over 450 years the Church Militant has failed to obliterate a considerable body of traditional lore and customs, particularly the use of the sacred hallucinogens. In marked contrast to the behavior of the church of the *conquistadores*, it was generally characteristic even of the stratified, militaristic, and expansionist Indian civilizations that conquest by one group of another, if it affected religion at all, typically resulted in accretion or synthesis rather than persecution, suppression, and forcible conversion. The latter blessings of civilized life had to await the coming of the Europeans.

I do not mean to idealize the pre-European situation as regards religion. Certainly there were aspects of such religions as that of the Aztecs, with its emphasis on human sacrifice to sustain the gods must at times have seemed more burdensome than beneficial—if not to the believers themselves at least to subject peoples. Nevertheless, most American Indians, from north to south and through all prehistory, seem to have valued above all freedom for each individual to determine his own relationship to the unseen forces of the universe. In many cases this process included personal confrontation in the ecstatic trance with the supernatural forces, often with the aid of plants to which mystical powers were ascribed. Significantly, there is no evidence that this ancient situation was fundamentally affected even by the rise of prehispanic political and religious bureaucracies, nor that it ever occurred to these bureaucracies to exercise police power over the individual's right to transform his consciousness. Early colonial sources on central Mexico certainly agree that use of the sacred hallucinogenic plants—from tobacco and peyote to mushrooms and morning glory seeds—permeated the whole pre-European religious structure, from the highest priests in the Aztec capital, Tenochtitlan, to the lowliest village curers. For obvious reasons, it was the latter who after the conquest were able effectively to conceal and to preserve the hallucinogenic pharmacopoeia and a surprisingly large body of other sacred traditions.

The fact that high states were central to much of aboriginal American Indian religion and have remained so where traditional systems have survived, even in truncated form, is especially noteworthy in view of Weil's (1972, p. 17) proposal that "the desire to alter consciousness periodically is an innate, normal drive analogous to hunger or the sexual drive." Although drugs are only one means of satisfying this drive, according to Weil, it is nevertheless this inborn biological (as opposed to socioculturally conditioned) need of the psyche for periods of nonordinary consciousness that accounts for the nearly universal use of intoxicants.

Although Weil makes a persuasive cross-cultural case, his argument that the desire for alternate states of consciousness is embedded in the neurophysiological structure of the brain must for the present rest on circumstantial evidence, strong though this is. On the other hand, La Barre's (1970) proposition that the earliest Americans probably brought their fascination for the psychedelic flora with them from their Asian homeland, as a function of ecstatic visionary shamanism, now has strong support from prehistoric archeology. (La Barre's and Weil's are not, needless to say, mutually exclusive hypotheses but complement each other.)

Archeological Evidence on Hallucinogen Use in the New World

Evidence for the great antiquity of the Amerindian hallucinogenic complex concerns one of the few physiologically hazardous hallucinogens known to have been employed by New World peoples. This is the so-called mescal bean, a misnomer since it has nothing to do with mescal, a distilled Mexican liquor produced from a species of agave, but is the red, beanlike seed of *Sophora secundiflora*, a leguminous flowering shrub native to Texas and northern Mexico. Like *Genista canariensis*, a nine-teenth-century import from the Canary Islands whose small, yellow flowers are now ritually smoked by Yaqui shamans in northern Mexico (Schultes, 1972, p. 51), *Sophora* seeds contain a highly toxic quinolizi-dine alkaloid called cytisine. In high doses cytisine is capable of causing nausea, convulsions, hallucinations, and even death from respiratory failure.

Notwithstanding these obvious dangers, *Sophora* seems to be the oldest and longest lived New World hallucinogen; at least it is the earliest for which we have direct and sustained archeological evidence. Historically, the potent seeds were the focus of a widespread complex of ecstatic visionary shamanistic medicine societies among the tribes of the southern Plains; in the final decades of the nineteenth century *Sophora* was replaced by the more benign peyote cactus. The cults in which *Sophora* played the central role were themselves supplanted by the new syncretistic pan-Indian peyote religion that was eventually incorporated as the Native American Church.

The first European mention of *Sophora secundiflora* dates to 1539, when Cabeza de Vaca reported the hallucinogenic seeds as an item of trade among the Indians of Texas. But its history and prehistory can be extended to the very beginnings of settlement of the Southwest by the early hunters who came down from the north. Caches of *Sophora* seeds and associated artifacts and shamanistic rock paintings reminiscent in subject matter of the historic red bean cults of the southern Plains were found by archeologists in a dozen or more rock shelters in Texas and northern Mexico, often alongside *Ungnadia speciosa*, another narcotic species. The cultural levels in which the seeds occurred yielded radio-carbon dates ranging from 8440 B.C., before the extinction of mam-moth, giant bison, and other Pleistocene big game, to A.D. 1000, when a new way of life based on the cultivation of maize, beans, and squash, replaced the long-lived Desert culture. In one site, Bonfire Shelter, the hallucinogenic seeds were found with Folsom and Plainview-type pro-jectile points and the bones of a large extinct species of Pleistocene bison, *Bison antiquus* (Adovasio & Fry, 1976).

It is certainly noteworthy that a single hallucinogen, the *Sophora* bean, apparently enjoyed an uninterrupted reign of over 10,000 years—from the ninth millennium B.C. well into the nineteenth century—as the focus of ecstatic shamanism, and, for but a few centuries of that enormous span of time, in the context of the archeologically well-docu-mented, homogeneous, conservative, and evidently highly successful Desert culture. This is all the more extraordinary in that of all the native hallucinogens only the genus *Datura* (jimsonweed) poses so great a physiological risk. Clearly, the individual, social, and supernatural benefits ascribed to the drug must have outweighed its disadvantages for it to have endured for so long. In any event, the proven contemporaneity of caches of S. *secundiflora* seeds with the cultural remains of early hunters, dated by C–14 computations at between 10,000 and 11,000 years ago, is strong circumstantial evidence in favor of La Barre's (1970) hypothesis of Paleolithic roots for the hallucinogenic complex in Indian America.

Without necessarily advocating unrestricted availability of every hallucinogen that is demonstrably less risky to health and life than S. *secundiflora* or *Datura,* I would hope that lessons will soon be drawn from the abundant cultural and psychopharmacological data available to us from ethnobotany, anthropology, and chemistry for most of the botanical hallucinogens that have played a major role in the context of magico-religious rites and curing practices, particularly among American Indians. Peyote, to mention but one hallucinogen, has a proven cultural history of more than 2,000 years in Mesoamerica and is likely to be even older than its first botanically recognizable representations in west Mexican archeological tomb art, dating to 100 B.C.–A.D. 200. Like the prehispanic Aztecs and their neighbors, more than 10,000 Huichols and many other Mexican Indians today continue to hold peyote sacred or at the very least possessed of great therapeutic powers for body and mind. The efforts of nearly 250,000 North American Indians, assisted by anthropologists and civil libertarians, over the past decades have finally made peyote use legal but only within the framework of the Native American Church.

Nonchemical Routes to High States

As I have stated, the foregoing discussion is not meant to imply that psychoactive plants or animal secretions (for there were some of these as well in the psychedelic tool kit of aboriginal populations) have always and everywhere been the only or even the principal means of achieving alternate states of consciousness. On the contrary, over vast areas of North America, many tribal peoples attained the same ends by nonchemical means: fasting, thirsting, self-mutilation, torture, exposure to the elements, sleeplessness, incessant dancing and other means of bringing on total exhaustion, bleeding, plunging into ice-cold pools, near drowning, laceration with thorns and animal teeth, and other painful ordeals, as well as a variety of non-hurtful "triggers," such as different kinds of rhythmic activity, self-hypnosis, meditation, chanting, and drumming. Some shamans may have used mirrors of pyrite, obsidian, or other reflective minerals to place themselves in trance states, as indeed some Indian shamans in Mexico still do.

Weil's report (Chapter 2) on the Indian sweat lodge ritual as a means of attaining high states further indicates the range of methods for inducing ecstatic states. In Mesoamerica the *temazcal* (sweat house) was of extraordinary significance in the religious life of many prehispanic peoples and this ritual still survives in Indian communities. Because of the great importance of solar eclipses in the Mesoamerican ritual calendar and in aboriginal cosmology, the possibility that high states may be triggered by the total eclipse of the sun (reported by Weil in Chapter 2) likewise raises all sorts of fascinating research possibilities.

THE MANDAN VISION-SEEKING ORDEAL

Most dramatic of other known consciousness-altering techniques were surely the spirit-quest ordeals of certain Plains tribes, such as the Oglala Sioux and the Mandan. I am particularly interested in this aspect of the well-known Sun Dance rituals because my own research into pre-Columbian art and iconography suggests that somewhat analogous self-torture, presumably for similar vision-quest purposes, may have been practiced even by the Classic Maya of southern Mesoamerica. This suggestion may come as a surprise to those who, in the face of evidence to the contrary, still prefer to think of the Maya as fundamentally different from the rest of Indian Mesoamerica, too intent on recording astronomical phenomena, computing time, and practicing astrology to commit violence on others in war or on themselves in pursuit of supernatural visions.

George Catlin, the Pennsylvania lawyer born in 1796, the dean of documentary painters of the American Indian and his culture, left us a vivid account as well as paintings and drawings of the vision-seeking ordeal practiced by the Mandan (cited in Donaldson, 1886). Catlin was one of the few white men of his time privileged to witness the entire ceremony, which was held in conjunction with the Plains Indian Sun Dance ceremony. (Catlin's description, incidentally, should be of special interest to Weil's [1972] discussion of children twirling or spinning as a deliberate technique of altering consciousness.)

Briefly, the Mandan ordeal proceeded as follows. Already greatly weakened from hunger, thirst, and four consecutive sleepless days and nights, the candidate had holes pierced by knives through the flesh of the shoulder and breast. Through these holes he was suspended by skewers and thongs from the center pole of the great medicine lodge. The vision seeker's shield, bow, quiver, and other belongings were suspended from still more skewers passed through other parts of his body, and in many instances a heavy bison skull was attached to each arm and leg. Attendants with long poles caused his body to spin ever faster, until the candidate, streaming with blood, passed out, his medicine bag dropping from his hands and his body hanging apparently lifeless. He was then lowered to the ground and allowed to recover. But the ordeal was far from over: There was still the sacrifice of the little finger of his left hand, which was chopped off and offered to the Great Spirit, followed by a furious race around an altar, with the bison skulls and other weights dragging behind the candidate, until he could endure no more and fell in a dead faint. With physical collapse the purpose of the ordeal, which took place at the end of the summer bison hunt, was accomplished.

Whites at best were wont to interpret the ritual as a test of courage and fortitude; at worst they preferred to see it as an example of Indian cruelty. In fact, the ritual belongs within the North American Indian tradition of the ecstatic spirit quest, however extreme an example it may be of the drugless vision-inducing ordeal and to whatever degree testing the young warrior's bravery and fortitude may have played a part in it.

The Mayan Tongue Mutilation Ordeal

Ordeals of this type, if not necessarily of the same intensity, were not uncommon even in ancient Mexico, notwithstanding the widespread use of psychochemicals of botanical origin to achieve alternate states of consciousness. Self-mutilation is depicted in the ritual art of different prehispanic cultures, from the Formative to the conquest in the sixteenth century, and bloodletting rites that presumably inflicted severe pain are described in the early colonial literature on the customs of central Mexican peoples as well as the Maya. These practices included perforation or laceration of the genitals, tongue, earlobes, arms, and legs with cactus thorns, stingray barbs, and other sharp instruments, as well as ritual dances in which the participants were strung together with ropes passing through their cheeks and even their penises.

The Maya may actually have practiced a vision-quest ordeal resembling that described by Catlin for the Plains Indians: A naturalistic clay figurine from a Classic Maya cemetery on the island of Jaina, in the Gulf of Campeche, depicts a man, perhaps a novice priest, with four perforated folds of flesh on his bare back, a pair on each side; body and arms are so positioned as to suggest that the figure was meant to be suspended from the holes pierced in the skin, very much like the vision seekers depicted by Catlin in his Mandan paintings and drawings.

Several well-known Maya stone monuments that depict self-mutilation of the most extreme sort appear to me to support the idea that such ordeals at least in some cases were similar in purpose to the vision-quest ordeal of the Great Plains. One famous carving dated ca. A.D. 780, Lintel 24 from the ceremonial center of Yaxchilán on the Usumacinta River in Chiapas, depicts a richly attired kneeling woman in the act of drawing through her protruding tongue a thick cord, presumably of agave fiber, set with pairs of large, sharp thorns or spines. Facing her is a standing man holding what appears to be a long smoking tube of the kind still used by the shamans of the Venezuelan Warao to place themselves into ecstatic trance states. Tongue laceration is depicted on other Maya monuments, although this is the only example in which the trauma is reinforced with spines.

In the literature such ordeals usually are discussed in terms of blood sacrifice alone—blood being the most precious gift to the supernaturals in ancient Mesoamerican ritual.[2] There can be no doubt that this was the primary purpose in ritual earpiercing, for example, especially since the earlobe is virtually without feeling and since there are good first-hand descriptions of the sacrificial disposition of blood drawn from the ears and other organs. (Blood taken from the male genitals also was sacrificial but, being fraught with generative potency and probably conceptually related to menstrual blood, was evidently of a different order, in that it played an important role in assuring the fertility of the earth. I discuss this aspect of blood sacrifice and symbolic dual sexuality among the Maya in P. T. Furst, 1976a.) The tongue ordeal, however, is unlikely to have had simple bloodletting as its sole or even primary purpose. In fact, an important object, the ceremonial receptacle for the sacrificial cord depicted on the carved scenes of this ritual, seems to provide the key. Invariably, these receptacles are shown as flat-bottomed, wide-rimmed, woven baskets or pottery bowls filled with

---

[2] At least one reason why blood assumed extraordinary value as a sacrificial offering must have been the widespread belief—which still survives here and there in Indian Mexico—that the blood circulating in the body is finite and any amount lost cannot be replaced. Hence, even the most minute amounts drawn for sacrificial purposes represented an irreplaceable part of the sacrificer's own life.

what are probably strips of bark paper (since ritual paper objects of this sort are known to have figured in blood sacrifice). In the scenes of the tongue ordeal on Lintels 17 and 24 at Yaxchilán the blood-soaked rope coils into the receptacle amid the paper strips. But on each of two companion monuments, Lintels 15 and 25 at the same site, a supernatural being in the form of a great twisting serpent or dragon rises from the selfsame sacrificial receptacle before a kneeling woman, her head upturned, apparently listening reverentially to an oracular human figure that emerges from the open jaws of the monster. These depictions suggest that the purpose and effect of the tongue ordeal was to conjure up, in an ecstatic state triggered by severe physical trauma, a deified ancestor, perhaps to give counsel, perhaps to validate priestly or royal succession.

In support of the above it should be noted that at least one important ethnohistorical source, the *Treatise on the Superstitions and Heathen Practices Prevailing Today Among the Native Indians of New Spain*, first issued in 1629 by Hernando Ruiz de Alarcon (a Mexican-born Spanish priest who investigated surviving indigenous customs in his native Guerrero and neighboring Morelos at the behest of the Archbishop of Mexico, Francisco Manso de Zuñiga), specifically cites the ecstatic trance as one effect of the blood-letting rite.

Describing sacrificial blood-letting in pilgrimages to hill-top sanctuaries, Ruiz de Alarcon (1892, p. 140) writes as follows:

> When he arrives at the place of the idol . . . he prostrates himself in the place where he leaves his offering, and makes his sacrifice by spilling his blood, to which end he has brought with him a needle, made from a small and sharp piece of cane, and with this pricks the ears in the place where women wear ornaments, until he has lost much blood. . . . They would also pierce themselves below the lip on the chin until it was open like a window, and they say that some even put holes in the upper part of their tongues. All this was done in sacrifice, and it is said that some of them would faint or become benumbed, and in this state of ecstasy they heard or thought they heard their idols speak, telling them that they were to become very happy, and certain to get what they wished for, which was usually children, wealth, long life, family or health. (translation mine)

A Northwest Coast Parallel

For the hypothesized magical and transformational explanation of the Maya tongue mutilation ordeal—as opposed to a purely sacrificial reason—we have a suggestive ethnographic parallel from the Northwest Coast of North America. Here there is no doubt that bloody trauma to the tongue has irresistible powers of conjuring up visions and of transmogrification.[3]

Among the better known Northwest Coast art motifs is a tongue-biting frog or raven depicted on elaborately carved shamans' rattles of such peoples as the Tlingit, Tsimshian, Haida, and Kwakiutl. The tongue mutilation motif occurs in various combinations. Of particular interest are those rattles on which a frog or bird bites into the protruding tongue of a reclining man. One of the earliest explanations that Seler (1892/1961) cited for this motif came from Captain Adrian Jacobson, who made a large collection of Northwest Coast art for the Berlin Ethnographic Museum: "It is by biting that medicine is administered" (p. 33).

This was correct, wrote Seler, provided that "medicine" is understood in the Plains Indian sense, embracing that which is mysterious, imbued with magical powers, miraculous, and divine. Citing myths collected by Franz Boas, Seler noted that biting the tongue or, more precisely, biting the tongue and spitting out the blood in the belief of Northwest Coast Indians confers supernatural powers. In one tale the culture hero of a Kwakiutl subtribe catches a fish whose real identity is the *sisiutl*, the great supernatural double-headed serpent that bears an uncanny resemblance to the well-known bicephalic cosmic snake of Mesoamerica and the Andes. As it is being pulled from the sea, the *sisiutl*-fish swells up to the size of a whale. To force the creature to reassume its proper shape, the hero slashes his own tongue and spits the spurting blood upon the fish, which, unable to withstand the superior magic, changes back to its serpent form. In another tradition, the young hero of the Nemkis, also a Kwakiutl subgroup, searches for a magical bone arrow. When he sees the arrow resting in a canoe floating on a mountain lake, he cuts his tongue and spits the spurting blood into his hand. In this way he is able to sneak up unseen and take the arrow from the boat. Without the magical blood from his lacerated tongue, we are told, the youth would have perished in the attempt.

However the Indians of the Northwest Coast might have come by such concepts, Seler noted similarities with certain ritual practices in Mesoamerica. Because tongue biting and blood taken from the injured organ are clearly identified with the acquisition of "medicine" power,

[3] I draw here on Seler's (1892/1961) discussion of symbolic themes in the art and cosmology of the Northwest Coast. As long ago as 1892 he noted the striking similarity between tongue mutilation on the Northwest Coast and in prehispanic Mesoamerica.

he suggested the term *medicine rattles* for the instruments on which this and related motifs are depicted.

A Dispute over Psychoactive Mushrooms

With respect to the Maya tongue ordeal, one question that must remain unanswered for the moment is whether or not psychoactive mushrooms of the species *Stropharia cubensis*, which still grow in profusion in the Usumacinta region, or some related variety was employed in the context of ritual self-mutilation. The possibility was first raised by Robertson (1972), but we simply do not have any definitive evidence pro or con.

One objection that could be made to a prehispanic role for *S. cubensis* is that as a dung fungus this species now is typically found in the droppings of domestic cattle, and cows of course were unknown in the New World prior to the coming of the Europeans. On closer examination of *Stropharia* ecology, however, the problem turns out to be more apparent than real. In order to fruit, *Stropharia* spores evidently require passage through the digestive system of ruminants in general, not cattle specifically. This species could have flourished in pre-European Mesoamerica in the droppings of a smaller indigenous ruminant, the deer being the most logical candidate. Not only were deer plentiful in the Maya environment, but they played an extraordinarily important role in the belief system of the Maya and other prehispanic peoples. Among the Maya the animal was especially prominent in the symbolism of death and the underworld. In several instances a close association is made between deer and a particular hallucinogen: The Huichols of western Mexico, for example, conceive of the divine deer as animal avatar of the peyote cactus and vice versa; in Peru ritual or supernatural deer hunts depicted on painted Moché ceramics of the fifth or sixth century A.D. invariably show the animal in association with a tree identifiable as *Anadenanthera colubrina*, from whose hallucinogenic seeds the ancient Andeans made their intoxicating *vilka* snuff (P. T. Furst, 1974).

In any event, that a dung mushroom such as *S. cubensis* need not have been introduced into Mexico after the conquest from some Old World locale but could have done perfectly well in the droppings of native deer is demonstrated by the fact that in highland Guatemala dung mushrooms described as resembling the psychoactive genus *Psilocybe* (presumably *S. cubensis*) have been observed in considerable numbers in the dung of sheep and goats. Both are ruminants of Old World origin whose droppings closely resemble in quantity and texture those of deer (Tedlock & Tedlock, 1976). Who knows—perhaps the deer's cosmological prominence was not wholly unrelated to its magical role as "progenitor" of *Stropharia cubensis!*

Whether or not we will ever find direct proof in the form of artistic representations that mushrooms actually were employed by the lowland Maya,[4] *S. cubensis* or one of its relatives could certainly have contributed to the transcendental experiences depicted on the monuments at Yaxchilán. *Stropharia* could also have played a role in alleviating the perception of pain during the tongue mutilation ordeals.

Non-Hurtful Pain

This suggestion brings up another question—whether all or some of the individuals depicted or described in the act of self-mutilation necessarily experienced physical hurt. Indeed, was pain a necessary precondition for triggering the ecstatic state? The fact is that despite trauma to the system sufficient to bring about a real alteration in the state of consciousness, the perception of pain can be blocked by a properly prepared individual. This phenomenon not only is well known from the practices of yogis and other mystics but also has been confirmed experimentally.[5]

For non-hurtful pain phenomena in ritual mutilation among the Maya, we have some sixteenth-century eyewitness statements; also, in Maya art depicting various kinds of physical trauma there is no suggestion of actual suffering. On the contrary, some of the people shown inflicting the severest sorts of injury upon themselves (for instance, tongue perforation with spiny ropes) appear composed and serene, not to say entranced. Here is an early colonial description by Fray Delgado of sacrificial genital mutilation among the Manche Chol Maya; it is quoted by Thompson (1938, p. 594):

> In Vicente Pach's [Pech's] ranch I saw the sacrifice. They took a chisel and wooden mallet, placed the one who had to sacrifice himself on a smooth stone slab, took out his penis, and cut it in three parts two finger breadths [up], the largest in the center, saying at the same time incantations and

[4] For highland Guatemala we have indirect, but highly suggestive, evidence for ancient mushroom cults in the more than two hundred stone effigies of mushrooms, some dating as far back as 1000 B.C.

[5] Presumably, the phenomenon of non-hurtful pain relates to the recently discovered highly specific opiate receptors in the mammalian brain, which chemically join opium-derived narcotics such as morphine and heroin and which have been found—and this is more to the point here—to fit together with substances, spontaneously manufactured in the body that are strikingly morphinelike in structure and in pain-alleviating effects.

words I did not understand. The one who was undergoing the operation did not seem to suffer, and did not lose a drop of blood.

Thompson commented that the "statement that no blood was lost would appear dubious. Apart from physical difficulties, the similar rite in Yucatán (as described by Bishop Diego de Landa) was definitely to draw blood." But that, of course, is just the point—bloodletting need not have been the chief motivation, at least not in every instance of described or depicted self-mutilation, and the experience of physical pain, as well as the flow of blood, could well have been suppressed through techniques of controlling the autonomic nervous system. Knowledge of this kind would hardly have been beyond the capabilities of the intellectual elite among the ancient Maya, whose brilliant achievements in mathematics, astronomy, hieroglyphic writing, architecture, and other arts made their civilization one of the most notable experiments in human history.

THE RITUAL SWEAT BATH

Andrew Weil's work has carried us considerably beyond the mere ethnographic recording of ecstatic phenomena within the indigenous cultures of the New World, especially inasmuch as he has recently focused on "techniques of ecstasy" other than hallucinogen use. For example, ritual sweat bathing in Mesoamerica has long been known to have served religious, purifying, and curing functions, but to my knowledge the kind of high experience reported by Weil in Chapter 2 (pp. 44–45) has not been seriously considered in relation to the *temazcal* complex. This lack seems surprising, especially since anyone who has had a traditional sauna bath must know that a kind of high state is very much part of the experience. The fact is that there are hints in the early literature and in the descriptions of sweat bathing by present-day informants that something of the sort of experience Weil had on the Sioux Rosebud Reservation must have occurred within—indeed, been one purpose of—the permanent, templelike masonry structures into which Mesoamerican peoples elaborated the simpler sweat lodges of North America and northern Eurasia (the sweat lodge is probably one of the Old World Mesolithic traits that early hunting bands carried with them into the New World).

As Weil notes in Chapter 2, among the Sioux the sweat lodge is consecrated ground on which man contacts the Great Spirit. The *temazcal* was widespread in prehispanic Mesoamerica—indeed, it still is important in many indigenous communities. Among the Mixtecs of Oaxaca it was considered to be so vital to the community that in the

Codex Vindobonensis, a major pre-conquest pictorial manuscript, for example, a conventionalized *temazcal* is repeatedly employed to symbolize a whole ceremonial and population center (J. L. Furst, 1975). In central Mexico, the *temazcal* was dedicated to the old Earth Mother Goddess, Toci, Grandmother, also called Heart of the Earth and Mother of the Gods. One of her appellations was Temazcaltoci, Grandmother of the Sweat Bath House. She was also special patroness of curing shamans and transformers, which fits well with the transformational, purifying, and therapeutic functions of the *temazcal*. To judge from the description of the *temazcal* by such early chroniclers as Durán (1971, pp. 269-271), the sweat bath ritual may have been experienced as a symbolic death and regeneration from the dark and fiery womb of the Great Mother, whose image was buried beneath the floor of the *temazcal* and to whom incense and other gifts were sacrificed both before the structure was actually erected on consecrated ground and each time people entered the bath house. Durán reported that he deliberately destroyed several prehispanic sweat bath houses, in part to cause fear among the people and in part to discover for himself one of the buried images of the goddess, which he said "turned out to be an ugly and monstrous stone face." This suggests that Toci may have been represented as Tlaltecuhtli, Owner or Lord of the Earth, the earth goddess in her animal manifestation as a toad with feline characteristics.

Bathers entered the *temazcal* on hands and knees through a low and narrow entrance. Upon emerging in the same manner, they were splashed and washed with cold water, the shock of which would have greatly intensified the experience of an alternate or high state (see Weil's remarks on p. 45). Durán reported that ten or twelve pitchers of very cold water were emptied over the overheated body of the ritual bather; he had been told, he wrote, that bathers became inured to the severe shock because they had been brought up in the traditional system: "If a Spaniard were to go through this, he would go into shock or become paralyzed." The cold bath seems also to reinforce the suggested symbolism of death, transformation (or incubation), and rebirth: Newborn infants were traditionally washed in cold water after emerging from the womb.

With respect to the intense heat within the sweat bath house, what Weil has to say about the relationship between one's state of mind and the experience or non-experience of physical hurt is very pertinent to the Mesoamerican *temazcal* ritual as well: "Burning occurs only when you lose contact with the psychic energy of the group and see yourself as an isolated individual trying to defend yourself against the onslaught of heat" (p. 45). Seen in this light, Durán's description takes on new meaning. The steam bath houses, he reported, were large enough to hold ten persons in a squatting position; standing was impossible and sitting virtually so.

What appalled him especially was what he called the "heathenish custom of mixed bathing," which he explained was based on a "diabolical superstition and belief" that no man could enter the *temazcal* unless accompanied by a woman and no woman without a man. When the *temazcal* was used for curing, a male patient had to be attended by a professional female "fanner" as bringer of health—i.e., a specialized curer—and a woman patient, a male curer. So highly regarded were these specialists that "they were esteemed as saints and whenever it was necessary to call them were showered with gifts: plentiful food, pulque, and ears of corn, depending upon the quality of each" (Durán, 1971, p. 271). But the main point was that the curer's gender always had to balance that of the patient—man for woman, woman for man. Durán and other priests tried valiantly to destroy this "diabolical superstition," but to no avail.

> To demonstrate clearly the faith which the natives had in this heathenish custom of mixed bathing, I wish to tell what occurred to me in a certain village where this evil custom or way existed. I insisted and demanded both from the pulpit and outside [the church] that males bathe by themselves and females by themselves, speaking sternly and threatening them with punishment. Then [the people] played a droll trick on me: in order not to break their heathen law and tradition, when the women went to bathe, they carried with them one or two of their male children, and the men a little girl or two. This was a feint so that if they were reprimanded they could answer that these were their own children and therefore were taken in. Actually, this is what they did answer, and it was all due to their remembrance of ancient paganism. (p. 271)

Of course it should have occurred to Durán that if small children of the opposite sex were a satisfactory substitute, sexual arousal could hardly have been the purpose of mixed bathing, as indeed it was not. Clearly, the "diabolical superstition" concerned unity and balance between the sexes and, in Weil's terms, the need for a balanced flow of psychic energy between them.

One additional point: Besides putting themselves in the proper mental state, the ancient Mesoamericans also dispensed herbal preparations to render the ritual bather invulnerable to the near boiling temperatures generated in the *temazcal*. Sahagún (1963, Vol. 11, pp. 151, 176–177) described one such infusion compounded from a small quantity of the leaves of a species of mesquite (*Prosopis* spp.) called *Quetzalmizquitl*, "precious mesquite," and the ground up, acrid root of the solanaceous tomato called *Coztomatl* (*Physalis costomatl* Moc.) As a member of the nightshade family, which includes the genus *Datura*, the tomato root was presumably the more effective ingredient in the mixture. Datura itself was commonly employed not only as a hallucinogen but also as a painkiller.

The fact that fragrances of various sorts, including smoke from hallucinogenic plants, play a role in the contemporary *temazcal* experience suggests that this was the case also in prehispanic times. In the Nahuatl-speaking pueblo of San Francisco Cuapa, in the state of Puebla, for example, *sinicuichi* (*Heimia salicifolia*) is sprinkled on the burning fuel in the *temazcal* fireplace so that its fragrant fumes may perfume the steaming interior (Knab, 1976). *Sinicuichi* is one of the most interesting of all the native hallucinogens of Mesoamerica: Its effects are said to be wholly auditory. Normally, *sinicuichi* is consumed in the form of a fermented, slightly intoxicating infusion made from the wilted leaves of the plant; according to Schultes (1972, p. 32), the effects include giddiness, drowsy euphoria, darkening of the surroundings, shrinking of the world around, altered perception of time and space, forgetfulness, removal from a state of reality, and sounds that are distorted and appear to come from a great distance. Knab does not think that the small quantities used in the *temazcal* are in themselves sufficient to bring about these effects; rather, the *sinicuichi*-perfumed steam may help to place the bather in a state of euphoric tranquillity. Perfuming is a well-known aspect of hallucinogenic ritual; indeed, many peoples consider fragrances to be absolutely essential to the total experience.

Sinicuichi itself, according to Schultes (1972), is considered to be sacred and endowed with supernatural powers among the indigenous peoples who still employ it ritually; it is said to assist the user to recall with great clarity events of the distant past, including even the prenatal state. Five quinolizidine alkaloids have been isolated from *H. salicifolia*, but the plant and its use are still not so well defined as one might wish. It is likely that yet other plants belonging to the aboriginal psychopharmacopoeia are in use everywhere in Mesoamerica as an essential constituent of ritual sweat bathing and also that fragrances play a widespread role in this as well as other rituals involving alternate or high states.

To summarize, psychochemicals are not required to place the ritual sweat bather in an extraordinary mental state; the intense heat and the contrast between hot and cold, in combination with the special mental preparation that the ritual bather who enters the sweat lodge has undergone, are themselves sufficient. Certainly among the major purposes of sweat bathing in North America and Mesoamerica were, and are, curing and purification. In addition, however, there are aspects to this ritual that place it squarely among the techniques of ecstasy that, as we have seen, range in the New World from physical and psychological ordeals to the hundred or so hallucinogenic plants discovered by American Indians, not to mention "spontaneous" shamanistic high states entered without the use of psychochemicals but phenomenologically indistinguishable from those triggered by psychedelics.

THE PEYOTE HUNT AS AN ORDEAL

Actually—and this applies to earlier remarks on the possible use of mushrooms in Maya self-mortification—some kind of ordeal, usually deprivation of food, drink, or sleep, is in the majority of cases the essential precondition even for the ritual use of hallucinogens (as it sometimes is in nonhallucinogenic rituals). Clearly, ordeals play a role in the intensification of the ecstatic experience. As an example from my own fieldwork, when the Huichol peyote pilgrims finally arrive in Wirikuta, the sacred country in the north-central Mexican desert where they are to gather the hallucinogenic cactus, they have already traveled some three hundred miles from their homeland (traditionally all the way on foot), having allowed themselves little or no sleep since setting out from the western Sierra Madre, and are close to exhaustion. They have kept themselves at a fever pitch of emotion by awareness of the gravity and sacredness of the enterprise on which they are embarked and its importance to the well-being of their people; incessant dancing and singing and the observance of innumerable rituals mark the journey. They have eaten virtually nothing, and little or no water has quenched their thirst. Salt is strictly prohibited for the duration of the pilgrimage and for many days before and after—no small sacrifice when one considers the high daytime heat of the desert even during the winter months, when most such pilgrimages are held. Finally, they have smoked many ritual cigarettes of potent native tobacco (*Nicotiana rustica*) wrapped in cornhusk, and they may also have purified themselves, literally and symbolically, by eating impressive quantities of the same tobacco. They are thus already at a very different level of consciousness, so much so that it is not necessary for them to be under the influence of the peyote alkaloids to perceive the plant in its animal form when the leader of the pilgrimage exclaims, at the sight of the very first cactus: "Ah, there he is at last, Our Elder Brother, the Deer who gives us our life!" or words to that effect. In the course of the rituals that follow, Huichols will literally saturate themselves with peyote, chewing it incessantly for days and nights on end (or drinking it in liquid form), getting little rest, and eating little normal food until the entire social and natural environment and the individual's relationship to it takes on a wholly mystical dimension. The metabolic system has been altered, and it is in that mystical union with otherworlds that the shamans interpret the visions—their own and those of others—in accordance with the traditional cultural norms on which they have been reared and the magical-animistic world view that permeates Huichol ideology.

A Biochemical Explanation of Non-Hurtful Pain

Before revising for publication my contribution to the Drug Abuse Council's workshop on alternate states of consciousness, I discussed with Joel Elkes ritual trauma as a technique for triggering high states. Since my own research into the cultural meanings of hallucinogens has focused largely on overt ritual behavior and its charter in the native cosmologies and mythological traditions, I am greatly indebted to him for clarifying the biochemical mechanisms involved and for permission to quote from some of our conversation. The following extract, then, represents Elkes' interpretation of some of the phenomena depicted on the Maya monuments or described by sixteenth-century chroniclers.

> Through the experience of biofeedback, which has been greatly developed and perfected in recent years, there is new experimental evidence to add to the experiences characteristic, for example, of yoga practice that the autonomic nervous system—so-called because it was thought to be not under voluntary control—can in fact be taught, that it can condition heart rate, blood pressure, temperature of the skin, perception of pain, etc. Through a series of exercises involving a relaxed state and the feeding back of signals, and through the individual's becoming aware of the functions and state of any component of the autonomic nervous system, one can in fact exercise controls on such things as skin temperature, pulse, blood pressure, and so forth. Skin temperature, it has been shown, can be raised by as much as 5°F even when the hand is immersed in very cold water. Beyond that are more extreme phenomena—for example, the response of the skin to physical or chemical injury, which can be changed in hypnotic trances, which

comes back to memory, the N-gram—the whole gestalt, so to speak—which is not just stored in microstructures in the brain but in fact is stored in the body itself. I recall an article in *Lancet,* for instance, that described the case of a sailor who had been shipwrecked and who relived the traumatic event in a hypnotic trance. The extraordinary thing was that as he went through the experience of hanging onto a rope, severe rope marks, real burns or weals, appeared on the skin, which was perfectly intact, and disappeared again when the hypnotic trance was over. The implication is that somehow the encoding occurs not only in the brain but in the tissues as well.

What actually occurs chemically in these systems we do not yet know. Now what happens with LSD and some of the other psychoactive structures is that—because they are so analogous to the naturally occurring compounds, perhaps just one methoxy group away—they evoke some of these memory traces through the release of a gating mechanism that normally shuts them out. Normally we gate constantly, a phenomenon one might compare to an internal Mount Palomar observatory, with one dome going up and one down, and a sweep that can be very narrow and that can be very wide. Outwardly it is scanning the environment, linear time, action-oriented planning; inwardly it is scanning memory stores, probably intuiting various kinds of new connections, which then have to be fed into an action plan.

Whether this "internal Palomar" is oriented to the right and left hemisphere I do not know, but I believe that light has a great deal to do with it, that some light-sensitive machinery was buried in the brain originally, light-sensitive machinery that had something to do with energy transformation and with scanning the environment. The pineal, the so-called third eye, is one of the *Ur*-organs involved here. In this connection it is interesting that the pineal is activated by an indole that is only one group removed from serotonin, which is activated by LSD. And then—and this is something that has intrigued me enormously—as I look at growth hormones in plants I find these selfsame substances in abundance as powerful growth activators. Clearly these compounds are one of the very, very early discoveries of nature in the evolutionary history of the planet.

In the specific case of a Maya priestess or woman of the elite drawing a rope, with or without spines, through her tongue and perhaps not feeling pain in the process, what is involved is the shutting off of the sensory pathways from the tongue, probably by some cognitive act, the superimposing of the image of a nonfeeling, even nonbleeding, tongue over the real, injured one. And that superimposed structure then becomes the real structure.

Now, if it is true that, as was reported by Fray Delgado, not only was there no pain but also no blood when the penis was lacerated, then probably there was also a command to the peripheral organs not to respond. And here what Andrew Weil suggests [Chapter 2] about the conduction of thermal energy in the case of heat, and kinetic energy in the case of a blow, becomes especially pertinent. Under certain specific conditions the peripheral nervous system might be able to receive unusually large amounts of physical energy, transmuting this energy electrochemically and conducting it away from the periphery—in the cases under consideration the mutilated tongue or penis of the Maya self-sacrificer—to the central nervous system. And there, in turn, it might be channeled into high states or alternate states of consciousness or otherwise discharged in a non-hurtful way. Perhaps, then, there is a gating mechanism that in some way instead of focusing or acting on the periphery simply deflects the energy. And this is something we know nothing about at the present time.

With respect to the possible use of psychoactive mushrooms within the ritual of self-mutilation, the same commands could also be triggered by the action of one or another hallucinogen, of which, as we know, the ancient Mesoamericans had a considerable number in addition to the sacred fungi. In fact, they clearly do that, and in that event, the superimposed images, especially if they are strongly felt, become the reality. Just how these structures are in fact superimposed upon one another I do not understand. All I am grappling with at the moment is a simple gating mechanism that exists in hypnogogic states, in dreaming, in the LSD state, etc.

What fascinates me about what we are now learning from the cross-cultural studies of anthropologists is that with the exception of ourselves every religion system, in every part of the world and in all times, seems to have incorporated these phenomena as an essential part of the healing arts. In other words, there is a healing quality about these states, and that is medically of great importance. And yet it is totally ignored in the sort of passive patient, active doctor kind of relationship that is the hallmark of Western medicine, in place of the self-mastery, self-help kind of model that so-called primitive peoples have mastered and that their shamanic curers employ, often with most remarkable therapeutic effects.

The answer, then, to whether actual physical pain, or the perception of pain, is essential to triggering alternate states of consciousness is clearly no. What you probably have in self-inflicted "painless mutilation" is massive sensory bombardment and probably massive release of chemical compounds in concentrations that are quite high. You therefore have a change, a switch in that automatic selector that rotates in-out, so to speak; so that you become much less aware of your surroundings. This probably involves a massive liberation of chemical compounds through this massive sensory bombardment, even though you do not experience it consciously. It is probably a question of ratio production and destruction. What has to be understood here is that these metabolites are so potent that they are handled in almost a quantal way. They are released, but they are so enormously powerful that they are immediately sucked back, taken up, bound in some way because otherwise they could play havoc with these very sensitive micromolecular systems. It is a matter of throwing the switch from the outward-directed to the inward-directed state. When you get the massive assault of the sort depicted in Maya art or described by the Spanish priests, you get a release not only of the major chemical compounds but also of some of these side compounds as well that normally, for good and necessary reasons, have a very short life but that now stay around not for their usual microseconds or milliseconds but for whole seconds. And so the switch is thrown, with the assistance of psychochemicals or without.

Summary

The entire subject of the discovery and utilization by so many peoples of psychochemicals in nature, and their relationship to alternate states of consciousness, is obviously vast and complex. Certainly it extends toward what Jung called archetypes, as it does to mythmaking and worldwide themes in oral tradition (especially the striking correspondences among different funerary, heroic, and shamanistic mythologies); art and iconography; traditional cultural systems of perceiving and ordering reality that differ more or less drastically from the so-called scientific or rational Western model; conceptions of otherworlds, death, and afterlife; mysticism; and, indeed, all that we subsume under the rubric "religion." Much as we think we already know—and we have learned a great deal in a very short time—the truth is that in these cultural areas we have made barely a beginning.

Yet it seems obvious that there is a need for an anthropological and culture-historical perspective. The ways in which, and the purposes for which, traditional societies have integrated psychochemicals into their intellectual culture and their social systems, and the fact that this kind of thing has been part and parcel of human behavior for thousands of years, are not irrelevant to our time and place. Granted, there are differences: In the preindustrial or tribal world, psychotropic plants are sacred and magical; they are perceived as living beings with supernatural attributes, if not indeed godlike, providing for shamans, and under certain special circumstances for ordinary folk as well, a bridge across the gulf that separates the known from the unknown spheres of existence. By common agreement, in the so-called primitive societies, the breakthrough in plane that the extraordinary chemicals in these plants facilitate is thought to be essential for the well-being of the individual and the community. As Elkes pointed out, the alternate or high states these plants and other techniques of ecstasy produce are widely considered through time and space to be of enormous therapeutic value and

are integrated as such in many non-Western religious and medical systems. It is no accident that in some Mexican Indian systems of this kind
both curer and patient partake of the sacred mushrooms or other hallucinogens in order to explore hand in hand, as it were, the otherworlds
in which the causes of illness are concealed—these "otherworlds" being,
as La Barre (1972) so astutely noted, nothing less than the subconscious.

It is true that such experiences—whether triggered by hallucinogens
or by nonchemical techniques—are fully consistent in the traditional
world with the religious-philosophical systems in which they became
institutionalized, systems that value and encourage personal encounters
with the supernatural and esteem the therapeutic properties of ecstatic
or high states. And this of course immediately differentiates them from
contemporary Western systems, religious and medical, although they
are perhaps not so far from Judeo-Christian practices of past centuries
and to some degree are akin to modern charismatic movements and sects.

We have seen the archeological, historical, and ethnographic evidence to be such as to endow the psychoactive flora of the world with a
respectable cultural history not only within present-day traditional cultures but also in Europe, where there survives at least a memory of
pre-Christian mushroom cults in folk traditions, fairy tales, riddles,
and nursery rhymes. In contemporary Mexican and South American
societies the sacred hallucinogens are accounted for in living religious
beliefs and customs in which all members share to a greater or lesser
extent and that validate the drugs' continued ritual use. We might go
so far as to say that in these instances the psychoactive plants actually
helped determine the history of the cultures in which they have played
a role, inasmuch as it is typically in the initiatory ecstatic trance that
the individual confirms for himself the validity of his group's religious
and social traditions and customs, which he has observed and heard
recited all his life. In the traditional, preindustrial context, then, the
magical plants have served to reify and validate the parental culture for
each successive generation—not, as comparable chemicals often do in
our own society, to afford a temporary means of escape from it or,
ideally, to provide insights into the self thought to be not ordinarily
available. The Mexican Indian who uses morning glory seeds or mushrooms already knows where his "trip" will take him; all he really requires the magical plants for is the essential breakthrough in plane, the
bridge, so to speak, across the gap between the everyday world and the
extraordinary (but no less substantial), supernatural one in which he
believes his social reality to have had its mystical origins. Like the

Tukano of Colombia, who returns from his *yajé* experience convinced of the truth of his traditional lifeway (cf. Reichel-Dolmatoff, 1972), so the Huichol wakes from his ecstatic peyote dream to exclaim, "It is as my fathers explained it to me!" One takes peyote, he says, "to learn how one goes about being Huichol." The identical enculturative aspect of the psychedelic experience has been documented among the Cahuilla of California, whose traditional hallucinogen is *Datura inoxia* (Bean & Saubel, 1972), and among many other native peoples of North and South America.

Whatever their objective or subjective effects, it is hardly for the purpose of enculturation that LSD or DMT is employed in our society, at least in the sense in which the traditional Indian learns to see himself as a functioning member of his society. And yet, objectively the chemistry of these modern drugs differs little from that of substances long employed in the "primitive" world; moreover, as noted earlier, as science has only recently discovered, the botanical psychochemicals used for millennia in ecstatic-religious and therapeutic rites and their laboratory equivalents are structurally very similar to compounds that occur naturally in the mammalian brain.

Still, the situation in which we as students of these phenomena find ourselves is that the same chemicals that many traditional peoples still value as sacred, benign, culturally integrative, and essential to the health of the individual and the community, chemicals we know to have a cultural history of millennia, are classified by our laws and social attitudes as inherently so dangerous, wicked, and alien to our ethic that their possession may be treated as no less a felony than possession of heroin. Clearly, then, it is society, not chemistry, that is the crucial factor: How but in terms of culturally generated stereotypes, not intrinsic characteristics or even measurable social and medical costs, can one explain the legal and moral approval of one social drug, alcohol, and the outlawing of another, marijuana?

Equally clearly, the veritable explosion of biological, pharmacological, and anthropological information on psychochemicals and high states has as yet had little effect on social policy. Even now, much that is written and legislated seems to be generated in a scientific vacuum rather than with reference to the considerable body of objective data as available to newspapermen and legislators as to the academic community.

In the face of all the evidence, as a people we still treat nonaddictive psychochemicals and the mental states they produce as brand-new and somehow alien phenomena, symptoms of our particular time and place, or, worse, prophetic of moral decay and social disintegration. Insofar as these chemicals occur in nature and alternate states of consciousness appear more and more to be intrinsic to being human, are not these fears and the policies they generate yet another reflection of the distance we have tried to place between ourselves and the natural world?

Amerindian peoples have not made this mistake. Some years ago a colleague, anthropologist Johannes Wilbert, told an Indian friend in Venezuela of the American astronauts who had landed on the moon, and he tried to explain the complex technology and vast sums of money this extraordinary feat required. His Warao informant was interested but not impressed. "It is strange," he said, "that you white people require such great effort to fly to the moon. Our shamans fly there all the time. All they have to do to get there is smoke and dream." What if we told this man of the discovery by modern science that it is precisely in the biochemistry of consciousness that we are related to the plant world? Considering how Indians have traditionally thought of themselves in relation to the natural environment, his reply might well be, "So, what else is new?" For what Western science is only just beginning to learn, indigenous Americans have never forgotten.

4

Ongoing Thought: The Normative Baseline for Alternate States of Consciousness

Jerome L. Singer

Stream of Consciousness as a Psychological Problem

IF WE ARE TO EXAMINE "altered" or "alternate" states of consciousness, should we not first respond to the challenge William James (1950) posed in his famous chapter "The Stream of Thought"? Even if one questions James' metaphor of the flowing river as a felicitous description of ongoing consciousness, a little careful introspection should raise questions about whether the traditional rubrics of perception, sensation, and imagery suffice to capture the complexity of private experience. To anybody but a psychologist it would seem amazing indeed that textbooks on thinking (Bourne et al., 1971; Johnson, 1955) can ignore the stream of consciousness and imagination, that books on personality (Mischel, 1971) or on adolescence (Seidman, 1960) can say so little about imagination or fantasy. After a half century of repression, at least imagery is back "in" and a fit subject for formal psychological research (Holt, 1964; Paivio, 1971; Segal, 1971; Sheehan, 1972). Ongoing thought remains, however, relatively neglected and primarily the domain of the fine artist.

Some of the research cited in the latter portion of this chapter was supported by Grant 1-R01-DA-00590-01, National Institute on Drug Abuse, to Bernard Segal and Jerome L. Singer.

Indeed, it was the creative personalities of literature, painting, and cinema who took up James' challenge initially. The excitement engendered in the first two decades of this century by the efforts of James Joyce to produce what Edmund Wilson (1922) called "perhaps the most faithful X-ray ever taken of the ordinary human consciousness" reflected the seriousness with which writers accepted James' insights. Writing in 1919, Virginia Woolf (1925/1953) said:

> Examine for a moment an ordinary mind on an ordinary day. The mind receives a myriad of impressions—trivial, fantastic, evanescent, or engraved with the sharpness of steel. From all sides they come, an incessant shower of innumerable atoms; and as they fall, as they shape themselves into the life of Monday or Tuesday the accent falls differently from the old . . . life is not a series of gig lamps symmetrically arranged; but an illuminous halo, a semitransparent envelope surrounding us from the beginning of consciousness to the end. (p. 154)

At the same time that James Joyce, Virginia Woolf, and T. S. Eliot, (1919/1950), in his discussion of the "objective correlative," were forming the basis for the use of the stream of consciousness as a literary and poetic medium, filmmakers like Sergei Eisenstein perceived an opportunity in motion pictures to capture even more effectively the ongoing thought stream. In his development of "montage" and in his effort to produce, by what he called "partial representations," images that would evoke for a viewer the same ongoing thought experience as occurred in the mind of the artist or of the character represented on the screen, Eisenstein (1942) made another great stride in providing an expression of ongoing thought.

The effectiveness with which cinema can capture the quick associations that characterize normal thought are manifest in some examples from recent films. In *The Pawnbroker* the tormented protagonist steps into a New York City subway train, and we see in briefest flash a scene from a cattle car crowded with Jews en route to a concentration camp, a memory from the pawnbroker's own experience. In *Midnight Cowboy* the cowboy and the woeful gamin, Ratso Rizzo, find themselves at a party. The ever hungry Ratso, standing before a buffet table laden with food, begins wolfing down sandwiches. Suddenly we see a quick shot of his long-dead father standing beside the table. In this poignant second or two of imagery the director has conveyed to us Ratso's fantasy: "If only my poor old dad could be here to enjoy this feast."

Overemphasis on Verbal and Directed Thought

Lacking the artist's freedom from the constraints of scientific method, behavioral scientists have focused much more on the products of specific directed thinking or on the study of isolated features of thought, such as the vividness of images, the effectiveness of imagery in paired associate learning, and other forms of problem solution. By their very nature, the methods of the experimental psychologist have led perhaps to an overweighting of the structured, directed, rational aspects of thought. Studies of concept learning or of abstraction abilities, of various forms of categorical thinking, and of arithmetic or spatial problem solution have predominated because they are easy to conduct and control. It has been only in recent years that the ethical thinking of individuals has been subjected to more careful study or that private judgments about human relationships have been examined systematically. Even these researches are generally cast within the very structured format of problem solution. The picture of the thought process that emerges therefore has a quality of organization and rationality that does not always fit either with the fine descriptions of writers or with our private experience if we take the trouble to observe it unfold in its natural course.

The contributions of psychoanalysis, significant as they have been in opening up a broader range of attention to the subtleties of thought and the irrational, wishful, and "selfish" side of private experience, have not fully addressed the nature of ongoing thought. As conscious as Freud was of the many persisting intrusions into adult mental processes of childlike, magical solutions or fantasies, he still tended to assume, it appears, that the well-analyzed adult would be characterized by much greater resort to secondary-process thinking. Indeed, it might be argued that Freud overplayed the logical and rational quality of mature waking thought and underestimated the adaptive and directed quality of wishful, imagery-laden thinking. Freud's theory of thinking represents perhaps the first elaborate effort to develop a comprehensive view of mental process (Rapaport, 1951b, 1960). Yet various structural characteristics of the theory—id, ego, superego; unconscious, preconscious, conscious; primary and secondary processes—are all too difficult to fit together since they were developed at different times and never were brought into correspondence (Gill, 1963).

Some attempted modification of this excessively rational view of mature thought processes was introduced by analysts such as Ernst Kris (1951), who proposed that at least for creative thought one had to look for "regression in the service of the ego." Again, the term *regression* seems to continue the earlier emphasis on the directed, rational, second-ary-process quality of mature adult thought. To assert that the poet who can recapture early childhood memories or fantasies but who can also make unusual and odd combinations from current experiences is relying on a more childlike mode of thought seems unsatisfactory. This ap-proach seems, for one thing, to emphasize verbal or language processes as being of a higher order than auditory or visual imagery content in adult thinking. Certainly this prejudice is pervasive among professionals, largely because they depend so much on the ultimate verbal expression of material in print. It would seem unlikely that the brain of a Beethoven or a Bach, teeming with melody, with novel and original combinations of themes, instrumental coloration, and interweaving lines of music, represents a somehow more primitive style of thought than that of a mathematician mentally solving algebra problems. Our recent height-ened awareness of the differential processing capacities of the brain and its functional asymmetry for verbal-quantitative and imagery-spatial representational capacities suggests that the process of effective thought is far more complex than has been recognized. In addition, if one frees oneself from the hydraulic energy model that has characterized so much of the theory about thinking in this century and opens the way for an information-processing model, one can be free also of the oversimplified primary/secondary process or regression views that have been a part of that model.

A basic problem in understanding ongoing human thought has to do, of course, with the fact that we inevitably rely on some aspect of language to determine the nature of private experience. This makes the report on thinking often very much subject to the demands of the given task. Most people who have written about thought in the past, with the exception of the psychoanalysts, have tended to value logic and analytic capacities and have attempted to adopt the most formal aspects of com-munication. This emphasis has led them almost inevitably to ignore the many intrusions of visual or auditory or other images into their thinking, in the interests of providing a refined product. Similarly, by the setting of tasks such as the forming of concepts, often using abstract geometric forms themselves alien to most people's day-to-day experience, they have seriously underestimated the degree to which most thinking has to do with *interpersonal* situations and human relationships. Indeed, one might assert that even Piaget, who has done so much to develop a cognitive or information-processing alternative to the drive model of thinking, has tended to a great extent to neglect the degree to which ongoing thought has reference to social interactions rather than simply encompassing the characteristics of the physical world. Questionnaire responses from hundreds of subjects have indicated that although there are sex differences in relative emphasis most people devote a good deal of time to speculation about human relationships and patterns of social interaction around them.

Again, it is only very recently that psychologists have addressed themselves more systematically to the important cognitive implications of thinking about people, their faces, their intentions, and the ethics of social situations (Kohlberg, 1966; Rosenthal, 1974; Selman, 1975; Tomkins, 1962–1963). A pet peeve of mine with respect to the psychoanalysts, who have done so much to focus our attention on the complexity of interpersonal relationships and their role in thought, has been their persistence in using the term *object representation* when talking about the way people are characterized in ongoing everyday thought.

Approaches to Studying Ongoing Thought

We are finally beginning to get some kinds of data that at least open the way for studies of ongoing mental processes. One group of approaches has involved questionnaires and inventories dealing with experiences of daydreaming and related imaginal experiences as they occur over one's life. These questionnaires, though on the whole yielding relatively consistent findings (Segal & Singer, 1975; Singer, 1966, 1975; Singer & Antrobus, 1972), are of course based upon retrospective reporting of dispositions to experience different types of daydreaming; the conditions under which these daydreams occur; and the relationship of the daydreams to other personality characteristics. Nevertheless, the large body of data accumulated makes it clear that most respondents report considerable amounts of ongoing thought, characterized by a variety of wishes, anticipations, and fearful expectations. Striking and apparently consistent individual differences in types and patternings of such ongoing thought are evident also.

Perhaps a more direct approach to capturing the ongoing stream of thought has emerged from a series of laboratory investigations that have the virtue of relatively strong control over external input but at the same time suffer from some of the inevitable artificiality of laboratory research. These studies have used as their approach the assignment of the subject to the task of detecting signals in a relatively circumscribed sensory environment so that the external cues available are more or less under experimental control. By interrupting people systematically while they are busily involved in detecting rapidly presented signals (e.g., sounds or lights), one can obtain estimates of the degree to which thoughts and images extraneous to the task occur spontaneously to the subjects. It is thus possible to measure within the limitations of these situations the extent to which other kinds of thinking are going on besides strict attention to a task that is not in itself intellectually demanding. Every fifteen seconds subjects report systematically the occurrence/nonoccurrence of "stimulus-independent" or "task-irrelevant" thought or provide verbal accounts of those thoughts that did occur. These reports can be recorded and later rated along appropriate classificatory dimensions. It is possible to build up considerable information on how much else is going on when an individual is presumably devoting primary attention to an assigned, externally derived task (Antrobus, Singer, Goldstein & Fortgang, 1970; Singer, 1975a).

These studies have indicated again and again that even when subjects are attaining 90 percent accuracy in the detection of auditory or visual signals they are nevertheless producing many extraneous thoughts. Indeed, one can relate the occurrence of such thoughts to a variety of parameters, including the information load of the detection task, the complexity of the task, the regularity of intervals between detection signals, the size of the gap between signals, the degree of unexpected information or stress presented to the subjects before entrance into the signal-detection booths (Antrobus, Singer, & Greenberg, 1966; Horowitz & Becker, 1971), and the personality characteristics of the subject. It seems likely not only that there is a good deal of task-irrelevant thought going on much of the time but also that such thought, although often somewhat fantastic or speculative, usually involves anticipations of future situations or reconstructions of past events that ultimately may have some value in guiding or steering behaviors for the future.

More recently there have been attempts to study ongoing thought even more directly, without the necessity for assignment of the subject to a signal-detection task (Singer, 1975a; Rychlak, 1973). An especially intriguing approach has been followed by Csikszentmihalyi (1974). This investigator and his collaborators have been concerned with studying the ongoing flow of behavior more generally and especially what he calls "autotelic behaviors," actions that are not in themselves clearly directed toward satisfaction of the more basic drives or the economic motives of the human condition. By having persons log their ongoing behavior, including mental activity, Csikszentmihalyi has been able to obtain some estimates of ongoing extraneous thought that bear on our present topic. For example, his data suggest that two-thirds of a group of twenty-one surgeons interviewed reported that they engaged in daydreaming particularly during the more routine aspects of the surgery, such as sewing up an incision. Their daydreams touched on music, food, wine, and women. In one phase of Csikszentmihalyi's research subjects were encouraged to inhibit regularly recurring autotelic activities. Those subjects who spent much time daydreaming and then attempted to inhibit such behavior subsequently reported extremely negative affective reactions.

If so much is indeed going on, it would seem that we ought to address ourselves more systematically to the stream of consciousness as a base for altered states of consciousness. It seems likely that the baseline or tonic characteristics of normal thought involve a range and variety of intrusions of images and interior monologues of retrospective or prospective scenes played out with greater or less vividness and that all of these are subject to different degrees of attention depending on the external task demands. I will elaborate on this suggestion in more detail below. I mention it at this point primarily to set the tone for a more intensive examination of the question of ongoing thought as a basic psychological problem.

Functions and Characteristics of Ongoing Thought

External and Internal Sources of Stimulation

As a baseline for consciousness, one may begin by taking into account the vast storage capacities of the brain and their special qualities. The vastness of the brain's storage capacity has been amply demonstrated in many recent experiments on the amazing effectiveness of recognition memory (Kagan & Kagan, 1970). This storage activity may involve not only sensory content but also, presumably, some degree of organization of material. Bartlett (1975) demonstrated ingeniously that environmental sounds that cannot easily be identified or labeled may still be stored as organizations rather than as purely sensory components for later recognition. I shall not attempt here to deal with the neurophysiological or neurochemical aspects of the storage process other than to suggest the likelihood that storage is not "in a place" (except perhaps within the left or right hemisphere, depending upon whether it is verbal-digital sequential or imagery-analogic) but rather is accomplished through some more active, relatively continuous recycling process. The brain is very likely fairly active at all times, and in a sense we must train ourselves not to heed the workings of its machinery just as we must learn not to notice the many gurglings of the stomach, the twitching of the toes, and the spontaneous firings of various nerve endings that occur all the time as we go about our day-to-day activities. The activity of the brain can be attested to by night dream research, which yields content reports from subjects interrupted at all stages of sleep.

In effect, then, this assumption leads to the likelihood that part of our sensory environment must include the ongoing activity of our own brain, which is expressed in the form of recurring (perhaps even randomly recurring) images in various modalities and bits and pieces of stored conversations. It seems conceivable that such activity represents a kind of noise in the system, an alternate source of stimulation to that produced by the physical stimuli of the external environment. Indeed, one might conceive of a continuum of stimulation fields in which clearly measurable external noises or lights or smells represent one pole. Further on the scale might lie bodily aches and pains or even more positive sensations that are less obvious to others but still referable on the whole to physically measurable characteristics—e.g., engorgement of the penis leading to a private sensation of sexual arousal.

Moving further internally, one might then have additional stimuli that are referable in part to the operation of peripheral processes. The "phosphenes," or entoptic lights and flashes, that characterize our experience when we shut our eyes and become aware of the fading of afterimages or of the play of lights and irregular geometric shapes on the "interior" of our eyelids have been relatively neglected until recent years. Horowitz (1970, 1974) has pioneered in studying these phenomena and reporting on their implications for hallucinatory behavior. Further along the internal dimension we may have more complex matching of externally derived stimuli to relatively recent stimulation held in short-term memory and some degree of organizational and coding activities. Still further along the internal dimension we might find rehearsal and replay activities from long-term memory, some of them set off by external stimuli as in the famous case of Marcel Proust's taste of madeleine crumbs in his tea, which brought flooding back a whole series of vivid images of the town of Combrai.

Perhaps most interior on this dimension would be associations primarily to the most private material drawn from long-term memory, as in the case of Proust's associations several steps removed from the initial taste of the madeleine to sets of associations gathered almost completely from long-term memory. For the most part, as best we can ascertain, our dreams, except those clearly referable to an outside noise such as an alarm going off, are responses to very private stimuli. A little introspection will make it clear how often our ongoing thoughts while we are performing other tasks represent a series of chained associations of varied degrees of vividness related only to material drawn from long-term memory. In some of our experimental work John Antrobus and I have used the phrase "stimulus-independent mentation" to describe reports of this kind obtained from subjects processing external signals. Nevertheless, in some respects even this phrase is misleading because the stimulus is itself some image or verbal sequence generated from long-term memory to which we respond with some of the same perceptual apparatus as if we were processing material clearly derived from an external source, such as the radio or the television set.

For practical purposes of communication I shall refer to this dimension as external/internal channels of stimulation, if the reader will keep in mind that we are really dealing here with a continuum rather than with two clearly differentiated or functionally dichotomous sources of stimulation.

DETERMINANTS OF ASSIGNMENT OF ATTENTION TO INTERNAL OR EXTERNAL CHANNELS

To what extent can we spell out the conditions under which a response, either overt or private, will be made to external or internal channels? Rapaport (1960) proposed for adaptive purposes there may be a "permanent gradient toward external cathexis." That is, external stimuli may demand more attention. Concepts such as energy expenditure or effort (Kahneman, 1973) have indeed been applied to the distribution of attention in relation to demands made upon some central executive within the information-processing mechanism of the brain. Clearly, it appears most adaptive for us to be more attuned to processing external cues when awake since there are so many potential hazards around us or since at least in man's earlier history alertness was necessary for the procurement of food. It seems to me, however, that a view of a limited channel capacity within an information-processing model is perhaps more appropriate to describe the demand character of external stimulation. To the extent that we are indeed awake, with eyes open, and moving around in an environment, the amount of feedback we get from external sources is likely to limit available channel space for processing internal material. If the same pathways appear to be used for processing private visual imagery as for processing externally derived visual stimulation (Antrobus, Singer, Goldstein, & Fortgang, 1970; Segal & Fusella, 1970), the active processing organs of the waking subject are likely to overload channels and limit internal processing. In addition, we undoubtedly train ourselves not to attend to private stimuli in much the same way that we learn to avoid noticing the nose on our face or the hundreds of twitches and gurglings of our active body machinery. Clinical observations of severely disturbed schizophrenic patients suggest that long-standing difficulties in body representation, associational control, and some of the withdrawal from attempts to involve themselves in social situations or to think about significant social situations all lead to their tendency to confuse these private bodily sensations with external stimulation (Angyal, 1944; Blatt, 1974; Singer, 1975b).

Given the greater demand character or, as we have elsewhere put it (Antrobus, Singer, Goldstein, & Fortgang, 1970), assignment of priorities to external or internal channels, can we order the conditions that will lead to relatively greater awareness and processing of material from long-term memory? Here we come to a new set of assumptions perhaps just as speculative but worth exploring for their implications.

Optimal Levels of Stimulation and Affect

Horowitz (1970) has attempted to generate a list of those circumstances that enhance the likelihood of an imagery experience. These include various pathological conditions, toxic states as well as circumstances of variations in external input, as in the case of different degrees of drowsiness or alertness. I believe it is necessary to add to these circumstances a combination of the notion of a central executive function with a concept of optimal levels of stimulation (Hebb, 1955).

Man is increasingly viewed by cognitive theorists as an image maker. That is, the human organism steers itself through its environment by schematizing its experiences into at least some relatively simple categories, then elaborating further on these categories through encoding processes that are also heavily intertwined with the language system. Each new set of environmental stimuli must be encoded and matched against some stored material. The various implications of the notion of the central matching processes based in part on anticipatory images or plans is a key feature of current cognitive systems (Miller, Galanter, & Pribram, 1960; Neisser, 1967; Tomkins, 1962–1963). The central matching concept is important on several grounds in the whole problem of the psychology of cognition and attention. Obviously, some selective process must be involved if man is to avoid being bombarded by the great range of external stimulation available. To some extent issues such as degree of structure or gestalt-like notions of inherent goodness (Garner, 1974) provide salience for certain external cues, but these in turn are already in part prepared for by the sets of plans or expectations we bring to each new environmental situation.

Let us focus here on the effect of matching, optimal stimulation, and affect on the salience of particular internal channel stimulations. Extensive work in sensory deprivation makes it clear that when there is dramatic reduction in novel material available for processing through our sense organs during otherwise alert or visual states of the organism, we will become increasingly aware of our own imagery or material drawn from long-term memory. But one does not require such an extreme condition of sensory deprivation to find oneself assigning a higher priority, at least temporarily, to processing material drawn from internal channels. There are many environments that provide ample external inputs but that because of their redundancy or limited complexity do not demand attention. Fiske and Maddi (1961) made this point well in their work on the functions of varied experiences. Optimal stimulation really means more than some simple quantitative measure of input.

Here I believe it is necessary to introduce Tomkins' (1962–1963) and Izard's (1971) notions of the critical role of affect as a primary motivator in our biological system. Moderate degrees of novel stimulation that requires central matching but cannot at once be assimilated to plans or expectations arouses, according to Tomkins, the affects of interest or surprise, which are positive emotions. As material is matched effectively following the search of the long-term memory system, the reduction of such novelty leads to the affect of joy or the smiling response. By contrast, rapidly occurring extreme amounts of novel stimulation, such as sudden loud noises or radio announcements of terrible disasters, may lead to startle reactions or to fear or terror responses. The expectations or plans brought to a given situation will determine in part the degree to which novel stimulation is likely to be viewed as interesting and therefore lead to further exploration or to be viewed as frightening and therefore lead to a distress response if it persists or to escape behaviors to avoid the stimulation. From this viewpoint, optimal stimulation is stimulation that is sufficiently novel that it can be gradually assimilated and thus holds our interest, keeps us exploring, but does not frighten or dismay us. Material that is extremely distressing and complex and persists for a long period of time will lead to the affect of aggression, if such stimulation is at a very high level, or to sadness, if the level of input is more moderate but still not readily tolerated. (See Singer, 1974, and Tomkins, 1962–1963, for a more detailed presentation of this view of the relation of information processing to separate affects.)

The position taken here bears similarity to other notions of the role of "discrepancy," for my intention is not to trace the notion of the matching process historically or to explore all of its various implications, including its relatively recent assignment of great significance in the conditioning process (Rescorla & Wagner, 1972). Rather, I would like to focus on the fact that this same process of central matching, expectation, discrepancy, or interest and joy as affects can be applied to material drawn from the internal channel. That is, we generally seek optimal levels of stimulation, and by and large these are available from external sources. When we find redundancy in our external environment (as in the case of being seated in a waiting room with only minimal novel external stimulation or during a lengthy train ride or under conditions of reduced sensory input in preparation for sleep), then we seek optimal levels of stimulation or matching of novel materials from the ongoing activity of the brain, which process is likely to become more salient as these conditions of external cue reduction are met.

From this vantage point, perhaps we can understand now why our night dreams seem so intriguing and odd to us. Here we have entered a phase of grossly reduced overt activity and processing of external material. We do not know for certain whether all that happens to produce night dream content is a heightened sensitivity to the "noise" of the system or our addition to sets of matches and expectations, even in sleep as well as on awakening, when we rehearse the dream material. Of course, to the extent that we are consciously aware of censorship operations in our dreams (as in the case perhaps of our committing a crime or an act of infidelity, when we literally feel or hear ourselves rationalizing or trying to undo the event), the effect of the dream is heightened by the relative discrepancy between our expectations and the stimulus content. When this discrepancy is especially great (as in the case of a dream of falling or of imminent death), we are less likely to go on with the dream and more likely to awaken, experiencing terror. But even our conscience may awaken us with a jerk in the former situation, depending on how well developed the superego is.

Night dreams, because they come during darkness, take on a figural quality that leads to their greater attributed significance. I would propose that daytime fantasy, more general ongoing interior monologues, and the private glosses that we put on a great variety of situations in which we find ourselves are perhaps even more characteristic of human consciousness. Because they occur in the midst of extensive processing of external material, they are less likely to be labeled as unique or "ticketed" for subsequent recall.

Attribution and Rehearsal Strategies

To the notion of the plans with which one approaches the external environment one must add a set of plans toward operating on internal channels. Here the notion of attribution derived from social psychology seems a key consideration as well. To what extent are we likely to identify our private events according to certain key rubrics? Much of the time we merely find our own fleeting thoughts and commentaries on passing events surprising or quaint, but because of the press of moving about in a physical environment or of reacting to others in social settings, we do not allow this novel stimulation to reverberate long enough in a short-term memory system for it to be stored effectively, unless we have already established a plan that this type of activity is worth rehearsing. A skilled novelist or poet is likely to value the odd or unusual associations he makes to an ongoing social situation. He may allow such thoughts to play themselves out more fully, even at the cost occasionally of appearing absentminded because he misses part of the concomitant conversation. He may, as a matter of fact, carry around a pad and pencil and write down some of this material for subsequent use since his experience indicates that often, because of information overload, he cannot recall interesting ideas without this technical help. Probably, some people in general adopt an approach that assigns somewhat higher priorities to reverberation and rehearsal of private associations, and this tendency increases the likelihood that not only will they identify and label particular material drawn from long-term memory but also they will, by rehearsing it further, increase the likelihood of its forming more complex connections with other categories of response. In a sense, then, the plans with which one approaches one's own awareness of ongoing private experience determine to a great extent the probability of increased complexity of associational structures.

The issue of attribution and expectancy about one's own private processes is important not only for the development of differentiated inner life. It also may play a role in the degree to which one is "comfortable" with private experiences. There is good reason to believe, primarily on the basis of clinical observation, that many people become frightened by their own thoughts or indeed consider their thoughts quasi-hallucinations simply because they have not approached these processes with a plan about their nature or general acceptability (Singer, 1975a; Horowitz, 1974).

Salience of Internal Stimulation

Let us next consider what factors contribute to the recurrence of certain images or contents generally in consciousness and also to their salience for the individual. If we assume the baseline of ongoing reverberatory activity, then we can make the next assumption that one approaches this material through the same modalities and with the same patterns of anticipations and expectations and plans that guide waking movement through the external environment. It is possible also that the ongoing stream of thought is somewhat randomly occurring, as part of the brain's storage system may reflect certain properties of structure or of "good gestalten" that will attract attention and lead to further rehearsal of the material. It remains to be seen whether such structures follow the same laws as materials in the external environment or whether for private experience unusual and odd combinations of associations produced perhaps randomly are more likely to attract attention and lead to further reverberation or rehearsal in the short-term memory system, thus increasing even further the likelihood that they will be later recalled. This seems somewhat more likely in the case of a night dream than a daydream, for often the latter is cast in a setting in which so many other preoccupations are occurring that one is quick to dismiss an odd thought.

Possibly there is a certain goodness of fit about particular structures such as well-known songs or snatches of melody that leads them, once noticed, to be replayed regularly, sometimes to the point of annoyance at the recurrence of the material. As Mark Twain once noted, a catchy rhyme may in effect take possession of one's consciousness. In this case one person after another is plagued by the little phrase "punch brothers, punch with care; punch in the presence of the passenjare!"—a jingle about trolley cars that individuals could not rid themselves of until they told it to others.

The stream of consciousness material in James Joyce's *Ulysses* includes many examples of well-turned or interestingly structured phrases that recur. Often the sounds as well as the meanings of the phrases are important. Alliterative phrases that may not have any special personal significance may remain in the attention longer or recur more frequently in one's interior monologue.

Structural characteristics that lead to salience are probably further enhanced by the search plan of the subject. The poet or composer may savor unusual phrases or musical connections that occur and play them out more extensively. In other words, such artists bring a set of their own private experiences that gives a higher priority to processing for further use unusual materials or materials that have a special "ring" to them. The obsessional neurotic whose plan is one that seeks the avoidance of confrontation with his own feelings of desire, anger, or pettiness may latch on to such structured phrases and repeat them again and again as a means of overloading consciousness and thus preventing even accidental awareness of the undesired thoughts.

Salience of what might be called "naturally occurring structures" is of course hard to demonstrate in respect to private conscious experience, and in any case it may play a smaller role than certain other principles that are more closely bound to the general set of the individual toward processing material in internal channels.

Persistence and Recurrence of "Novel" Stimulus-Independent Thought

A special feature of internal activity may be the somewhat more vague and less vivid quality (except in night dreams) of our imagery in the awakened state. It may be more difficult therefore to make a match to novel material that one notices in stimulus-independent mentation than to material that one confronts in the external channel. A sudden loud noise may startle one, but in most cases it can quickly be identified and matched with some material from long-term memory so that the result is a sense of relief or even laughter as the match is made. A strange face that attracts one can often be matched eventually to the face of a relative or childhood friend. Images and phrases that occur without obvious external referents may be so vague that one is less likely to identify them, and to the extent that one is initially attracted to them they may be harder to assimilate into established schema and therefore may persist longer. A snatch of melody or a landscape image may attract our notice and interest us sufficiently to be reverberated in short-term memory but because we cannot find an easy match or because its associational network is itself so complex it may continue to recur and hold our interest for a much longer time before it can be fully assimilated into established cognitive schema. This notion can be applied to the regular recurrence of wishes or fantasies that have not been satisfied. They continue to be of interest to us (particularly those that relate to already ongoing sets of plans that are part of an individual's general search system) since they cannot be matched to actual memories.

Consider also the differences between certain external events that may have occurred and the complexity of the labeling processes and associational frameworks of the ongoing storage system. If we hear news of the death of a stranger, even under unusual or dramatic circumstances, we may think about this event for a little while, but before long we will have forgotten the event; that is, it loses probability of recurrence in the "buffer" storage system (Broadbent, 1971). The death of a person close to us is a subject of recurring images and fantasies because so many other events in the physical environment and so many of our own ongoing associations are already linked with that person that we cannot dismiss the thought and linkage so readily. We have in the past built so many wishes and fantasies or specific memories around that particular individual that a high percentage of naturally occurring thoughts will be associated with him or her. They remind us of the individual's death and thereby further provoke a high level of discrepant matching or unassimilability and the affects of anger or distress and sadness.

Some examples of how this process may work can be given. During a Palestinian airplane hijacking news reports indicated that one of the hostages, a Swiss businessman, had been murdered. I am certain that I would never have thought any further of this particular event were it not for the fact that a few days later my research assistant told me that this man had been a close friend of her father's and that her father was very much upset about his death. This information made the incident real to me and led to some further imaginings, at least while my assistant was telling me about possible associations between her father and the dead man. Again, however, I had no further thoughts about this event to the best of my knowledge until I began casting around while writing this account for examples of recurrent fantasies. Probably, this situation came back to mind primarily because once it became linked with people I knew and was further rehearsed its likelihood of recurrence was tremendously increased. It seems quite possible that had I not had further discussion with my research assistant about this event I would never again have thought about the man's death.

Consider another situation: the death of a man's wife after thirty or so years of marriage. There are innumerable connections between a husband and wife, experiences that have been shared, fantasies as yet unresolved, wishes for the two that are likely to recur. Suppose that the husband had been unfaithful to his wife during the period of her fatal illness. To the extent that he already has a sense of guilt about his infidelity, the husband's inability to resolve the conflict between his active involvement with another woman and his wife's subsequent death may lead to an even greater likelihood that material from their shared life will recur in a varied set of associations, subsequently leading to a high level of unassimilability of the material and to a heightened affect of either self-directed anger or depression and grief. Indeed, it would be interesting to study the possibility that extended mourning and grief reactions may in part reflect not only a closeness of association and strong attachment but also a greater mixture of feelings toward the person (ambivalence), so that assimilation of the associations is less likely and we see what on the surface looks like a reaction formation or an excessive response. To the extent that wishes have indeed the vagueness and probability of recurrence suggested above, then unresolved wishes or conflicts of desires may account for much longer depressions.

One need not in this formulation posit a recurring appetitive drive system (Rapaport, 1960) to explain why certain fantasies or images recur throughout one's life. It seems more likely that early childhood wishes and desires that have remained at the level of fantasy cannot easily be assimilated and although practiced and repracticed they were never effectively organized into structured cognitive schema that can be matched effectively with memories. The result is that each time these images recur they continue to arouse some mild interest and are therefore repracticed and persist for longer periods in the short-term memory system.

Current Concerns and Unfinished Business

The principle of matching and its connection with the arousal of surprise and interest as well as joy when the final match is made may also be related to the increasing indications that recurring thoughts or dream contents are related not only to childhood wishes and drives but also to current unfinished business or current concerns and unresolved immediate stresses (Breger, Hunter, & Lane, 1971; Klinger, 1971; Singer, 1975a, 1975b). The power of the notion of the Zeigarnik effect has never been fully explored as a psychological principle despite its development in Kurt Lewin's laboratory in the 1920s. It seems to me that a great deal of our conscious experience can be characterized by the recurrence of thoughts about tasks initiated but as yet uncompleted; plans set in motion but as yet far from execution; actions taken quite recently that one realizes were inadequate to a task or incorrect; deadlines in work assignments still to be met; and promises in relationship to others still to be kept. Freud recognized this principle, of course, in his notion of the day residue that forms a basic component of the dreamwork, but he underestimated the effect such daily occurring events have on ongoing mentation and fantasy. The awareness of a host of incompleted tasks can bring severe pain and undoubtedly accounts for many headaches and for the development of devices to avoid thinking, such as the use of barbiturates or alcohol.

It may well be that certain types of job situations differ dramatically from others in the degree to which they inevitably involve many unresolved issues. A man whose work involves primarily extensive long-range planning and a variety of investment activities for others may find himself reverting in thought to such material much more frequently and perhaps having greater difficulty falling asleep at night than a truck driver or factory worker, whose particular assignment may be completed within the space of a day and who does not have the responsibility for long-range planning in connection with his work. Of course, the driver or skilled laborer may have all kinds of other unfinished business in the form of tasks around the home that remain to be done, bills to be paid, and family responsibilities that cause him insomnia as well. Nevertheless, it would be intriguing to see whether we could get samples of ongoing thought, through some of the techniques previously described, from persons whose work involves different degrees of relative completion of the activity within limited time spans to determine to what extent ongoing thought does indeed reflect recurrent images and scenes or interior monologues related to such incomplete tasks.

STYLISTIC DIFFERENCES IN INTERNAL/EXTERNAL RESPONSES

We must now consider the question of the plans with which one approaches one's own internal experience. It seems clear that situational factors such as the relative redundancy of a physical environment, the tedium of a long wait in drab surroundings, the particular task demand set (as in the case of psychoanalysis, in which the patient is encouraged to catch hold of the train of thought) all play key roles in one's awareness of private fantasy. Nevertheless, there seem to be striking individual differences in the extent to which we set up expectations for recalling our ongoing fantasy activity. A good deal of the time during any day we simply fail to label our passing thoughts for recurrence. That is to say, we do not assign them sufficient attention and indeed add to them a kind of intention that they be thought about again so that they simply do not have a sufficient basis for recurrence within the other complex material being processed. By failing to set up formal labeling or retrieval routines we may often be surprised when such thoughts do reach our awareness in periods of preparation for sleep, when there are fewer competing stimuli, or during our dreams.

Still, some people are practiced daydreamers. That is, they adopt a conscious attitude of attention to their ongoing stream of thought; therefore, symbolic materials and novel combinations are much more accessible to them. Such persons may be more likely to gain relatively quick insight into the transformations from normal English sentences that may occur in their dream images. Indeed, to some extent psychoanalysis trains an individual to perform this very act of transformation. It alerts the patient to noticing dreams and replaying them mentally several times or writing them down so as not to forget them, and then gives him a labeling or coding system that will increase the likelihood of recall. Needless to say, the coding system varies considerably as a function of the particular school of psychoanalysis, and we may never catch hold of the veridical content of the dream because of the overlay of the special labels different schools propose.

There is increasing evidence that there are striking individual differences in the extent to which persons learn to approach and to interpret their ongoing conscious experience (Singer, 1975b). Indeed, situations seem also to be closely related to processes of control and attribution. To some extent an individual who has learned to be comfortable with make-believe and playful activities, perhaps from childhood (Singer, 1973), also may become comfortable with, and feel some degree of control over, his own ongoing thought activities. Willingness to explore internal activities and to accept their diversity and oddity may make an individual less likely to be distressed or confused about what is fantasy and what is real. There are indications from studies of sensory deprivation, for example, that those persons who are already more comfortable with private fantasy activity are less likely to report gross discomfort with sensory deprivation or to be susceptible to hallucinatory experiences. There may be, in addition, different degrees of explanation and role attitudes that come into play in relation to one's own ongoing fantasy activities. Indeed, there may be habitual or recurrent styles of daydreaming that are hard to alter. Our own research, using factor analytic approaches, brings out the recurrence of three patterns of daydreaming, one a guilty-dysphoric style characterized by many fantasies involving guilt and self-recrimination, others involving hostile and aggressive wishes, and still others involving fears of failure as well as wishes for achievement. A second factor is characterized more by fleeting and uncontrollable fantasies, generally of an anxiety-laden nature, considerable distractibility, and mind wandering, which includes the inability to hold fast to thoughts or to inhibit visual or auditory attention to external events.

A third factor seems to be associated more with positive contents of fantasy, vivid visual and auditory imagery, future-oriented and planful fantasies, and in general acceptance of daydreaming as a worthwhile activity (Giambra, 1974; Isaacs, 1976; Segal & Singer, 1975; Singer & Antrobus, 1963, 1972; Starker, 1974). While an individual, if a great fantasizer, could show all of these patterns, it seems likely that some individuals are more given to one or another of them and in a sense become habituated to approaching their search of internal material with a view to organizing it in relation to these patterns. I shall return a little later to further questions about stylistic patterns in processing internal material. For the moment the point I wish to stress is that the approach of an individual to examining private processes, dwelling on them, and rehearsing them generates an entirely new set of consequences and creates an entirely different internal environment that needs to be understood.

FEEDBACK CHARACTERISTICS OF ATTENTION TO INNER STIMULI

In effect, private experience has its own set of feedback characteristics. In attending to our ongoing dreams and daydreams we are practicing new private responses and making new combinations, new labels, and also viewing ourselves in relation to this material in a different perspective. Here we have the entire range of "as if" responses recognized as a significant part of the individual's behavioral repertoire. The introspective individual carves out a fairly differentiated realm of schema and generates new labels and new rubrics. Retrieval processes become more organized in many ways since there is considerable evidence that the most efficient retrieval involves a combination of imagery and labeling (Paivio, 1971; Seaman, 1972). The extensive work now being done on the use of imagery in various psychotherapeutic approaches (Singer, 1974) suggests that a conscious approach to producing and examining one's own imagery or using it in connection with behavior modification or psychotherapeutic activities may increase one's general self-awareness, heighten one's sense of control over ongoing inner processes, and possibly lead to greater empathic capacities. Style differences in emphasis on verbal versus imagery or concrete representations need also to be explored as well as relative emphases on sequential-logical thought processes compared with spatial and visual or auditory imagery processes. Brain asymmetry in relation to these functions has yet to be fully explored, especially with regard to pinning down more precisely how the *interaction* of verbal chaining sequences with representational materials in the ongoing thought stream is produced.

Stylistic Patterns of Internal/External Processing

DAYDREAMING AND STIMULUS-INDEPENDENT THOUGHT

Somehow or other, despite the many vicissitudes of personality research, we find ourselves returning again and again to some form of an introversion/extraversion dimension as a major feature of human difference. Carrigan (1960), reviewing the literature to that date, concluded that the notion of introversion/extraversion was still viable. Although Jung's classification system has never gained extensive empirical support, there are psychometric indications of stylistic patterns involving introversion and extraversion at least along two dimensions, sociability and thoughtfulness (Guilford, 1959). Here we will concentrate primarily upon introversion/extraversion in relation to the area of thoughtfulness or the assignment of priorities to processing internal versus external stimuli (Singer, 1966).

The extensive literature on the Rorschach inkblot method continues to provide evidence that at least moderately supports Rorschach's own delineation of introversion/extraversion by the use of scores for movement and color responses associated with the blots (Singer, 1960, 1968). Factor analyses of self-reports concerning daydreaming and related imaginal processes generally indicate that individuals do vary in the degree to which they emphasize private processes or are aware of such processes. At the opposite pole, or distributed along a separate dimension, are subjects less concerned with such internal processing and much more involved in obtaining experiences or information from the external environment (Giambra, 1974; Isaacs, 1976; Segal & Singer, 1975; Singer & Antrobus, 1963, 1972; Starker, 1974).

If we move beyond self-report consistencies on questionnaires, the question arises as to whether such reports are related to other behaviors. Antrobus, Coleman, and Singer (1967) found that subjects classified as high daydreamers on both the Guilford Thoughtfulness Introversion Scale and the Singer daydreaming scale were more likely to report the occurrence of stimulus-independent thoughts during an extended signal-detection task watch. The internally oriented individuals did not make any more errors initially because of their preoccupation with private content. As time went on, they seemed to become more and more involved with stimulus-independent thought, with the consequence that their error rate increased in comparison with that of subjects low in introversive tendencies. Using a quite different format,

Fusella (1972) studied persons participating in the so-called Perky phenomenon experiment (Segal, 1971)—that is, projecting the subject's own imagery onto a blank screen while (unknown to him or her) the experimenter actually flashed a picture of that same fixation point at a low but discriminable level of illumination. Subjects high in questionnaire measures of daydreaming and internal sensitivity tended to rate their images as more vivid than did subjects who scored low on those scales. They also missed more of the externally produced signals. That is, they were less likely to be aware that an actual picture had been flashed at the fixation point where they were imagining their own private scene.

Meskin and Singer (1974) also found support in a quite different type of format for differences in daydreaming style. We studied laterality of eyeshift during processing of reflective questions in a dyadic interview situation. Internally oriented subjects were found, again on the basis of daydreaming questionnaires, to be more likely to be "left-shifters" in processing thought material and also more likely to produce complex private materials.

An important step has been taken by Isaacs (1976), who was able to differentiate daydreaming style from mind wandering rather clearly. Using subjects representative of orthogonal dimensions of daydreaming and mind wandering, he was able to show that persons high on daydreaming tended to produce much more stimulus-independent thought, responses made to material derived more from the long-term memory system than from cues or signals in the external environment. Subjects differing in mind wandering did not show differences so much in the processing of private materials as in the degree to which they manifested *control* over the processing of either private or external material. Subjects who showed strikingly high patterns of daydreaming style on questionnaire scales tended to produce more analogic or metaphoric types of content in their stimulus-independent mentation during periods of silence or signal detection. More recent findings (Huba, Segal, & Singer, 1977) also indicate that daydreaming patterns as measured by the Imaginal Processes Inventory (Singer & Antrobus, 1972) are related to other personality dimensions with measurable behavioral correlates. Canonical analyses of the Imaginal Processes Inventory and the Personality Research Form for more than five hundred male and female college students from northeastern and border-state colleges indicated that patterns of daydreaming do indeed relate to other personality characteristics. I shall deal further with some of these issues in the next section.

While one must always keep in mind the fact that for any given behavioral situation a great portion of the variance is often attributed to the demands of the situation and its context, as Mischel (1968) has warned, there is nevertheless ample support for the likelihood that stylistic patterns of assignment of priority to private thoughts and awareness of the ongoing thought stream do contribute to the total variance. An introversive orientation may itself represent at least three modes of concern or style: positive-vivid, guilty-dysphoric, anxious-distractible. Still, some people on the whole seem more inclined to pay a good deal of attention to the ongoing thought stream and to give it, if not absolute priority, then relatively more weight even in the face of fairly demanding external tasks.

EXTERNALIZATION AND ADDICTIVE BEHAVIORS

There is a growing body of evidence that many kinds of addictive behaviors or at least manifestations of excess in drinking, eating, and drug use bear some relationship to a marked desire for (or a habitual pattern of) processing externally derived experiences. A study of more than six hundred college students (Segal & Singer, 1975) examined scores for drug and alcohol use along with data obtained from the Jackson Personality Research Form, the Singer-Antrobus Imaginal Processes Inventory, the Rotter Internal-External Locus of Control Scale, and the Zuckerman Sensation Seeking Scale. Factor analyses, multivariate analyses of variance, and discriminate analyses were carried out for all of these groups by sex, college (Ivy League or border-state rural college), and drug use.

General findings of the different analyses indicated clearly that the primary dimension separating drug and alcohol users from non-users in these samples might best be termed *externalization*. Those college subjects who showed emphasis on the use of drugs and alcohol were much more likely to be characterized as individuals who were constantly striving for new experiences or stimulation derived from *external* sources. These findings also bear close correspondence to reports by Zuckerman, Neary, and Brustman (1970) and Zuckerman, Bone, Neary, Mangelsdorff, and Brustman (1972).

The distinctive personality profile that seemed to characterize particularly the multiple-drug and frequent marijuana user in our sample was that of a physically active person searching for novel experiences, eschewing group participation and conformity, striving for autonomy, minimizing the importance of formal achievement, and continually desirous of external stimulation. Daydreaming and fantasy patterns,

contrary to some expectations, were not found to be particularly related to multiple-drug or frequent marijuana use. Rather, the data
indicated that persons who emphasized the use of drugs showed little
development of their own private fantasy capacities. If anything, there
was a tendency for heavier alcohol use to be associated with an attempt
at disinhibition and release from guilty and aggressive fantasies, particularly in the rural, predominantly Southern Baptist, male college
sample. On the whole, drug use more than alcohol use reflected the
externalizing tendencies. Discriminate function analyses also can clearly
separate drug users from non-users, with the latter subjects tending to
be people little interested in taking overt risks, persons who emphasize
greater control over their behavior and show greater interest in processing private fantasies or thoughts. In our research, drug users tended to
place greater emphasis on externally oriented attitudes or behaviors such
as seeking new kinds of experiences from the outside world, attempting
to establish a sense of freedom from social or moral constraints, and
playing down the importance of conformity to social norms or achievement and competence development.

The external orientation that emerged from our study seems to have
a strong cognitive quality to it and may represent the fundamental information-processing style in which excessive reliance is placed on reacting to content from the physical or social environments with too
little emphasis on the adequate matching of material from the long-term
memory system. In this sense "externality" bears a resemblance to a
cognitive style such as Broadbent's (1958) "short processors"—that is,
persons who are inclined to make a match of new information only with
the most immediately preceding information rather than scanning the
long-term memory system more widely before producing an output response. Recent research on obesity (Schachter & Rodin, 1974) has
also supported the notion that persons given to addictive eating are
inclined to be externally oriented and find it difficult to ignore cues from
the physical environment. A study by Rodin and Singer (1976) has
indicated that overweight subjects are less likely to report visual
imagery in their daydreaming and are strongly drawn to look at the
interviewer's face. They have great difficulty, too, engaging in complex
thought in a face-to-face social situation. The data of this study support
other findings concerning the strong external pull of the environment
for obese individuals. Pliner (1973a, 1973b) has reported that obese
individuals differ strikingly in their pattern of thinking from normal-
weight subjects, depending much more heavily upon external cues to
guide them in the organization of their thought and in their pattern of

response. In the Rodin and Singer (1976) study, overweight subjects seemed to be more predominantly right-shifters. Their responses to questions indicated the predominance of verbal-sequential thought processes over spatial representations or visual imagery. They also found it difficult to carry on extended thinking without looking away from the interviewer or shutting their eyes since apparently the pull of external cues and particularly the complex stimulus configuration of the face (Tomkins, 1962–1963) imposes a heavy demand on their information channel capacity.

Although much work yet remains to be done on pinpointing the nature of the externalization process, we seem to be on the verge of a new reexamination of the behavioral implications of the differential processing of material from external sources and that from long-term memory. It would appear from our data that addictive behavior grows not so much out of excessive involvement in private fantasy as out of a desire to seek some novel experience because one has failed to develop such an inner capacity. It seems likely that this approach is worth pursuing. An additional complication that is at the same time challenging has to do with the possibility that individuals are differentially specialized in the emphasis they have placed on verbal versus spatial representational processing. Although we have no evidence at present that such differences represent genuine constitutional differences in the functional capacities of the left and right hemispheres, it is worth exploring more extensively whether habitual styles lead to differential storage and reliance on the functions presumably governed by the left hemisphere (verbal-sequential) and the right hemisphere (spatial-imagery parallel processing).

Some Needed Research

PERSONALITY STYLES

The large-scale nomothetic data gathered by Segal and Singer (1976), Zuckerman and associates (1972), and Jessor and associates (1973) emphasize the external orientation of drug or marijuana users among late adolescents; yet we require further information on the specific processes that underlie this externality. Few studies have examined subjects representing extremes on dimensions of externality or on combinations of externality and actual drug use in laboratory situations, where specific attentional functions can be explored. We need also to know much more about the ways in which relative emphasis on the verbal-sequential as against the imagery-spatial representational modes of thinking or information processing intersect with externality, as some of the data cited previously suggest. To the extent that habitual styles of processing reflect differential degrees of lateral specialization, laboratory studies might tease out more precisely the degree to which a person who lacks skill in visual imagery or who is not accustomed to making extended searches of long-term memory in the face of new stimulation may be inclined to become more dependent on increasing external resources. Is it possible that an absence of skill in attending to the ongoing thought stream or a failure to develop adequate labeling devices for such internal processes so that one can take joy from them and use anticipation in a constructive fashion may contribute to the excessive dependence of drug users on the external environment? Lacking the ability to shift flexibly between internal and external poles, do drug users suffer from "stimulus hunger"?

A recent examination of our own data from about a thousand college students averaging just over eighteen years of age emphasized also the interaction of two major dimensions defining the reasons these young people offer for their use of alcohol or marijuana. One dimension represents the affective response sought from the drug; for example, certain drugs are employed to heighten and sustain good feelings. Other subjects emphasize drug or alcohol use to reduce negative affects such as guilt, depression, and anxiety. The second dimension along which subjects varied might be termed the relative role of contingency factors in the use of drugs or alcohol. Thus, many young people drink beer simply because it is the thing to do in hot weather after hard work. They may take some marijuana at a party because it is a sociable response rather than because it affects their mood or cognition. But others drink or use marijuana because it reduces feelings of anger, loneliness, and tension in the group situation—social contingency is here mixed with a need to reduce negative affects (Huba, Segal, & Singer, 1977).

The use of drugs or alcohol either to enhance positive emotions and widen cognitive experiences or to reduce negative emotions resembles the reports by Silvan Tomkins and his collaborators on the smoking patterns of adults. Tomkins has pointed out that the treatment of smoking has markedly different prognoses for positive-affect smokers, who can quit easily, and negative-affect smokers, who can rarely stop smoking for long. One might predict the same results for drug users or drinkers. Those whose drinking or use of various drugs hinges heavily on the social situation or who use drugs merely for a mild mood uplift during otherwise pleasurable circumstances (as most college students now use marijuana) may be less likely to show drug abuse patterns later on. Those young people for whom drinking or drug use is perceived as a means of reducing strong negative affects, anxiety, guilt, sadness, or anger may be more susceptible to abuse or addiction. This position is supported by clinical data of Khantzian, Mack, and Schatzberg (1974), who reported that heroin addiction is strongly tied to an attempt to reduce the negative feelings experienced from coping or competency failures. Although Platt (1975) interpreted his findings from a comparison of heroin addicts with non-user delinquents as failing to support the Khantzian report, the significant differences he noted compare well with those of Huba, Segal, and Singer (1976) for multiple-drug users in college freshmen samples. The heroin addicts show the sensation-seeking needs for autonomy and counterculture orientations found in the college student "heads" but also show greater evidence of "death concerns" and a need for abasement.

An increasing body of literature based on the cognitive model of Piaget as elaborated by Turner emphasizes the development of social competence and must include in role taking the role rehearsal behaviors. A willingness to examine alternative role possibilities in imagination and to lay out privately various alternatives in one's future behavior may be an important part of mature thinking in the Piagetian postoperational period. Our own research has suggested that multiple-drug users are individuals who have, despite their assertions of striving for autonomy, failed to develop a sufficient sense of self-awareness, of anticipatory imagery and social role-taking skills to provide them with "immunity" from the pressures of each new environmental contingency.

There is by now a very sizable body of information and clinical anecdotes emphasizing the useful features of imagery in the processes of psychotherapy and behavior modification (Singer, 1974). Recognition seems to have come within the past decade or less that the private stream of thought and the possibilities of what Freud long ago called "experimental action" through the medium of thought represent one of man's major skills. The power of imagery to produce changes not only in fear responses but also in subsequent overt exploratory behaviors or in the modification of severe symptomatologic or unwanted behavior patterns represents an encouraging advance in behavioral technology. It remains to be seen whether drug or alcohol users who are characterized by strong externalization patterns can be trained to make more effective use of their own ongoing thought stream thereby to modify their dependence on external gratifications. Research of this kind is currently under way in our laboratories, and some data may soon be available. Certainly some of the promising results obtained in individual case studies with obese and alcoholic individuals are encouraging, but more extensive research with drug abusers has yet to be carried out (Singer, 1974). Work by Csikszentmihalyi (1974) has pointed out the extent to which persons oriented around autotelic activities involving chewing, biting, smoking, and eating are inclined to report feelings of alienation from society and are to some extent self-alienated because of a lack of resources in imagery and fantasy. Indeed, when individuals who showed strong tendencies to rely on their own fantasy activity were systematically deprived of such activity for a couple of days, they showed much greater distress and difficulty than individuals who were deprived of social activities or other kinds of autotelic behaviors. Clearly, fantasy and awareness of one's ongoing thought stream may have a valuable feedback and balancing effect on how one steers oneself through day-to-day life.

STATES OF CONSCIOUSNESS

The emphasis in this chapter thus far has been on establishing the importance of understanding the ongoing thought stream and some of its implications for personality. What of the question of alternate states of consciousness? It seems possible that what we consider alternate states of consciousness depends to a great extent on attribution and labeling processes. I believe that individuals who are practiced daydreamers— that is to say, persons who can readily shift to a more extended processing of private material compared to that of material from the external world—may find little that is novel in drugged or various hypnotic states. They have defined a range of possible situations in which they can, because of redundant processing demands from the outside, redirect their attention to private exploration with reasonable comfort and without serious danger of missing important external cues. Also, they may be less likely to look to externally derived substances such as drugs, tobacco, or alcohol, or to related activities in order to provide themselves with intense novel and attractive stimulation. For the practiced daydreamer listening to music may involve very extended reverie; he does not need the so-called slowing-down effect that is presumably produced for many people by marijuana. The situation is perhaps a bit more complex, since, as indicated earlier, not all persons who rely extensively on private events are positive in their orientation toward their fantasies. Subjects who are prone to guilt-oriented daydreams, at least in recent studies by Segal and myself, seem likely to move toward alcohol as a means of blotting out private experience and encouraging themselves to more uninhibited overt action. By contrast, college students, in their anticipation of what marijuana will do for them (according to our research), turn out to expect the marijuana effect to lead to a kind of extended passive observation of the environment. The interesting thing from our studies is that in neither drug nor alcohol anticipation does reliance on the externally derived substance lead to an expectation of the development of a truly richer "inner" life, as is sometimes reported.

With respect to meditative states, there is no really conclusive evidence as yet as to how these mesh with internal or external stylistic patterns. People experienced in transcendental meditation tend to report that they do indeed generate considerable fantasy during their trance exercises. There seem to be differences between yoga and Zen adherents, with the former more inclined to follow daydream and thought patterns and the latter more oriented toward abolishing extended thinking and focusing primarily on a perceptual response (Barber, 1970). Still, Maupin (1965) found that persons already inclined toward acceptance of inner experience and fantasy were more likely to profit relatively quickly from Zen meditation exercises.

The close relationships between the capacity for generating self-oriented imagery or awareness of private imagery and hypnosis has been extensively discussed by J. Hilgard (1970). The links between hypnotic susceptibility and a history of daydreaming or childhood imaginary companions are documented in her research. Creative personalities studied by Helson (1965) and by Anastasi and Schaefer (1969) also reported more childhood emphasis on daydreaming and imaginary playmates. As suggested at the outset, the so-called regression in the service of the ego attributed to the artist by psychoanalytic theorists may represent an early expansion of the repertoire of imaginal responses, a style carried with functionally adaptive effectiveness into adult life as a skill that all mature adults could benefit from, rather than a dip into "childlike" thought. The seeming distraction, absent-mindedness, and trancelike behavior of the creative scientist or artist may represent not so much a shift to an "altered state of consciousness" as a well-trained capacity for assigning a high priority to attending in concentrated fashion to the private, ongoing stream of thought when, after all, so much of our external environmental information is redundant.

ALTERNATE STATES, ONGOING THOUGHT, AND DRUG CHARACTERISTICS

Recent research on neurotransmitters suggests that a surprising number of chemical compounds involved in the so-called psychoactive drugs are secreted in small quantities at nerve endings in the brain. Work on catecholamines and on morphine transmission in animal brains has pointed to a confrontation, perhaps in the next decade, between neurophysiology and behavioral science over the old mind/body problem. Can some of the research methodology and theoretical approaches to the study of ongoing thought contribute to fusing the data from the two fields? What follows is a fantasy, but one that may be able to generate some feasible research.

Suppose we assert the possibility that certain neurotransmitters are differentially specialized to activate groups of nerve cells and to produce more or less broadly ramifying or activation effects. Suppose, too, that such effects interact with the specialized characteristics of the brain structures—e.g., sensory areas, motor areas, perceptual or synthetic organizing areas, and (based on left/right-hemisphere specialization) analogic and digital processing areas. One way we might approach a *psychological* understanding of these processes with intact human beings might be to study the nature of ongoing thought in individuals who have ingested specific psychoactive drugs under controlled conditions. Although we have many anecdotal reports on the effects of drugs, we have not availed ourselves systematically of consensual reporting techniques and operational definitions for scoring such reports. Researchers on night dreaming are relying increasingly on detailed ratings, matching methods, and common dimensions for scoring reports obtained upon awakenings from various sleep stages. These methods are being applied also to reports of ongoing thought and to samples of thought obtained during signal-detection procedures (e.g., Isaacs, 1976).

Reports might be assembled from individuals experienced in the use of specific drugs. By training them to be alert to certain differentiations that might be critical—e.g., sensory from perceptual or cognitive from affective or motor processes—we might get a group of reports relatively free of private metaphor. Such reports could then be rated by "blind" judges along such dimensions as imagery modality, vividness, attribution versus direct effect, realism versus fantasy, verbal versus spatial imagery representation. A cluster or factor analysis of a series of reports from a large sample might yield a limited number of dimensions along which all reports varied for a given drug. Such dimensions might then be examined for their tie to the known or presumed brain level involved and the possible operation of neurotransmitters in that region. One might then examine several other drugs and the factors emerging from statistical analyses of correlation matrices between ratings of reports of experience following ingestion.

Perhaps a more precise approach would be to use relatively naive subjects with, of course, double-blind procedures and control drugs or placebos. Subjects could be assigned experimenter-controlled tasks such as signal-detection or vigilance procedures. One could thus obtain not only reports of "yes or no" for extraneous thought every fifteen seconds (Antrobus, Singer, Goldstein, & Fortgang, 1970) but also verbal accounts of thought every minute or so and thus accumulate as many as forty-five to sixty reports per subject for an hour's task. The accuracy of signal detection reflecting perceptual effectiveness and motivation could be studied also. Again, one might use this method to test specific differential hypotheses about drug effects—e.g., one drug affecting sensory response, another affecting attention to inner or outer channels, another influencing emotionality or motivation rather than information-processing capacities. In addition, ratings of verbal reports and related data such as mood ratings, physiological reactivity, and detection accuracy patterns could be included in a correlation matrix for factor analysis. The dimensions that emerged, if replicable on other samples, should suggest the major characteristics of the psychological impact of the drug; these might be more perceptual or sensory for some, more mood oriented for others, more motoric for others. These results could then be related to animal research findings pinpointing neurotransmitter relations to level of cortical region and suggest some important theoretical and research directions.

It might be argued, especially by phenomenologically oriented drug researchers, that such experiments would be too artificial and not readily extrapolated to drug effects in more typical social situations. But unless one eschews experimentation or systematic data collection entirely, even day-to-day life situations may be susceptible to some comparable analysis of ongoing thought. The use of daily logs, as demonstrated in Csikszentmihalyi's (1974) work, is but one instance of such an approach. Or relatively naturally formed groups could be assigned group tasks and provide periodic reports on experience; communication would of course be controlled. Once we accept the fact that the systematic analysis of reports of ongoing thought can be carried out by methods of coding and rating, a methodology is available for training self-observation as well as for training "blind" raters of reports. It takes only the ingenuity of behavioral scientists and the cooperation of informed volunteers to approach the useful scientific study of alternate states of consciousness.

In conclusion, then, the way beckons for us to explore more fully the structural characteristics of ongoing consciousness. Such an exploration may go far toward debunking the mysticism of altered states of consciousness while exciting us with new possibilities for using man's basic information-processing capacities in an ever more creative and adaptive fashion.

5

A Framework for Describing Subjective
States of Consciousness

Caryl Marsh

What Is Consciousness?

CONSCIOUSNESS IS A SUBJECT that has been much debated by scholars and writers interested in unraveling the essential nature of human capacities. The word *conscious*, a Latin compound that can be translated as "knowing things together," was first used in English early in the seventeenth century by Francis Bacon. Later, John Locke (1690) defined consciousness as "the perception of what passes in a man's own mind" (p. 138).

Over the centuries following Locke, the concept of consciousness has been used in several different ways. Each of these uses enlarges our thinking about the concept but at the same time leads to a certain amount of confusion.

In the early nineteenth century, psychology was trying to develop as a natural science, apart from philosophy. At that time, psychology was often defined as the "science of consciousness." Consciousness included all the contents of awareness: sensations, mental images, thoughts, desires, emotions, wishes, and the like. It was thought of as a kind of "mental stuff," a peculiar substance, different from the material substance of which physical objects are composed (Burt, 1972).

Consciousness has also been used as an attribute or quality, signifying the difference between lifeless, mindless stuff such as the earth and an

121

alive, alert human. Consciousness described the awake state of human beings or animals as contrasted with their asleep state, which was then called unconscious. In comparing the contents of awareness in the fully awake state with the contents of awareness in a drowsy, somnolent state, we note a dimension that can be called "levels of awareness" or "levels of consciousness."

James (1890/1950) described consciousness as a continuous stream, ever moving, never the same from moment to moment. This continuous stream or flow of awareness seemed an important and legitimate subject for psychological study by introspection and experiment.

Toward the end of the nineteenth century and in the first decade of the twentieth, at several laboratories in Germany and in the United States psychologists were hard at work exploring the contents of their subjects' awareness, using the method of introspection (G. Humphrey, 1963). They found consciousness and its elements elusive. Reported results were contradictory. Besides, looking inward was not in tune with the spirit of the times. Watson (1913), the founder of behaviorism in the United States, proclaimed: "The time has come when psychology must discard all reference to consciousness . . . its sole task is the prediction and control of behavior; and introspection can play no part of its method" (p. 158). Many American psychologists followed Watson, abandoning the study of consciousness and the human mind along with it. Others attempted to "explain" the phenomena of consciousness by relating them to neurophysiological events (Boring, 1932). The dimensions of consciousness were equated with neurophysiological operations within the brain. Consciousness was placed within the framework of stimulus-response theory.

Meanwhile, in Vienna, Freud (1900/1938), was proclaiming the power of the *un*conscious. Freud thought that a major part of the stream of mental activity is unconscious. Selected portions of this stream enter conscious awareness when we are awake and also when we are asleep: "In psycho-analysis, there is no choice for us but to declare mental processes to be *in themselves unconscious*, and to compare the perception of them by consciousness with the perception of the outside world through the sense-organs; we even hope to extract some fresh knowledge from the conparison" (Freud, 1915/1960, p. 104).

The writings of Freud and his followers have been very persuasive. Today, many of us use the unconscious as an explanatory concept with the same degree of certainty and casualness with which members of another culture might use spirits and demons to explain thoughts or behavior.

During the past several decades, while psychoanalysts and psychologists have been probing the unconscious, neuroscientists have been probing and analyzing the brain and also speculating about the nature of human consciousness (Eccles, 1973; Pribram, Nuwer, & Baron, 1974; Sperry, 1969). Neurobiologists, neurophysiologists, neurochemists, even neuromathematicians have explored the brain intensively from their several points of view. They have investigated the electrochemical activity of the individual nerve cell, mapped neuronal pathways and functions, and studied what happens when the two halves of the brain are partially separated (Gazzaniga, 1972; Sperry, 1966).

From earliest times, people have thought that the brain is closely related to what we experience as consciousness. The problem has been to describe the relationship. Different scholars who have pondered the problem have had different solutions. For example, the seventeenth-century French philosopher Descartes located the connection between mind and body in the pineal gland, deep in the brain. Others saw no separation between the psychological mind and the physical brain; both mind and brain were considered to be different aspects of one unity. This position is referred to as the identity hypothesis as contrasted with Descartes' view, which is referred to as dualism.

There are a variety of positions on both sides of the mind/body question. A detailed discussion of this debate is not my purpose, but it is important to stress that although the issue is often ignored it is by no means resolved.

Indeed, neuroscientists disagree among themselves about the relations between the brain and consciousness. Steven Rose (1973), a British neurobiologist, challenged traditional distinctions between mind and brain, which he regards as essentially semantic. He suggested that the term *consciousness* is itself a source of confusion.

> [It is] a portmanteau word of many meanings. Thus it may simply imply a state different from that of being asleep or in a coma; that is, the reverse of being "unconscious." Or it may be used to relate to the private world of the mind in contrast with a presumed "public" world of observed behavior.
>
> In this book my use of the word perhaps owes more to the Marxist than to the Freudian tradition. I relate it specifically to the sum total of brain activity, the brain state, as affected by both the internal development of the individual and the external events impinging upon him. (p. 22)

On the other hand, Sir John Eccles (1973), a Nobel prize–winning neurobiologist, adheres to the mind/brain distinction.

There is something very special about the human brain. It has a performance in relationship to culture, to consciousness, to language, to memory, that uniquely distinguishes it from even the most highly developed brains of other animals. . . . We shall see that it is beyond our comprehension how these subtle properties of the conscious self came to be associated with a material structure, the human brain, that owes its origin to the biological process of evolution. I can state with complete assurance that for each of us our brains give us all our experiences and memories, our imaginations, our dreams. Furthermore, it is through our brains that each of us can plan and carry out actions and so achieve expression in the world as, for example, I am doing now in expressing my ideas. I am able to do this because my stream of conceptual thinking can somehow or other activate neuronal changes that eventually result in all the complex movements that give writing. (pp. 1–2)

Eccles further described himself and his co-author Karl Popper as "very strong dualists and interactionists in our new understanding of the brain-mind problem. We have come to appreciate that it is only a strong dualism that has a tenable position."

During the past decade, interest in the widespread experiences of chemically induced changes in consciousness and in the accumulating evidence that the two halves of the brain are not completely identical in structure or function (Gazzaniga, 1972; Kimura, 1973; Sperry, 1966), as well as a general dissatisfaction with the behaviorist focus of mainstream psychology, have led some psychologists to propose new ways of studying and explaining consciousness.

Tart (1972a) pointed out that "experiences of ecstasy, mystical union, other 'dimensions,' rapture, beauty, space-and-time transcendence, and transpersonal knowledge, all common in altered states of consciousness, are simply not treated adequately in conventional scientific approaches" (p. 1204). He proposed a "state-specific science" for the careful study of the different states of consciousness that result from meditation, hypnosis, and consciousness-modifying chemicals. Essential to this method is that the scientist be trained to investigate a particular state of consciousness while he is himself experiencing it. Tart advocates the development of a far more imaginative approach to the study of all aspects of consciousness, at the same time that we maintain the canons of scientific method.

Ornstein (1973), too, is very critical of psychology's neglect of the study of consciousness. His view of consciousness has been heavily influenced by the evidence that the two halves of the brain seem to function in somewhat different ways. Ornstein's thesis is "that two major modes of consciousness exist in Man, the intellectual and its complement, the intuitive. Contemporary science (and, indeed, much of Western culture) has predominantly emphasized the intellectual mode, and has filtered out rich sources of evidence: meditation, 'mysticism,' non-ordinary reality, the influence of 'the body' on 'the mind' " (p. xi). Ornstein (1972) has noted that we are not equipped to experience the world as it fully exists. The human eye sees only a very limited band of the entire electromagnetic spectrum. The human ear hears only a limited range of all the possible sound waves. What we select from the available stimuli for the content of our consciousness at any particular moment is influenced in part by our own biological receiving mechanism, as well as by our momentary needs, and our whole past history, which includes the way in which Western culture has defined and structured reality to exclude the intuitive perceptual mode. Ornstein believes that for a full, accurate description of consciousness and human capacities, we need more exploration of our nonverbal, intuitive side.

Radford (1974) summarized a point of view that may influence future research on consciousness.

> Introspection gives us information about experience. It yields some data otherwise inaccessible. It may besides bring to light facts that might otherwise be overlooked, or stimulate us to ask new questions. Like any technique, it has peculiar difficulties, especially when used in odd circumstances. These, however, are the natural hazards of science. I would suggest that the battle that began over 60 years ago, and which some are apparently still fighting, might now be amicably concluded. (p. 250)

Consciousness, defined by Locke as "the perception of what passes in man's own mind," is recognized today as a multifaceted, multidimensional concept. There is no agreement about its boundaries or how it works or how to study it. The various interpretations of consciousness can be held in mind as potentially fruitful hypotheses pending the accumulation of convincing evidence that supports one particular view.

A Framework for Describing Contents of Consciousness

For most of us, the images, thoughts, and feelings of consciousness are difficult to describe. They are complex, continually changing. Skillful artists—poets, filmmakers, painters, photographers, novelists, musicians—often capture and communicate vividly the unique contents of their awareness.

Despite the unique contents of each person's awareness, there are underlying similarities, a discernible common framework. This common framework enables us to characterize the contents of our awareness at any particular moment and to distinguish among different states of awareness.

Focus

By *focus* I mean the direction of one's attention, outward to external objects and conditions or inward to one's own thoughts, feelings, images, awareness of oneself. Focus of attention can be thought of as a continuum. One end is deep within us, as in meditation when we totally block out all external stimuli. The other end is complete absorption in something outside ourselves, as when we are engrossed in reading a book, listening to someone, solving a puzzle, watching a film, or playing a game.

Focus of attention is like a spotlight that we move about. It has also been compared to a tuning system. We constantly tune in or out whole segments of stimuli, much as we switch channels on a television set and then adjust the images and sound. Often, we are unaware of the extent to which we are shifting the focus of our attention from outside to inside and back out again or from one set of stimuli to another. Hence, we tend to be unaware of how and to what extent we control consciousness by refocusing attention and what the full potential of this capacity might be.

Structure

By *structure*, I mean foreground, background, and overview or aerial view. In the *foreground* of awareness are the sense impressions, thoughts, feelings, memories, plans, wishes, strivings that capture our attention at any particular moment. In the *background* are the more general, persistent awarenesses of time, place, social reality, and personal identity. We know roughly what time it is, the date, how long we have been awake, how soon we will be going to sleep. We know where we are, in what place, what city or area, what country. We have our culture's frames of reference for assessing reality. In the background of our awareness, there is also a constant sense of the steady, silent workings of the body.

By *overview or aerial view*, I mean one's awareness of oneself being aware. You can observe yourself observing your own consciousness. Philosophers call this the reflective mode.

An important characteristic of this structure is that the relationships of foreground and background can change at any time, more swiftly than we can talk about them. The sensation of a sudden pain in your body will immediately move to the foreground of your awareness. Any unfamiliar change in the background of awareness tends to draw attention to itself and thereby shift the patterns of your awareness so that what was background becomes foreground. What was foreground may shift to background or fade away entirely. In some states of consciousness, there may be only foreground. Background awareness may vanish, as in dreams or intensive activities that have no sense of time or place.

ATTRIBUTES

By *attributes*, I mean the qualities that describe the perceptions, images, thoughts, feelings, and memories of awareness. Any of the qualities may be present in varying degrees or may be completely absent. Some qualities, combined with structure and focus, distinguish one state of consciousness from another.

Sample attributes are:

- clear/blurred
- whole/fragmented
- organized/jumbled
- familiar/unfamiliar
- meaningful/meaningless
- colorful/colorless
- real/imagined
- like/dislike
- expanded/contracted
- purposeful/purposeless

Attributes of one's role are:

- Within one's own images during a daydream or sleep dream, one sees oneself anywhere along the continuum from active and involved to passive spectator to helpless victim in regard to the events taking place in the images.
- One also perceives one's role in relation to the degree of control one has over initiating the images. For example, in studies of the hypnagogic imagery that some people experience as they are falling asleep, subjects report that the images just seem to produce them-

selves automatically like a series of lantern slides (McKellar, 1957).
- Sleep dreams, too, are often seen as foreign to the dreamer, who finds it difficult to accept them as the product of his own mental life.

Perceptions are:

- Perceptions of sensations and changes in one's body, of size and shape, and of the myriad distinctive changes triggered by psychological and physical activities or chemicals.
- During intense physical activity, one's body and the tangible environment occupy all of one's awareness. Intensity of feeling increases, and background awareness fades.

Attributes of time are:

- past, present, future, timeless

Attributes of space are:

- inside one's body
- outside one's body
- spaceless

The foregoing lists do not exhaust the possible ways in which one may describe the contents of one's own awareness in any particular state of consciousness. Our language lacks precise terms for describing some of our most strongly felt experiences. Several contemporary filmmakers are trying to move beyond this word barrier.

> A lot of my films are felt, hopefully, as one feels movement, as it were, the kinesthetic quality of life and scale relationships, time dimensions. These are all in a way musical or architectural or choreographic concepts. . . . We all respond to them although we don't have the words for them. We don't have ways in which we can articulate all of these things. (Emshwiller, 1973, p. 14)

FLOW

The most noticeable characteristic of consciousness is that it is continually changing. Earlier, I quoted William James' well-known description of consciousness as a continuous stream, ever moving, never the same from moment to moment. There have been some notable efforts to analyze the subjective experience of the flow of consciousness. Henri Bergson, the French philosopher (1907/1946), wrote:

> I find, first, that I pass from state to state. I am hot or cold. I am gay or I am sad. I work or I do nothing. I look around me or I think of something

else. Sensations, feelings, volitions representations, these are the modifications among which my existence divides itself and which color it, each in turn. I am changing, then, ceaselessly. But more must be said. The change is far more radical than one would think at first. . . .

Let us take the most stable internal states, visual perception of a stationary external object. Even though the object stays the same, even though I eye it from the same side, from the same angle, in the same light: the vision I now have nonetheless differs from the one I just did have, even if only because it is an instant older. My memory is there, pushing something of this past into this present. My state of mind, advancing along the highway of time, inflates itself continually with the duration it picks up; it snowballs, as it were. So it is even more strongly with the more profoundly interior states, sensations, affects, desires, etc., which do not correspond like a simple visual perception, to some invariable exterior object. But it is convenient to pay no attention to this uninterrupted change, and to notice it only when it becomes big enough to impress on the body a new attitude, or on the attention a new direction. At that precise moment one finds one has changed state. The truth is that one changes ceaselessly, and that the state itself is already change. (pp. 1–2)

Among the best known descriptions of the flow of consciousness are those by James Joyce and Virginia Woolf. These stream of consciousness novelists created a literary style in which emphasis is placed predominantly upon exploration of pre-speech levels of awareness. Their accounts tried to include everything—"sensations and memories, feelings and conceptions, fancies and imaginations, intuitions, visions, insights, processes of association. They try to record passages of an individual's entire psychic life" (R. Humphrey, 1954, p. 7).

The following excerpt from Joyce's *Ulysses* (1934) illustrates the flow of consciousness by recording its precise content rather than by analyzing the process, as Bergson did.

Perhaps they get a man smell off us. What though? Cigary gloves Long John had on his desk the other. Breath? What you eat and drink gives that. No. Mansmell, I mean. . . . That diffuses itself all through the body, permeates. Source of life and it's extremely curious the smell. Celery sauce. Let me.

Mr. Bloom inserted his nose. Hm. Into the. Hm. Opening of his waistcoat. Almond or. No. Lemons it is. Ah no, that's the soap. . . .

Howth. Bailey light. Two, four, six, eight, nine. See. Has to change or they might think it a house. Wreckers. Grace darling. People afraid of the dark. Also glowworms, cyclists: lightingup time. Jewels diamonds flash better. Light is a kind of reassuring. Not going to hurt you. Better now of course than long ago. Country roads. Run you through the small guts for nothing. Still two types there are you bob against. Scowl or smile. Pardon! Not at all. Best time to spray plants too in the shade after the sun. Some light still. Red rays are longest. Roygbiv Vance taught us: red, orange, yellow, green, blue, indigo, violet. A star I see. Venus? Can't tell yet. Two, when three it's night. Were those nightclouds there all the time? Looks like a phantom ship. No. Wait. Trees are they? An optical illusion. Mirage. Land of the setting sun this. Homerule sun setting in the southeast. My native land, goodnight.

Dew falling. Bad for you, dear, to sit on that stone. Brings on white fluxions. Never have little baby then less he was big strong fight his way up though. Might get piles myself. Sticks too like a summer cold, sore on the mouth. Cut with grass or paper worst. Friction of the position. Like to be that rock she sat on. O sweet little, you don't know how nice you looked. I begin to like them at that age. Green apples. Grab at all that offer.[1] (pp. 368–370)

Some filmmakers and painters also try to express the continually changing nature of consciousness by showing the many images that flow through awareness at any particular moment. The different sets of perceptions that accompany the flow have been referred to as states of consciousness.

Alternate States of Consciousness

Alternate states of consciousness, a term introduced by Zinberg (1974), refers to the fact that the different states of consciousness follow one another by turns. So-called ordinary waking consciousness easily flows into daydream or reverie and back again into alert, awake consciousness.

The ambiguities about consciousness itself spill over into the definitions and delimitations of states of consciousness. When James (1890/ 1950, 1902/1929) referred to different *"states* of consciousness," two of his examples were mystical states and hypnotic states. The Würzburg psychologists used the term to describe the rapidly changing awareness reported by their subjects, who tried to observe themselves thinking (G. Humphrey, 1963). Freud's use of the term implied that there might be an almost infinite number of different states. States of consciousness

---

[1] From James Joyce, *Ulysses.* Copyright 1914, 1918, by Margaret Caroline Anderson, and renewed 1942, 1946, by Norah Joseph Joyce. Reprinted by permission of Random House, Inc.

has been used to refer to elation, depression, or rage and to pathological or psychotic states (Rapaport, 1951).

The term *altered ego functioning* has also been used to describe some of the changes in self-awareness reported by people undergoing hypnosis combined with psychotherapy (Gill & Brenman, 1959).

Finally, the term *altered states of consciousness* has been given an all-embracing definition by Ludwig (1969).

> For the purpose of discussion I shall regard altered state(s) of consciousness . . . as any mental state(s), induced by various physiological, psychological, or pharmacological maneuvers or agents, which can be recognized subjectively by the individual himself (or by an objective observer of the individual) as representing a sufficient deviation in subjective experience or psychological functioning from certain general norms for that individual during alert, waking consciousness. This sufficient deviation may be represented by a greater preoccupation than usual with internal sensations or mental processes, changes in formal characteristics of thought, and impairment of reality testing to various degrees. (p. 225)

Ludwig's (1969) list of altered states includes daydreaming, sleep and dream states, hypnosis, meditative states, sensory deprivation, and chemically induced altered states. In addition, Ludwig mentioned specific alterations of consciousness such as highway hypnosis, "Kayak disease," occurring in Greenlanders forced to spend several days in a kayak while hunting seals, ecstatic trance, such as experienced by the "howling" or "whirling" dervishes during their religious dance, and the changes in consciousness that may occur following bilateral cataract operations.

Tart's (1969) definition of altered states of consciousness stresses the individual's perception of a *qualitative* shift in his pattern of mental functioning. Included in Tart's list of altered states are the hypnogogic, which some people experience as they are falling asleep, the hypnopompic, a transitional state that occurs as we awaken from sleep, sleep and dreams, meditation, hypnosis, minor psychedelic, and major psychedelic.

Altered states of awareness is a term used by Teyler (1972) to refer to "the fact that our awareness of the world about us is not constant" (p. i). The term is the title of a collection of classic scientific papers that summarize the many physical and psychological factors that may influence changing awareness. The starting point for these papers is the brain itself and its continual electrical activity, awake or asleep, as measured by the electroencephalogram. This continual activity is considered to be significant supporting evidence for the hypothesis that psychological processes are going on constantly, whether or not they enter awareness. Other papers in the collection discuss research on the different areas of the brain that appear to influence sleep and arousal activity. The psychological experiments thought to be directly relevant to understanding altered awareness deal with sleep and dreams and with sharp changes in the external environment such as major distortions of, or total deprivation of, stimuli.

Today, biofeedback research also is included in discussions of different states of consciousness. The basic hypothesis of biofeedback is: If one can observe in oneself a biological event of which one is normally unaware, such as one's blood pressure, one can be trained to modify some aspect of that event. Biofeedback research may help to clarify to what extent the ability to control an autonomic process such as blood flow may be related to the capacity to change one's state of consciousness (Miller et al., 1973).

DISTINGUISHING CHARACTERISTICS OF FAMILIAR ALTERNATE STATES OF CONSCIOUSNESS

The most familiar state of consciousness is so-called ordinary waking consciousness. The most familiar alternate state is daydreaming, followed by sleep and awareness of the psychological processes that accompany the various stages of sleep. Meditation, trance, and hypnosis have an exotic sound in our culture. Yet, 600 out of 1,500 American adults surveyed recently reported having had something resembling a "mystical" experience (Greeley & McCready, 1975). The mild changes that result from consuming substances like coffee, tea, or aspirin probably do not qualify as alternate states of consciousness. The changes that come from substantial quantities of alcohol and all the other consciousness-changing chemicals represent additional, more clearly definable, familiar alternate states.

Alert, awake, ordinary consciousness has a *structure*, with foreground and background. The *focus*, or direction of attention, is tilted toward external stimuli, with some sensations coming from inside as well. The *attributes* we usually apply to the contents of ordinary awake consciousness are: organized, meaningful, clear, real, with a familiar sense of time and place. And there always is the impression of *flow*, or movement.

Yet, the direction of focus is as subject to change as a seesaw. It may be almost completely weighted with external stimuli if we are listening carefully to someone or completely engaged in an activity outside ourselves. The next moment, the balance may tilt completely inward, and we suddenly realize we have missed an entire segment of a speech or a symphony, not grasped several paragraphs of a page we were reading, walked past the intersection we intended to turn into, or driven through a red light. The focus of attention wandered from outside stimuli to stimuli inside us.

Daydreaming

The word *daydreaming*, according to Singer (1966), is generally used to mean

> a shift of attention away from an ongoing physical or mental task or from a perceptual response to external stimulation towards a response to some internal stimulus. The inner processes usually considered are "pictures in the mind's eye," the unrolling of a sequence of events, memories, or creatively constructed images of future events of various degrees of probability of occurrence. Also included as objects of daydreaming are introspective awareness of bodily sensations, affects, or *monologues intérieurs*. While wish fulfillment is a frequent feature of the content of waking fantasy, common usage and the sparse scientific literature have also noted daydreaming's planful or constructive aspects, as well as its anxiety-ridden or obsessional character in particular individuals or at different periods for a given person. (p. 3)

Some object to such an all-inclusive description of daydreaming, preferring to reserve the word for an interior fantasy in which the "dream" content is totally nonrealistic. For imagined problem solving or planning activity, they consider "thinking" to be a more accurate label. For some people, the shift from attention focused outward to attention focused inward and back again is so frequent and automatic that much psychological activity that might be classified as daydreaming using one set of criteria is regarded as part of ordinary waking consciousness using a different set of criteria.

The distinguishing characteristics of daydreaming can be summarized using the framework proposed earlier to describe subjective consciousness.

The *focus* of attention is turned inward. We do not respond to stimuli outside ourselves, such as a red light or a knock at the door. We are likely to say we did not "see" the light or "hear" the knock, that we were "lost in thought" and unaware of the passage of time.

The *structure* has both foreground and background. In the foreground are the imagined daydream events unfolding. The background awareness of time and place has not totally faded, as happens in sleep dreams, but it is much more faint than it is in an alert, awake state.

Attributes applied to the contents of daydreams are likely to be: imagined, unreal, impossible. But the unrealness is not bizarre, as it may be in a sleep dream. The story line is coherent although improbable. Often, there is a planful element in the daydream. It is clear, organized, meaningful, familiar. It may be fragmented in the sense that the images are incomplete, blurred around the edges. Daydreams are sometimes called "dreamlike thoughts," for they combine both the inner imagery of the dream with elements of logical thinking. But the wish-fulfillment quality of the daydream supplants the reality-testing activity of ordinary awake consciousness.

The following paragraphs from Thurber's (1942) *The Secret Life of Walter Mitty* capture the essence of a full-blown, escape/wish-fulfillment/heroic daydream.

> "We're going through!" The Commander's voice was like thin ice breaking. He wore his full-dress uniform, with the heavily braided white cap pulled down rakishly over one cold gray eye. "We can't make it, sir. It's spoiling for a hurricane, if you ask me." "I'm not asking you, Lieutenant Berg," said the Commander. "Throw on the power lights! Rev her up to 8,500! We're going through!" The pounding of the cylinders increased: ta-pocketa-pocketa-pocketa-*pocketa-pocketa*. The Commander stared at the ice forming on the pilot window. He walked over and twisted a row of complicated dials. "Switch on No. 8 auxiliary!" he shouted. "Switch on No. 8 auxiliary!" repeated Lieutenant Berg. "Full strength in No. 3 turret!" shouted the Commander. "Full strength in No. 3 turret!" The crew, bending to their various tasks in the huge, hurtling eight-engined Navy hydroplane, looked at each other and grinned. "The Old Man'll get us through," they said to one another. "The Old Man ain't afraid of Hell! . . .
>
> "Not so fast! You're driving too fast!" said Mrs. Mitty. "What are you driving so fast for?"
>
> "Hmm?" said Walter Mitty. He looked at his wife, in the seat beside him, with shocked astonishment. She seemed grossly unfamiliar, like a strange woman who had yelled at him in a crowd. "You were up to fifty-five," she said. "You know I don't like to go more than forty. You were up to fifty-five." Walter Mitty drove on toward Waterbury in silence, the roaring of the SN202 through the worst storm in twenty years of Navy flying fading in the remote, intimate airways of his mind. (pp. 72–73)

The *flow* of the daydream may not seem as swift as the flow of ordinary waking consciousness. When we are absorbed in a daydream we seem to lose the sense of the passage of time. As contrasted with external clock time, daydream time may seem very slow. The filmmaker uses a slow motion sequence to convey the idea of a daydream or reverie. One has the impression of time standing still in some daydreams. Yet the contents continue to flow as in other states of consciousness.

Meditation

In meditation, the individual actively seeks to change his or her state of consciousness. The person deliberately blocks out attention to external sensations. There is a careful focus of attention inward. Meditation instructions stress four essential ingredients: (a) a quiet, calm environment; (b) a passive attitude, not trying to force any particular mental event; (c) a comfortable position, so that one's muscular activity is reduced to the minimum; and (d) a mental device such as a one-syllable word or sound repeated over and over again either silently or in a low, gentle tone, so as to halt meaningful activity. (The mental device may simply be focusing awareness on one's own breathing.)

The subjective contents of awareness vary with the individual and the goals of meditation. The following account by Maggie Scarf (1975), a writer on scientific subjects, describes an experience fairly typical of the nonreligious meditator.

> I meditated alone for ten minutes. To my surprise, I began responding immediately. The hysterical urge to laugh receded; I started breathing deeply and began sinking into a restful, almost "floating" state. I wondered, even as I experienced a sort of calm emptiness, whether this could be a placebo reaction on my part: I felt funny, tingling sensations in my jaw, and this seemed an odd coincidence—my jaw is one place that usually gets taut when I feel generally tense. And there was a similar small tingle in a particular back muscle, a muscle I had been aware of only twice before in my life— both occasions when it had knotted into a painful ball following upon an acutely stressful incident. Did this tingling represent, then, the "release of stress" that the Transcendental Meditation people had said one was very likely to perceive physically? It was certainly strange that the tingling should occur in those particular places. . . . That first session ended with a huge yawn. I felt refreshed and relaxed. (pp. 12, 52)

An earlier account of a deliberate, inward focused experience is by the nineteenth-century English poet Tennyson. James (1902/1929) quotes him:

> I have never had any revelations through anaesthetics, but a kind of waking trance—this for lack of a better word—I have frequently had, quite up from boyhood, when I have been all alone. This has come upon me through repeating my own name to myself silently, till all at once, as it were out of the intensity of the consciousness of individuality, individuality itself seemed to dissolve and fade away into boundless being and this not a con-

fused state but the clearest, the surest of the surest, utterly beyond words—where death was an almost laughable impossibility—the loss of personality (if so it were) seeming no extinction, but the only true life. I am ashamed of my description. Have I not said the state is utterly beyond words? (p. 374)

James, who classified Tennyson's account as a "mystical experience," characterized such an experience as follows:

1. Ineffable: The subject of the experience immediately says that it defies expression, that no adequate report of its contents can be given in words.
2. Noetic: The experience is overwhelming, providing knowledge and understanding, revealing new relationships.
3. Transient: Mystical states cannot be sustained for long. Except in rare instances, half an hour, or at most an hour or two, seems to be the limit beyond which this sort of experience fades into the light of common day. The memory of the experience, however, may persist throughout one's life.
4. Passivity: The oncoming of mystical states may be facilitated by preliminary voluntary operations—fixing one's attention or going through certain bodily performances or other procedures that mysticism prescribe; yet when the characteristic sort of consciousness has set in, the mystic feels as if his own will were in abeyance, and indeed sometimes as if he were grasped and held by a superior power.

James quoted the contents of awareness reported by Saint Teresa, a Spanish mystic, as typical of reports by religious people actively seeking a mystical experience via meditation. An important ingredient of Saint Teresa's meditation was "orison," a devotional prayer intended to achieve the mind's detachment from outer sensations, which interfere with its concentration upon ideal things.

In the orison of union, the soul is fully awake as regards God, but wholly asleep as regards things of this world and in respect of herself. During the short time the union lasts, she is as it were deprived of every feeling, and even if she would, she could not think of any single thing. Thus she needs to employ no artifice in order to arrest the use of her understanding: it remains so stricken with inactivity that she neither knows what she loves, nor in what manner she loves, nor what she wills. In short, she is utterly dead to the things of the world and lives solely in God. . . . I do not even know whether in this state she has enough life left to breathe. It seems to me she has not; or at least that if she does breathe, she is unaware of it. Her intellect would fain understand something of what is going on within her, but it has so little force now that it can act in no way whatsoever. So a person who falls into a deep faint appears as if dead. . . . (p. 400)

Some religious manuals on meditation recommend that the disciple expel sensation by a graduated series of efforts to imagine holy scenes. The acme of this kind of discipline would be what James called a semi-hallucinatory mono-ideism—an imaginary figure of Christ, for example, coming fully to occupy the mind. This kind of preparation for focusing attention inward can lead to seeing visions. Underhill (1911/1961), in her classic study of mysticism, quoted the well-known account, also by Saint Teresa, of a hallucinatory experience while meditating.

> I saw an angel close by me, on my left side, in bodily form. This I am not accustomed to see unless very rarely. Though I have visions of angels frequently, yet I see them only by an intellectual vision, such as I have spoken of before. It was our Lord's will that in this vision I should see the angel in this wise. He was not large, but small of stature, and most beautiful—his face burning, as if he were one of the highest angels, who seem to be all of fire: they must be those whom we call Cherubim. . . . I saw in his hand a long spear of gold, and at the iron's point there seemed to be a little fire. He appeared to me to be thrusting it at times into my heart, and to pierce my very entrails; when he drew it out, he seemed to draw them out also and to leave me all on fire with a great love of God. The pain was so great that it made me moan; and yet so surpassing was the sweetness of this excessive pain that I could not wish to be rid of it. The soul is satisfied now with nothing less than God. The pain is not bodily but spiritual; though the body has its share in it, even a large one. It is a caressing of love so sweet which now takes place between the soul and God, that I pray God of his goodness to make him experience it who may think that I am lying. (p. 292)

The foregoing description resembles the usual account of a sleep dream. Can we suppose that Saint Teresa fell asleep during her meditation?

Physiological studies of subjects during the practice of transcendental meditation show a pattern of alert, wakeful relaxation. Wallace and Benson (1972) found in such states reductions in oxygen consumption, carbon dioxide elimination, and the rate and volume of respiration. There was a slight increase in the acidity of the arterial blood, a marked decrease in the blood lactate level, a slowing of the heartbeat, and a considerable increase in skin resistance. The electroencephalogram patterns of the meditators showed an increase of alpha brain waves with occasional theta wave activity. Wallace and Benson pointed out that the physiological pattern of meditation is different not only from that of sleep and of hypnosis but also from the pattern their subjects showed when sitting quietly, prior to beginning meditation.

The contents of awareness during meditation may be characterized using our four dimensions. The *focus* is directed deliberately inward. *Structurally*, in the foreground of awareness, the person concentrates upon the psychological device he or she has chosen as the aid to induce the desired state: a word, a prayer, awareness of breathing, a visual image. There is a conscious effort to clear the mind of everything else. Theoretically there is no background awareness. The *attributes* applied to the experience of meditation for relaxation are "restful, floating, empty." The attributes applied to the contents of awareness when the goal of the meditation is mystical seem to be "ineffable, indescribable, joyful." As in daydreaming, in meditation there may be a sharply reduced awareness of *flow*.

HYPNOSIS

Hypnosis is not thought of as a familiar alternate state of consciousness. Yet, it has been pointed out that "the commonest light-trance induction technique is called 'a TV commercial' in our culture" (Musès & Young, 1974, p. 3). We allow ourselves to be hypnotized by the commercial and then follow its suggestions. The building blocks of the hypnotic effect seem to be part of the basic equipment of ordinary awake consciousness: the capacity to become completely absorbed in something outside ourselves and the capacity to follow suggestions made to us by another person.

The phenomenon of total absorption in something outside of us is illustrated by the following quotation from one of J. Hilgard's (1970) young subjects in a hypnosis experiment.

> Julie observed that hypnosis was like reading a book. . . . She said, "When I get really involved in reading, I'm not aware of what is going on around me. I concentrate on the people in the book or the movie or in imagination as it is in hypnosis. Reading a book can hypnotize you."
>
> "After each book, I'm completely washed out. After hypnosis, it was the same. I was completely washed out and couldn't keep my eyes open. I lacked the ability to communicate."

Shor (1959/1969) illustrated the phenomenon of total attention and absorption outward with an example from his own experience.

> I was reading a rather difficult scientific book which required complete absorption of thought to follow the argument. I had lost myself in it, and

was unaware of the passage of time or my surroundings. Then, without warning, something was intruding upon me; a vague, nebulous feeling of change. It all took place in a split-second, and when it was over I discovered that my wife had entered the room and had addressed a remark to me. I was then able to call forth the remark itself, which had somehow etched itself into my memory, even though at the time it was spoken I was not aware of it. (p. 241)

The extreme suggestibility of the hypnotized subject is considered by some researchers to be the only justification for calling hypnosis a state (Hull, 1933; Orne, 1972). Subjects are described as passive, losing initiative, and lacking the desire to make and carry out plans on their own.

E. R. Hilgard (1968) has called this quality of extreme suggestibility "subsidence of the planning function," describing it as follows:

If a subject is told to circulate around a room, trying to fool the people there into believing he is not hypnotized, he does this successfully for a while, but eventually seeks a comfortable chair in a remote place, closes his eyes, and resumes his inert planlessness. (p. 6)

One of Hilgard's subjects described the experience thus:

Once I was going to swallow, but decided it wasn't worth the effort. At one point I was trying to decide if my legs were crossed but I couldn't tell, and didn't quite have the initiative to find out.... (p. 6)

Under the influence of hypnosis, subjects seem to have a greater ability for fantasy production and for recalling long-forgotten memories and a greater tolerance for reality distortion. They enter readily into role-playing and display posthypnotic amnesia. In addition to the feeling of passivity and compulsion to follow the hypnotist, subjects report perceiving "changes in size or appearance of parts of their bodies, feelings of floating, blacking out, dizziness, spinning."

J. Hilgard (1970) cited an example of a young subject who was told that she would awaken from hypnosis to find that she had no hands but that this discovery would not bother her. When her "absent" (invisible) hands were then given a rather strong electric shock, the subject reported that she felt nothing although there had been no specific analgesia suggestions. Her account follows.

Dr. H. told me that I didn't have any hands. He had a little shocking machine that kept floating around in the air. I was very interested in the fact that I didn't have any hands and I really felt I didn't. He told me it would be funny and I thought it amusing to see Dr. H. poking around in the air. My silly looking long sleeves with only circles at the end where the hands would be. Only those ridiculous ruffles were there.

Asked why she was not troubled by the absence of her hands, the subject replied:

Somewhere else I absolutely know I have hands. I know they're not cut off. I'm exploring the sensation of not having them. There's no anxiety. He said they would appear gradually at the count of five. He asked me how they came back and I didn't know. I had quit doing what I was doing that was keeping me from seeing them. But whatever it was I was doing was inside me, and I couldn't observe what I quit doing when my hands were again there. It's as though they were there all the time but I hadn't noticed them. They didn't suddenly appear as though they had come from nowhere, and they didn't appear gradually as though there were a film being developed.

Physiological studies of bodily changes that take place during hypnosis reflect whatever state has been suggested to the subject by the hypnotist (Wallace & Benson, 1972). Brain wave activity, heart rate, blood pressure, skin resistance, and respiration all show the patterns characteristic of the behavioral or emotional state suggested to the subject by the hypnotist. There is also evidence that under hypnosis subjects are able to control autonomic functions such as skin temperature (Roberts, Kewman, & Macdonald, 1973). And, the evidence is overwhelming that hypnosis is quite different from ordinary sleep (Evans, 1972; Hull, 1933; Wallace & Benson, 1972).

Hypnosis theory and research has moved far beyond the notions of "animal magnetism" proposed by Mesmer in the eighteenth century. Authors today stress the importance of analyzing the phenomena of hypnosis in terms of familiar psychological processes. Some have compared hypnotic suggestibility to role-playing and all the other ordinary influencing of one another's behavior that goes on between adults and children, leaders and followers in everyday life (Sarbin & Coe, 1972). Others tracing the origins of individual differences in suggestibility have found patterns in early child and parent relationships that seem to bear upon the intertwining of attention, imagination, and suggestibility that characterizes hypnosis (E. R. Hilgard, 1968). Research designs combining hypnosis with biofeedback are being used to study the mechanisms involved in voluntary control of autonomic bodily functions. Posthypnotic suggestion has been used to study the modifiability of dream content (Tart, 1965/1969).

Although some writers think that neither the necessary nor the sufficient conditions for hypnosis have been delineated (Orne, 1972), hypnosis seems to involve a decision by the subject to give over his initiative to the hypnotist or to the hypnotic situation. The *focus* or direction of attention is outward. The *structure* of awareness, as in meditation, has only foreground; the background fades. Shor (1959/1969) has referred to the background as the "generalized reality-orientation" and has suggested that any state in which this background has faded out of awareness can be called a trance state. The *attribute* characteristically applied to the contents of awareness in hypnosis is the attribute of one's role: passive—the feeling of compulsion to carry out the suggestions of the hypnotist. Depending upon these suggestions, there may be a slowing down, a speeding up, or an unawareness of *flow*.

SLEEP DREAMING

It seems paradoxical to refer to the dreaming that occurs during sleep as an alternate state of consciousness. Sleep has long been viewed as a condition "in which there is a greater or less degree of unconsciousness" (McKendrick, 1911, p. 238). Dreams have been described as a series of thoughts or images and feelings passing through the mind in sleep. They constitute a kind of awareness that is very different from the awareness of ordinary waking consciousness. This difference and, above all, the strangeness of the contents of dreams have intrigued and puzzled people for thousands of years.

The oldest documents on sleep dreams are Babylonian and Assyrian clay tablets dating back to 2500 B.C. These tablets attempted to answer the same questions about dreams that remain unanswered today. What do dreams mean? How shall we interpret them? People at different times and in different cultures have developed a wide range of answers to these questions. Dreams have been considered to be obscure messages from the gods, views of the future, voyages to the true reality, or signs of having eaten too much (Woods, 1947).

Freud (1900/1938) tried to bring the interpretation of dreams into the domain of psychology, using dream associations as a way of calling into awareness thoughts and memories that are "unconscious." However, prior to the discovery of rapid eye movements (REM) during sleep and their use as an indicator of dreaming, scientific research on dreams was thought to be "like trying to lasso a cloud on a windy day while perched in wet sneakers on a mountaintop" (Van de Castle, 1971).

Since the discovery of rapid eye movements and their correlation with sleep dreaming and with a distinctive brain wave pattern, there has been an avalanche of research on sleep and dreaming (Rechtschaffen &

Eakins, n.d.). The accumulated evidence on sleep and dreaming supports the statement that "all phases of sleep are associated with some kind of subjective experience or mental activity" (Dement, 1965, p. 192). Subjects awakened from rapid-eye-movement sleep predominantly report dreams that can be described as "adventures," a series of connected events with a variety of sensory imagery that seemed real at the time. Dream reports from rapid-eye-movement sleep become longer, more detailed, more vivid, and more emotional as the night progresses. A subject awakened from *non*-rapid-eye-movement (NREM) sleep will often describe his subjective experience as simply "thinking" about something (Van de Castle, 1971). His recollections tend to be abstract, vague, brief, and fragmentary, with few lengthy adventures, very few characters, and a minimum of sensory imagery. Typically, situations from the very recent past are reported.

Normal dream content is wildly unpredictable (Dement, 1965). There is a striking lack of critical judgment on the part of the dreamer. The most incongruous, illogical, and impossible happenings are accepted as real and are invested with emotion. At the same time, at some other level of awareness, we seem to know that we are dreaming (Freud, 1900/1938). Missing from dreams is a sense of free will (Hartmann, 1973).

The physiological measures of the rapid-eye-movement state—brain waves, heart and respiratory rates, blood pressure—seem most like those of a highly active, awake state. In fact, if it were not for his closed eyelids, the subject in this state would appear to be awake and looking about (Dement, 1965). On the other hand, non-rapid-eye-movement sleep is characterized by an overall low level of physiological activity similar to that typical of a voluntary, relaxed, quiet, awake state.

A vast amount of information about the physiology of sleep exists, but "we seem to have remained fixated at the level of fascination with the ups and downs of the ink tracings and have neglected to study how these squiggles relate to the ebb and flow of phenomenological dream experience" (Van de Castle, 1971). Tart (1969) urges more research on the experimental control of dreaming. Since some subjects incorporate into dreams such external stimuli as sounds and bright lights, and since some sleeping subjects are able to perform simple motor acts in response to external stimuli, Tart has asked whether it might be possible to train subjects to carry out more complex behaviors at specified points during a dream state.

Witkin and Lewis (1967) also have tried to study the influence of external events upon the formation of dream images. They have shown people films with emotional and with neutral content prior to the subjects' going to sleep. They have then traced the way in which these stimuli become incorporated into, and represented in, the dreams of that night. The dream transformations appear to be related to the person's cognitive style in dealing with other situations. Ullman and Krippner (1970) have tried to influence dream content by telepathy. Several studies have now been reported in which statistically significant results support the hypothesis of a possible telepathic capacity during dreaming. Other researchers are studying the role of chemical changes within the brain cells. Hartmann (1973) has sought to integrate subjective experiences of dreaming with neurochemical changes in the brain.

Although our understanding of dreaming is still very incomplete, there is enough evidence of a special kind of awareness during sleep dreaming to warrant calling it an alternate state of consciousness. Given the possibility that rapid-eye-movement dreams and non-rapid-eye-movement "dreams" may have different unconscious meanings and motivations, as well as different levels of physiological functioning, eventually there may be reason to specify more than one sleep dream state of consciousness.

During sleep dreaming the *focus* of attention is inward. Under certain circumstances, external stimuli can be perceived by the dreamer and incorporated into the dream or acted upon. The dream *structure* has only foreground. The dream seems to be the total reality. Background awareness has faded. When there is an awareness that the dream is a dream, that awareness is like the overview of waking consciousness. It is a form of concentrated knowing about what one is doing or experiencing. Sleep dreams have two sets of *attributes*. One set applies to the dream while it is in progress. The attributes will characterize the visual, emotional, and thought content of the dream as it is experienced: vivid or vague, terrifying or peaceful, colorful or bland. The second set of attributes applies to our awake evaluation of the dream as incongruous, illogical, bizarre. Sleep dreams *flow*, but often the scenes seem to flash by as a series of unconnected events. They lack the transitions we are accustomed to in an awake state.

Summary

1. Consciousness is a complex concept, with unresolved psychological and philosophical implications regarding the fundamental nature of human beings.

2. In this chapter, consciousness is defined as the awareness of what passes in one's own mind.
3. Consciousness is continually changing. The contents of awareness at any particular moment constitute a *state of consciousness*.
4. A simple, unified framework is proposed for describing the contents of awareness at any given moment. The dimensions of the framework are: *focus* of attention, *structure* (foreground, background, overview), *attributes*, and *flow*.
5. An *alternate state of consciousness* is one that is perceived as markedly different from the preceding state. Significant differences as well as similarities between alternate states of consciousness can be clearly characterized using the dimensions of *focus*, *structure*, *attributes*, and *flow*.
6. Familiar alternate states of consciousness are described. These states are: ordinary awake consciousness and daydreaming, meditation, hypnosis, and sleep dreaming. Meditation, trance, and self-hypnosis are seen as variants of daydreaming. Attention is directed to the role of the individual's decision to change his consciousness from one state to another.

This overview does not cover chemically induced alternate states, shamanistic trance states, psychotic states, or other identifiable states of interest. I believe, however, that the framework for describing the contents of awareness applies to those states as well as to the more familiar ones.

6

A Biofeedback Strategy in the Study of Consciousness

David Shapiro

Can Consciousness Be Altered?

WHEN THE TERM *altered states of consciousness* first came to my attention (Tart, 1969, 1972a) it seemed to imply a fundamental shift in consciousness away from naturally occurring experiences. The idea of an "altered" state suggested that a new kind of conscious experience was being created in the individual, one that had never existed before. This meaning of an altered state is probably derived from psychoactive drug-induced modifications of experience and behavior. Through this means, prolongations of subjective moods, feelings, images, and thoughts can be brought about. Although drugs do not act in isolation from other causal factors, such as the individual's expectations and attitudes and the social circumstances in which the drug is used, they have the important capability of eliciting long-lasting changes in conscious and behavioral processes. Moreover, the effects can be initiated simply and terminated predictably. In our culture, other internal and subjective states such as affects, moods, fantasies, and daydreams tend to be viewed, in contrast, as relatively short-lived and are not as definable or predictable.

The author's research was supported by Grant MH-26923, National Institute of Mental Health, and Contract N00014-75-C-0150, Office of Naval Research. Some of the ideas in this chapter were stimulated by discussions with Norman Zinberg, Gary Schwartz, and Richard Davidson on the use of psychophysiological methods in assessing drug-related states of consciousness.

The ability to generate a given psychophysiological state with drugs and to maintain it over the course of time appears to facilitate a process whereby the associated conscious experience can be more readily identified or labeled. With repeated experiences, the individual can refine the nature of the subjective state and compare his experiences with those of others who are similarly involved. A subculture or a set of ideas about the experience often develops around the use of particular drugs, and a new norm of consciousness may evolve for the participants, who may not previously have experienced such states, recognized them as such, or labeled them precisely in these ways.

What is altered in consciousness is the extent to which varieties of conscious experience can be reliably identified and specified, the degree to which defined experiences can be maintained over time and the distribution of such states within the total experience of the individual. Critical to an understanding of these processes is research on the transformation of raw experiences into identified conscious states. As we learn more about this process of transformation and the variety of states that can be achieved we have to consider the individual's potential to exercise a degree of voluntary control over the variety and time course of his own experiences of consciousness without the use of drugs.

Whether or not the anatomy of the nervous system is still evolving, there is meaning in the evolution of consciousness. It is a social process in which naturally occurring tendencies are selected out of a total set of possibilities. It is a matter of individual experience and cultural definition which can probably alter the nature of consciousness considerably in the same sense that social views, intuition, and language usage are constantly producing new conceptions of reality.

Psychophysiology and Consciousness

The quest to define and understand the nature of consciousness is no different in essence from the classic problem in psychophysiology concerning the nature of emotional behavior and experience. For example, one research approach is to contrive certain situations believed to be associated with fear, anger, euphoria, or depression—e.g., threat of pain, harm, or danger; frustration of goal-directed behavior; achievement of positive goals; or helplessness in the face of aversive events. Having set up such eliciting conditions, we try to appraise the individual's behavioral reactions, sensations, and perceptions, reported moods or feelings, cortical, autonomic, and other physiological functions, and biochemical changes. The success of this research strategy depends on the degree to which the participant subjects have similar and consistent ways of appraising and responding to these eliciting situations. The classic studies of fear and anger (Ax, 1953; Funkenstein, 1955) attempted with some success to delineate specific patterns of physiological response associated with certain provocative conditions. Related changes in consciousness were more difficult to evaluate.

The addition of cognitive factors in this research, such as expectancy, set, or attitude (e.g., Schachter, 1964), makes it possible to broaden the scope of investigation by considering the complex interaction of physiological, cognitive, and situational factors. This strategy includes the use of injected substances (e.g., epinephrine or chloropromazine) as a means of inducing physiological processes assumed to be related to particular emotional reactions. The research suggests that subjective states such as anger and elation depend on both bodily reactions and cognitive appraisal of the circumstances.

Direct manipulations of bodily processes can be achieved in animal subjects, too, by lesions, ablations, or electrical stimulation which result in alterations of neural or chemical functions. Human subjects with existing neurological damage or other disorders also provide a basis for investigation of subjective states. In research on emotional states such as anxiety, terror, euphoria, depression, or elation, we may begin to characterize subjective qualities associated with these states.

Meditation and Related Approaches to the Control of Consciousness

In current thinking, greater attention is being paid to a variety of meditative disciplines and practices, many of which have their origin in Eastern cultures, primarily because of their implications for physiological as well as conscious process. These practices include transcendental meditation, Zazen, various yogic disciplines, attentional states in the martial arts, diverse forms of prayer and meditation as practiced in Western religions, and various forms of concentration in the arts and in athletics. Of particular interest is the detailed specification in some disciplines of different modes of attention and concentration—whether on internal or external events or objects, on the breath or different parts of the body, or on various internal sensations. In my laboratory we made an intensive study of an experienced yoga teacher, and observed more than twenty sustained breathing patterns that were part of his discipline and that were associated with unique cardiovascular response patterns. These were highly practiced bodily maneuvers. The teacher also demonstrated a variety of procedures to facilitate concentration and various levels of attentiveness and sleep. On a par with the physical maneuvers, highly practiced psychological practices such as these may shape conscious experience in the same way that drugs do.

In transcendental meditation, the practitioner is in a relaxed physical position, breathing slowly and deeply while focusing attention as much as possible on a single sound or word (mantra). The practice seems to result in large reductions in certain physiological responses—e.g., electrodermal activity, oxygen consumption, respiratory rate, blood lactate (Wallace, Benson, & Wilson, 1971)—and with apparent reductions in reaction to stress-related stimuli (Goleman, 1974). The nature of the state of consciousness in transcendental meditation is not exactly clear, but it seems to resemble a passive, peaceful, untroubled mental state that is associated with bodily and subjective relaxation.

As in the case of drug-induced changes in consciousness, I have called attention to various practices that result in clear patterns of physiological processes. These practices seem to fix within the individual associated states of consciousness. But it is not necessary to allude to the more exotic Eastern practices to make the same point. Similar procedures for the regulation of consciousness, behavior, and bodily functions have been examined in Western psychology and have attained a respectable status in established scientific research. I refer to research on hypnosis and suggestion, and more generally to the role of cognitive factors in the regulation of perception, attention, and bodily processes. The more radical the procedure—for example, prolonged sensory deprivation and extreme social isolation—the more predictable the outcome: In this case, distortions in time perception and body image, delusions, and hallucinatorylike mental activities take place. In research on the physiological and subjective effects of suggestion, the susceptibility of the subject has been shown to be an important ingredient (Engstrom, 1976).

In autogenic training (Luthe, 1963), a major technique is the direction of the individual's attention to internal sensations as a means of altering bodily responses and thereby coping with symptoms. Subjects or patients are coached in using imagery and other means of increasing the warmth of the fingers or the feeling of heaviness in the limbs to achieve passivity and complete relaxation. In common with certain yoga techniques, autogenic procedures attempt to achieve or increase awareness of particular bodily sensations. The achievement of relaxation in autogenic therapy is also the goal of other meditation practices. The major significance of the study of meditative practices has been in exploring the plasticity of physiological and conscious processes and the potential for self-regulation of these processes.

Biofeedback and Physiological Self-Regulation

The newly emerging field of Western research on the regulation of physiological responses and states of consciousness by means of biofeedback (and operant conditioning) techniques is of special relevance to the study of consciousness. In biofeedback training, the individual is fed back information about his own biological response or about a number of responses, occurring simultaneously. The information is a sensory (auditory or visual) analogue of the actual physiological response or responses, and it is provided to him at the same instant that the physiological activity is occurring, or after a very brief delay. Hence the term *biofeedback*—"bio" meaning that the information is biological and "feedback" meaning that it is precisely coupled in time with the ongoing biological events. Biofeedback is another means of manipulating specific patterns of physiological responses and consciousness, and may be the most precise of all the purely psychological (nonchemical, nonsurgical) methods that have been developed so far.

Biofeedback may be conceived of as either positive or negative in its function. That is, the feedback stimulus may be rewarding to the subject and serve to enhance the activity. Or the feedback stimulus may be aversive and serve to dampen the responses. In other words, the feedback stimulus has reinforcing properties. Such an operant conditioning framework has been employed widely in biofeedback research to account for the modification of the ongoing physiological responses by the feedback stimuli. This framework provides a clear notation and a huge body of prior facts about somatomotor operant learning against which to examine the phenomena of biofeedback and visceral learning (for reviews see Miller, 1969; Shapiro & Schwartz, 1972; Shapiro & Surwit, 1976). The framework also provides numerous experimental test procedures— intermittent reinforcement, effects of different schedules, comparison of reward, punishment, escape and avoidance learning, and so on.

Other researchers have taken their point of departure from electronics and cybernetic control theory. The biological systems involved are not closed, and all the critical functions are not understood or specified. However, a good example of a relatively closed system is the feedback loop developed by Mulholland (1968) to study properties of electroencephalographic (EEG) rhythms. For example, it is arranged that occurrence of the EEG alpha rhythm (8–13 Hz) results in increase in light stimulation, which in turn blocks the alpha rhythm, and occurrence of non-alpha results in decrease in light stimulation. In this framework, the feedback stimuli are thought to have direct consequences for the behavior.

Other writers have employed cognitive models of biofeedback learning. A theory of voluntary control relevant to this model has been developed by Brener (1974). He has proposed that the externalized sensory feedback is used by the individual as a means of calibrating the afferent feedback of his own visceral responses against the external referent (the feedback) as a means of facilitating awareness of visceral activities and thereby achieving greater control. Brener gives the analogy of a deaf person learning to talk by calibrating the responses of his own muscular vocal apparatus against the vibratory sensations talking can produce in the fingers. These sensations substitute for the usual auditory sensations in normal people. After practice and learning, the individual can dispense with such a feedback crutch. Visceral learning and self-regulation may be analogous processes. Thus, in this framework, the feedback is a symbolic representation of the physiological event or events, and the individual engages in some behavior either to augment or to diminish the feedback and therefore the activity. In this sense, the feedback in and of itself is neutral with respect to its direct influence on the physiological activity.

Biofeedback contrasts with other behavioral procedures, such as hypnosis, in an important way: The output of the system, in this case the desired response, is constantly being monitored by the individual subject, providing the impetus to "correct" his own efforts in whatever way possible to bring about the desired response. For example, feedback in the form of meter deflections may be given for relative changes in heart rate on each successive heartbeat, using a cardiotachometer visual display in which deflections of the indicator are directly proportional to changes in heart rate. By watching the meter the individual can determine whether or not he is successful in changing the meter in a given direction and what he may be doing to facilitate this change. The process may involve awareness of changes in the rhythm of the heart, including sensing of heartbeat or heart rate, changes in circulation, physical maneuvers such as changes in breathing or in the state of tension of various muscles, particular forms of thinking or imagery, or variations in attention and perception.

Other writers have considered physiological self-regulation as comparable to the learning of complex motor skills (Lang, 1974) and have attempted to explore analogies between biofeedback learning and known facts about skill learning.

Biofeedback: A General Proposal of Relevance to Consciousness

Biofeedback is a purely behavioral means of achieving certain levels of physiological response in the individual. It is also a voluntary or self-regulatory procedure that can be initiated or terminated at will. More important, biofeedback is also a means by which the individual can bring about a given, precisely defined pattern of physiological responses. To the extent that the physiological pattern can be maintained over time with biofeedback, this procedure can be used to examine accompanying alterations in consciousness.

The significance of a biofeedback strategy is dependent on knowledge of patterns of physiological response. Over the past several decades advances have been made in delineating specific physiological response patterns associated with different kinds of human behavior and cognition—mental effort, orienting and attention, performance in different kinds of tasks (see Lacey & Lacey, 1974; Sokolov, 1963; Greenfield & Sternbach, 1972). The patterns of responses include the electroencephalogram, evoked potential, contingent negative variation, heart rate, digital skin temperature, blood pressure, respiration, electrodermal activity, eye movements, and other functions that can be measured with noninvasive procedures. More recently, research on cerebral specialization has grown rapidly, attempting to relate differences in electrical activity of the two hemispheres of the brain to different kinds of task performance (Doyle, Ornstein, & Galin, 1974; Galin, 1974; Galin & Ornstein, 1972; Morgan, Macdonald, & Hilgard, 1974). To the extent that the individual can regulate particular patterns of cortical and peripheral neural and visceral functions by means of biofeedback techniques it should be possible to study a variety of associated states of consciousness, including the simulation of states occurring under the influence of psychoactive drugs. Before suggesting any specific proposals for research, I must define *state of consciousness* and summarize the literature on biofeedback effects relevant to this strategy.

What Is a State of Consciousness?

I have suggested that the individual can regulate patterns of his own physiological responses, the patterns to be selected on the basis of promising findings of current psychophysiological research. Then by maintaining these patterns over reasonably long periods of time, he can begin to identify and assess associated conscious experiences. Unlike other attempts in this area (to be reviewed subsequently), I have emphasized the control of the *patterns* of physiological responses rather than of single responses in line with assumptions about the functional significance of such patterns for behavior and consciousness.

I have made the simplifying assumption that a state of consciousness is a biological function, albeit one that is difficult to objectify and quantify. It is no different from other complex biological functions that are the product of numerous interacting biological processes. Blood pressure is an example of a much simpler but still complex biological function. As we have learned about the various constituent factors, we can specify and predict how blood pressure will vary in relation to properties of the blood vessels, heart, kidneys, and other internal organs, activities of autonomic nerves, endocrine changes, feedback from pressure receptors, changes in muscles and so on. Fortunately, there is a single index of blood pressure which is easy to measure and quantify. In the case of consciousness, we have no satisfactory single index although many have been proposed—e.g., alterness, clarity, intensity, extensity, and focus.

To study consciousness, we have little choice but to measure a number of different constituent activities of the body. It is reasonable to assume that what is happening in different brain structures may be more critical to understanding consciousness. But what is happening in the brain is not distinctly separate from what is happening in other peripheral systems. Controlling and regulating processes exist throughout the body, and central and peripheral functions are constantly interacting.

Given this assumed specificity of bodily activities in relation to consciousness and the further assumption that all bodily activities are pertinent, a state of consciousness may be defined as a specific pattern of physiological and subjective responses—cortical, autonomic, and somatomotor functions on the one hand, simultaneously occurring imagery, ideation, and fantasies on the other. By pattern, I mean a simultaneously occurring pattern of events—e.g., alpha EEG activity in the right hemisphere, beta EEG activity in the left hemisphere, elevation in heart rate,

increase in electrodermal activity, and particular ideation such as manipulation of symbols in solving an arithmetic problem. This conception
provides a basis for research on states of consciousness, as it does for inquiry into other psychological or behavioral processes.

It has to be asked, finally, whether there is an enormous number of
possible psychophysiological patterns and associated states of consciousness. Obviously, great care must be exercised in the selection of particular patterns for study. Moreover, in order to define and identify
complex patterns, it is necessary to process large amounts of data. How
can this goal be accomplished? These questions will be taken up later.

Biofeedback: Relevant Findings on Consciousness and Physiological Patterning

Some of the earliest research in biofeedback was stimulated by questions about conscious correlates of EEG activity. Kamiya (1969) was
concerned with subjective properties of the alpha rhythm, and he asked
the question, "Can people be trained to discern the comings or goings of
brain rhythms—say, the EEG alpha rhythm—just by using the standard
learning procedures that have been developed for use with rats and
pigeons?" His procedure was to signal the subject at times when the
alpha rhythm was occurring and at times when it was not, asking the
subject to guess which state he was in. After each guess, the subject was
told whether or not he was correct. With training, subjects improved in
their ability to discriminate their brain rhythms. Not only could subjects
learn to identify their own brain rhythms, but also they could produce
relative increases or decreases in the cortical activity as a result of feedback training.

Kamiya's subjects reported various conscious experiences associated
with EEG rhythms. Non-alpha was related to visual imagery, the more
intense the better; alpha was associated with mental relaxation and a
"noncritical attitude" toward the environment. In a subsequent report,
alpha was found to be associated with reports of relaxation, "letting go,"
and pleasant affect; whereas non-alpha was associated with alertness or
visual attention (Nowlis & Kamiya, 1970). Similarly, Brown (1970b)
reported that the "greatest achievement of enhanced alpha activity
appeared to be related to narrowing of perceptual awareness and pleasant
feeling states" (p. 442). In extending this means of investigating what
she termed "recognition of aspects of consciousness," Brown (1970a)

studied associations between beta, alpha, and theta EEG rhythms and subjective thought or feeling activity. Among the predominant subjective reports were the following: beta—worry, anger, fear, and frustration; alpha—pleasant feeling, well-being, pleasure, tranquility, and relaxation; theta—memory of problems, uncertainty, problem solving, future planning, switching thoughts, solving mechanical or financial problems, daydreaming. For further research along these lines see Budzynski (1973a,b); Green, Green, and Walters (1971); Hefferline and Bruno (1971); Mulholland (1973); and Peper (1972).

The degree to which relations between EEG changes and consciousness are unique has been questioned by a number of investigators, as discussed by Walsh (1974). In one study subjects never reported typical "alpha experiences" while resting in total darkness even though they were producing large amounts of alpha EEG activity at that time (Paskewitz, Lynch, Orne, & Costello, 1970). Furthermore, whether or not alpha activity can increase beyond levels occurring in resting baseline conditions has been disputed (see Paskewitz & Orne, 1973). Walsh (1974) hypothesized that suggestion could play a major role in eliciting the verbal reports associated with alpha biofeedback training (see Beatty, 1972). Using a design derived from drug research (Schachter, 1964), Walsh compared four conditions: (1) alpha instructions with alpha feedback; (2) alpha instructions with no alpha feedback; (3) neutral instructions with alpha feedback; and (4) neutral instructions with no alpha feedback. It was found that alpha activity must be present in the records *and* the appropriate cognitive set must be induced in order for subjects to report the typical alpha experience. Walsh concluded that neither set nor physiological change as a single factor could be considered primary in explaining the reports of consciousness. Both are necessary.

A similar conclusion was arrived at in a cardiovascular biofeedback study (Sirota, Schwartz, & Shapiro, 1974). In this study, subjects were instructed to increase or decrease their heart rate voluntarily in anticipation of receiving aversive stimuli. They were also given heart rate feedback and rewards for criterion changes. Voluntary slowing of heart rate was reported to lead to a relative reduction in the perceived aversiveness of the stimuli. However, the effect was observed mainly in those subjects who reported experiencing cardiac reactions to fear situations in daily life. A *combination* of physiological and cognitive factors would seem to be necessary if instrumental learning of a physiological response is to transfer effectively to a related perceptual change.

These findings suggest that the analysis of combined *patterns* of physiological, behavioral, and cognitive events is required in elucidating states of consciousness. A similar position has been espoused by Stoyva and Kamiya (1968) and Stoyva (1973) in proposals for the study of consciousness, dreaming, sleep-onset imagery, and hallucinations. As Stoyva and Kamiya (1968) conclude:

> The major point to be made here is that the use of operant technique in combination with the physiological indicator (alpha) and the verbal report provides substantial construct validation for the hypothetical internal state by means of converging operations. . . . For example, it may prove possible for Ss to discriminate and control other types of EEG waves in addition to the alpha rhythm; for instance, beta, delta, and theta waves, rhythms characteristic of alertness, rhythms characteristic of drowsiness. If such a degree of discrimination and control proves possible, it could give psychologists a means of exploring and mapping a variety of conscious states, thus providing a powerful tool for the introspective method. It may also develop that, if S's ability to report about a limited number of private events can be sharpened in this way, then this new skill may transfer to other private events as well; so that S becomes more generally reliable—and sensitive—in the reporting of private events. (pp. 202–203)

The position I have taken here is that self-regulation techniques can be employed to generate *patterns* of different kinds of physiological events (central *and* peripheral) and that through the induction of such *patterns*, still more refinement may be attained in the scrutiny of private events or states of consciousness. Evidence for the biofeedback control of patterns of autonomic nervous system events is now available (Schwartz, 1972; Schwartz, 1975; Schwartz, Shapiro, & Tursky, 1971). For example, when subjects were given feedback for heart rate or blood pressure alone, it was found that the reinforced function could be either increased or decreased, while the other function did not change. However, when feedback and reward were given for simultaneous change in *both* heart rate and blood pressure, the two functions could be deliberately associated or dissociated to some degree. More recent research indicates that various combinations of EEG and autonomic responses can also be shaped up with biofeedback training (Hassett & Schwartz, 1975).

The present proposal for research builds on the proposition put forth by Stoyva and Kamiya for the study of private events utilizing more recent findings that patterns of physiological events can be self-regulated. Study of such self-regulated patterns plus reports about consciousness experience provide the basis of the present strategy of research.

Biofeedback and Consciousness: Suggestions for Research

Using a biofeedback monitoring approach, the individual can produce a criterion amount of a particular physiological response or pattern of responses over some sustained period of time, and then, through reports of ideation and imagery, the associated state of consciousness may be examined. Simultaneous occurrences of conscious experience *and* physiological event should be most informative. In addition, by suggesting to the individual that he engage in some particular mental process—concentrate on a particular thought or image, generate a conscious state such as detached passive attention, adopt a feeling set of sadness or happiness—while at the same time maintaining the particular physiological activity, investigators may obtain interesting results that suggest new directions for study. The congruence of a particular mental set and a given physiological response may be significant to the total experience. Particular combinations of set and physiology may be more compatible than others, and this may provide further leads for investigation. As in the Walsh (1974) study cited previously, specific cognitive instructions *plus* physiological patterns induced by means of feedback provide a model for this research.

The pattern strategy is a critical innovation in this research. For example, the pattern of left-hemisphere beta EEG–right-hemisphere alpha EEG–increased heart rate–increased electrodermal activity could be associated with a state of consciousness related to a general set of logical problem solving and manipulation of symbols. The occurrence of such a pattern in association with particular ideation or imagery may be indicative of unique subjective states.

The procedure would be for the individual subject to verbalize during the experimental session; in this way congruences of specific verbal reports and physiological pattern could be examined. Clearly, reliable introspective reports are difficult to obtain, although experience in these procedures may increase the usefulness of individuals' reports. One problem is that introspection itself may distract the individual or interfere with the states of consciousness that we want to observe. "Automatic" verbalizations or other automatic motor responses related to experience can possibly be achieved with training and experience (Hilgard, Morgan, & Macdonald, 1975).

Biofeedback techniques may be adapted also to research on the evaluation of psychoactive drugs. First, psychophysiological patterns known to be associated with particular drugs may be induced using the feedback method. That is, subjects can be asked to self-regulate these same patterns without the aid of drugs, and the consequent effects on consciousness evaluated. Will the effects be at all comparable? Second, the ability of subjects to regulate certain physiological patterns can be assessed while they are under the influence of particular drugs. The question, then, is the extent to which such self-regulation is affected by the particular drugs. Are subjects more or less sensitive to internal changes? Is self-control enhanced or diminished? What does this tell us about the nature of conscious experiences with particular drugs?

Finally, the technology for the assessment of physiological response patterning is largely available in current laboratory minicomputer systems. These systems include a number of capabilities—analogue to digital conversion, on-line assessment of simultaneously occurring events in different input channels, data storage, and facilities for on-line production of feedback displays. A major remaining problem concerns the availability and future development of methods for interrelating spontaneous verbal reports with the ongoing physiological events and for assessing patterns of physiological *and* verbal events.

Conclusion

Although there are inherent difficulties in definition, objectification, and quantification, the study of states of consciousness is seen as no different in essence from the study of other properties of biological systems. The assumption made in this chapter is that states of consciousness can be defined by unique patterns of physiological responses and reports of subjective experiences. To the extent that such states can be maintained and prolonged within the individual, greater knowledge about the nature and transformations of consciousness may be obtained.

New developments in biofeedback research suggest that patterns of physiological activity can be regulated by the individual. The strategy I have proposed is to select particular patterns of response for the individual to regulate and sustain with the aid of biofeedback and then to examine associated changes in ideation, imagery, and feeling. Biofeedback procedures can also be used in conjunction with particular cognitive, situational, or instructional sets. The justification for such an approach derives from evidence on the specialization of biological structures and functions in different kinds of cognitive, perceptual, and motor tasks. Whether or not the proposal is workable or can yield new insights into states of consciousness remains to be determined.

7

Putting the Pieces Together: A Conceptual Framework for Understanding Discrete States of Consciousness

Charles T. Tart

I OFTEN BEGIN LECTURES on states of consciousness by asking the audience, "Is there anyone here right now who *seriously* believes that what he is experiencing in this room this morning may be something he is just dreaming? I don't mean picky philosophical doubt about the ultimate nature of experience or anything like that; I'm asking whether anyone in any seriously *practical* way thinks this might be a dream he's experiencing now, rather than his ordinary state of consciousness. Put your hand up if you think this may very well be a dream."

I have asked this question of many audiences, and I have almost never seen a hand go up. To answer this question, one quickly scans the contents and quality of one's experiences and finds that some specific elements of it, as well as the overall pattern of one's experiences, match very well those qualities one has come to associate with ordinary waking consciousness and do not match the qualities one has come to associate with being in a dreaming state of consciousness.

I ask audiences this question in order experientially to remind them

I am most obviously indebted to such thinkers as Roberto Assagioli, John Bennett, Carlos Castaneda and his teacher don Juan, Arthur Deikman, Sigmund Freud, David Galin, George Gurdjieff, Arthur Hastings, Ernest Hilgard, Thomas Kuhn, Carl Jung, John Lilly, Abraham Maslow, Harold McCurdy, Gardner Murphy, Claudio Naranjo, Maurice Nicoll, Robert Ornstein, Peter Ouspensky, Idries Shah, Ronald Shor, and Tarthang Tulku.

of a basic datum; namely, that people sometimes scan the pattern of their ongoing experience and classify it as being one or another *state of consciousness*.

In this discussion, I shall briefly describe a conceptual framework I have been developing for the past decade about the nature of consciousness, and particularly about the nature of states of consciousness, with the hope that this theoretical framework will help our understanding of a vitally important area of knowledge, an area of knowledge that currently can only be called messy. Although the things we loosely call altered states of consciousness are often critically important in determining human values and behavior, and although we are in the midst of a cultural evolution (or revolution, depending on your values) in which experiences from altered states of consciousness play an important part, our scientific knowledge of this area is just at its beginning. We have thousands of bits of unrelated data, a few relationships here and there, a small-scale theory here and there, but mainly a mess. The theoretical framework I shall describe attempts to give an overall picture of this area and to guide future research. Space limitations will force me to be very sketchy about many aspects of the theory, but detail and elaboration can be found in Tart (1975b). And, our scientific ignorance in this area will force me to be sketchy about many more details.

The background ingredients of the theory are diverse, ranging from my personal experience, to experiential reports of experimental subjects and of colleagues, to hints and ideas from the traditional psychologies of other cultures.

I shall emphasize a *psychological* approach to altered states of consciousness, as that is the approach I know best, and I believe it is adequate for building a comprehensive science of consciousness. The conceptual framework I shall present, however, is basically a *systems* approach to looking at consciousness; it can be quite easily translated into behavioral or neurophysiological terms. I find the neurophysiological framework presented by Karl Pribram in Chapter 8 and in his other writings and by Joel Elkes in Chapter 10 and elsewhere closely paralleling this psychological approach.

Ordinary Consciousness Is a Construction

The basic point I shall try to make as a prelude to discussing what *discrete states of consciousness* (d-SoCs) and *discrete altered states of consciousness* (d-ASCs) are is that our ordinary consciousness it not at all a natural *given* but only a *construction* and, in many important ways, a rather arbitrary construction. This point is difficult to comprehend even on an intellectual level, much less a practical level, because, after all, we *are* our ordinary state of consciousness, and each of our egos tends implicitly to assume that the way *it* is, is the natural, given standard of how an ego, a state of consciousness, *should* be. We shall work our way up to this conclusion more systematically.

ATTENTION/AWARENESS

1. We begin with a concept of some kind of basic *awareness*, some kind of basic ability to "know" or "sense" or "cognize" or "recognize" that something is happening. This is a fundamental theoretical and experiential given. We do not know scientifically what the ultimate nature of awareness is, but it is our starting point. It is beyond conceptual definition; it may be the "missing center" that Deikman so brilliantly discusses in Chapter 9.

In further discussion, I shall speak of *attention/awareness* to refer to a further basic given that we have *some* ability to direct this awareness from one thing to another.

This basic attention/awareness is something we can both conceptualize and experience as distinct from the particular *contents* of awareness at any time; that is, to varying degrees, we can talk about attention/awareness as an experiential reality independent of any particular content of awareness. I am aware of a plant hanging in front of me at this moment of writing; if I turn my head I'm aware of a chair. The function of basic awareness remains in spite of incredibly varied changes in its content.

2. Another basic theoretical and experiential given is the sometime existence of an awareness of being aware, self-awareness. The degree of self-awareness varies from moment to moment. At one extreme, I can be very aware that at this moment I am looking at the plant in front of me. At the other extreme, I may be totally immersed in viewing the plant, but I am not aware of being aware of the plant. That is, there is an experiential continuum at one end of which attention/awareness and the particular content of awareness are essentially merged,[1] at the other end of the continuum there is awareness of being aware, in addition to the particular content of awareness. The lower end of the self-awareness continuum, relatively total absorption, is probably where we spend most

---

[1] Something that we can know only retrospectively.

of our lives even though we like to credit ourselves with high self-aware-ness. I have elaborated this idea elsewhere (Tart, 1975a; 1975b). The higher end comes to us more rarely, although it may be sought deliber-ately in certain kinds of meditative practices, such as the Buddhist Vipassana meditation.

The ultimate degree of separation of attention/awareness from con-tents of self-awareness that is possible in any final sense varies with one's theoretical position about the ultimate nature of the mind. If one adopts the conventional view that mental activity is identical with brain functioning, there is a definite limit as to how far awareness can "back off" from particular contents: Awareness is itself a product of the structure and contents of the individual brain. This is a psychological manifestation of the principle of relativity (Tart, 1975b). Although the feeling of being aware of being aware has an "objective" quality to it, a conservative commentator would say that this objectivity is only relative and basically illusory.

A more radical view, common to the spiritual psychologies (Tart, 1975c), is that basic awareness is not just a property of the brain but is (at least partially) something from "outside" the workings of the brain. Insofar as this assertion is correct, it is conceivable that most or all content associated with brain processes could be "stood back" from so that in this view the degree of separation between content and atten-tion/awareness, the degree of self-awareness, is much higher than in the conservative one.

Whichever view one takes, what is psychologically important for studying consciousness is that the degree of self-awareness varies con-siderably from moment to moment, and it strongly affects other aspects of mental functioning.

3. Attention/awareness can be volitionally directed to *some* extent. If I ask you to become aware of the sensations in your left knee now, you can do so. But few would claim anything like total ability in directing attention. If you are being burned by a flame, it is well-nigh impossible to direct your attention/awareness to something else and not notice the pain at all, although this redirection can be done successfully by certain people and by many more people in certain states of con-sciousness. As the degree of separation of attention/awareness from con-tent seems to vary quite frequently, so does the degree to which we seem able volitionally to direct our attention/awareness.

Stimuli and structures (subsequently we shall deal with structures) attract or capture attention/awareness: The sounds and sight of an ac-cident and a crowd suddenly gathering capture your attention as you are walking down the street. Similarly, ongoing mental activity, activated structures, tends to attract any loose, contentless attention/awareness and bind that attention/awareness to it. This attractive pull may outweigh volitional attempts to deploy attention/awareness elsewhere. For example, we worry over and over about a particular problem though we know we're just wasting our energy going around in circles and should redirect our attention.

The ease with which particular kinds of structures and contents capture attention/awareness will vary with the state of consciousness and the personality structure of the individual. Indeed, we could partially define personality as the structures that habitually capture a person's attention/awareness.

4. Attention/awareness constitutes the major phenomenal energy of the consciously experienced mind. *Energy* is here used in the most abstract sense of the term—the ability to do work, the ability to make something happen. Attention/awareness is then energy in the sense that structures having no effect on consciousness at a given time can be activated if given attention to, or structures may draw attention/awareness energy automatically, habitually, as a function of personality structure, thus keeping a kind of low-level, automated attention in them all the time (these are our long-term desires, concerns, phobias), or attention energy may inhibit particular structures from functioning. The selective refocusing of attention/awareness energy on desired ends is a central part of innumerable systems that have been developed to control the mind.

5. The total amount of attention/awareness energy available to a person varies from time to time, but there may be some fixed upper limits on it for a particular day or other time period. Some days we simply cannot concentrate well; other days we seem to be able to focus clearly. We talk about "exhausting" our ability to pay attention, and phenomenally the total amount of attention/awareness energy available under ordinary conditions may be fixed for various time base periods.

Let us now look at basic theoretical postulates about the mental/psychological structures that utilize the energy of attention/awareness.

STRUCTURE

6. This theory postulates that the mind, from which consciousness arises, consists of a myriad of structures. A psychological *structure* refers to a relatively stable organization of component parts that performs one or more related psychological functions.

We infer (from "outside") the existence of a particular structure of observing that a certain kind of input information reliably results in a certain kind of transformed output information under typical conditions. We ask, "How much is fourteen divided by seven?" We are told, "Two." After repeating this process, with variations, we infer the existence of a special structure or related set of structures we might name something like "arithmetical skills." Or we might infer (from "inside") the existence of a particular structure when, given certain classes of experienced input information, we experience certain transformed classes of output/response information. For example, I overhear the question about fourteen divided by seven and note that some part of me automatically "answers": "Two." Thus, I infer an arithmetical-skills structure as part of my own mind.

We hypothesize that structures generally continue to exist even when they are not active, not functioning, since they operate again when appropriate activating information is present. I again know that fourteen divided by seven is two, even though I have not thought about this problem for a while.

The emphasis here is on the structure forming or doing something that has a recognizable shape, pattern, function, process. Ordinarily in dealing with a structure, we are interested in its overall properties as a complete structure, as a structured system, rather than in the workings of its component parts. Insofar as any structure can be broken down into sub-substructures, one can do finer analyses ad infinitum. The arithmetical-skills structure could be broken down into adding, subtracting, multiplying, and dividing substructures. Such detailed analyses, however, may not be profitable in understanding the properties of the overall system—say, a state of consciousness—that one is examining. The most obvious quality that characterizes an automobile *as a system* is its ability to move passengers along roads at high speed; a metallurgical analysis of a car's spark plugs is not very relevant to understanding the vehicle's primary functioning and nature. Our concern, then, is with psychological structures that show functions useful to our understanding of consciousness. Such structures might be given names like sexual needs, social coping mechanisms, and language abilities.

7. A psychological structure may show variation in the intensity and/or the quality of its activity, both overall and in terms of its component parts, but still retain its basic patterns, its basic gestalt qualities, its basic system function, and so remain recognizably the same. A car is usefully referred to as a car whether it is traveling at five miles an hour or twenty-five miles an hour, whether it is red or blue, whether the

original spark plugs have been replaced by spark plugs of a different brand.

8. Some structures are essentially permanent; they cannot have their important aspects of functioning modified in any significant way; they are biological/physiological givens. They are the "hardware" of our mental system, to use an analogy from computer programming; they are programs built into the machinery of the nervous system.

9. Some structures are mainly or totally given by the individual's developmental history. That is, they are created by, programmed by, the learning, conditioning, and enculturation processes to which the particular individual is exposed. This is the "software." Because of the immense programmability of human beings, most of the structures that interest us, that we consider particularly *human*, fall within this software category.

10. Permanent structures create limits on, and add qualities to, what can be done with programmable structures: The hardware to an extent constrains the software. The physiological parameters of the human being place some limits on his particular mental experience, his possible range of programming.

Our interest now is in relatively permanent structures, ones that are around long enough for us conveniently to observe and study, hours or weeks or years. Still, all the theoretical ideas in this essay should be applicable to structures that are not long-lasting, even though investigation may be more difficult.

Structures, then, are hypothesized explanatory entities based on experiential or behavioral or psychological data.

Let us next consider the interaction of attention/awareness and structures.

INTERACTION OF STRUCTURE AND ATTENTION/AWARENESS

11. Many structures function totally autonomously of attention/awareness. Such are basic physiological structures like the kidneys. We infer their integrity and nature as structures from other kinds of data, as we do not have any direct awareness of them.[2] Such structures do not utilize attention/awareness as an energy, but some other form of physiological activating energy. Structures that cannot be observed by

[2] We should be careful about any a priori definitions that certain structures must be out of awareness. Data from the rapidly developing science of biofeedback (see Chapter 6 of this volume) and traditional data from yoga and other spiritual disciplines should remind us that many processes long considered totally outside conscious awareness can be brought to conscious awareness with appropriate training.

attention/awareness are of incidental interest to the study of consciousness, except for their context-forming, indirect influences on other structures that are accessible to conscious awareness.

12. Some structures must use a certain amount of attention/awareness energy in order to: (a) be formed or created in the first place (software programming); and/or (b) operate; and/or (c) have their operation inhibited; and/or (d) have their structure or operation modified; and/or (e) be destructured, dismantled. We shall call these *psychological structures* when it is important to distinguish them from structures in general. Thus, many structures require some amount of attention/awareness energy for their initial formation: the attention originally required to learn arithmetical skills being an excellent example. Once the knowledge of structure we call arithmetical skills is formed, it is usually present only in an inactive, latent form. When an arithmetical question is asked, attention/awareness is put into that particular structure, and we exhibit (experience) arithmetical skills. If our original learning, structuring, programming was not very thorough, a fairly obvious amount of attention/awareness energy is necessary to call this skill into use. Once the structure has become highly automated and overlearned, only a small amount of attention/awareness energy is experienced as being needed to activate and run the structure. We solve basic arithmetic problems with little awareness of the process involved in so doing.

Note that although we have distinguished attention/awareness and structure for reasons of analytical convenience and faithfulness to certain experiential data, ordinarily we infer the existence of *activated* mental structures; i.e., we get data about structures when the structures are functioning, utilizing attention/awareness energy.

13. Although we postulate attention/awareness energy as capable of activating and altering psychological structures, as being the "fuel" that makes many structures run, observation indicates that affecting the operation of structures by the volitional deployment of attention/awareness energy is not always easy. We may attempt to alter a structure's operation by attending to it in certain ways but to no avail. We may even achieve effects contrary to those we desired. We may be unable to stop a certain structure from operating although we try to withhold attention/awareness energy from it. The reasons for this failure may be twofold.

First, if the structure is operating (at least partially) on kinds of energy other than attention/awareness energy, such as physiological energy, it may no longer be possible to affect the operation given the amount of attention/awareness energy we are able to focus on it. (We need to consider other kinds of psychological energy—for instance, emotional energy—but space does not allow that here.) Second, it may be that the structure does operate with attention/awareness energy but, because of automatization and/or because of very vital connections with the reward and punishment system of the personality structure—there may be secondary gains from the operation of the structure in spite of our apparent dissatisfaction—the amount of attention/awareness energy we can use to try to alter the structure's functioning is not sufficient to do so. Indeed, it seems clear that among ordinary people in ordinary states of consciousness, the amount of attention/awareness energy subject to conscious control and deployment may be quite small compared with some of the relatively permanent investments of energy in certain basic structures comprising the individual's personality and his adaptation to the consensus reality of his culture.

14. Insofar as the amount of attention/awareness energy available at any particular time has a fixed upper limit, there should be some decrements found when too many structures draw on this energy simultaneously. If the available attention/awareness energy is greater than the total used, no decrements will occur with the simultaneous activation of several structures.

15. Once a structure has been formed and is operating, either in isolation or in interaction with other structures, the attention/awareness energy required for its operation may be automatically drawn on either intermittently or continuously. That is, the personality and "normal" state of consciousness are operating in such a way that attention is repeatedly and automatically drawn to the particular structure. Personality may be partially defined as the set of interacting structures (traits) that habitually are activated by attention/awareness energy. A person may not realize that his attention/awareness energy is being drawn to this structure, unless he develops the ability to deploy attention in an observational mode, the self-awareness mode. Again we must distinguish the case in which the structure learns to operate with an energy other than attention/awareness energy. Some of these latter kinds of structures may still be capable of de-automatization with the proper deployment of attention/awareness energy to them although this process may be difficult.

There is a fluctuating but generally large drain on attention/awareness energy at all times by the multitude of automated, interacting structures whose operation constitutes our personality, our "normal" state of consciousness, our perception of and interaction with consensus reality. Because the basic structures comprising this normal state of consciousness are activated most of our waking life, we do not perceive this activation as a drain on attention/awareness energy but simply as the "natural" state of things. We have become habituated to it. The most important kinds of data supporting this observation come from reports of the effects of meditation, a process that in many ways is a deliberate refocusing of attention/awareness energy, taking it away from its customary structures and either putting it in nonordinary structures or trying to maintain it as a relatively pure, detached awareness. From meditative experience it can be seen that attention/awareness energy must be used to support our ordinary state of consciousness. Too, from these kinds of experiences of great clarity, the automatized drain of attention/awareness energy into habitually activated structures is seen as attenuating the clarity of basic awareness, so ordinary consciousness is seen as blurred and dreamlike.

Let us now consider the interaction of structures themselves.

INTERACTION OF STRUCTURES WITH STRUCTURES

16. Although the interaction of one structure with another structure depends on the structures' being activated by attention/awareness or other kinds of energy, this interaction is modified by an important limitation; namely, *individual structures have various kinds of properties* that limit and control their potential range of interaction with one another. That is, structures are not "equipotential" with respect to interacting with one another but have important individual characteristics.

Consider that any structure has one or more ways in which information can be put into it, and one or more ways in which information is outputted from the structure. (For more complex structures, we probably should distinguish also between inputs and outputs that we can be consciously aware of with suitable deployment of attention/awareness, between inputs and outputs that we cannot be consciously aware of but that we can make inferences about, and between inputs and outputs that are part of feedback control interconnections between structures but of which we cannot be directly aware. We can say in general that in order for two structures to interact they must have either a direct connection between them or some connections mediated by other structures; their input and output information must be in the same kind of "code" so that the information output from one "makes sense" to the input of another; the output signals of one structure must not be so weak that they are below the threshold for reception by the other structure, nor must the output signals of one structure be so strong that they overload the input of the other structure.

Let us consider ways in which psychological structures may *not* interact, with a possible example of each.

First, two structures may not interact because there is no direct or mediated connection between them. I have, for example, structures involved in moving the little finger of my left hand and sensing its motion, and I have structures involved in sensing my body temperature, say, in telling whether I have a fever or a chill. Although I am moving my little finger vigorously now, I can get no sense of having either a fever or a chill from that action. Those two structures seem to be totally unconnected.

Second, two structures may not interact if the code of output and input information is incompatible. My body, for example, has learned to ride a bicycle. Although I can sense that knowing in my body, in the structure that mediates my experience of my riding a bicycle when the bicycle is actually in motion, I cannot verbalize this knowing: The knowledge encoded in that particular structure does not code into the kinds of knowledge that constitute my verbal structures.

Third, two structures may not interact if the output "signal" from one is too weak, below the threshold for affecting another. I may be quite angry with someone and arguing with him. During the argument a "still small voice" in me is telling me that I am acting foolish, but I have very little awareness of this still small voice and it cannot affect the action of the structures involved in feeling angry and arguing.

Fourth, two structures may not interact properly if the output signal from one overloads the other. I may be in severe pain during a structural integration session, for instance, and I "know" (another structure tells me) that if I could relax the pain would be lessened considerably. Nevertheless, the structures that are involved in relaxing are so overloaded by the intense pain that they cannot carry out their normal function.

Fifth, two structures may be unable to interact properly if the action of a third structure interferes with them. An example is neurotic defense mechanisms. Suppose, for instance, your boss is a despicable character and constantly humiliates you. Yet part of your personality structure has a strong respect for authority and a belief in yourself as a very calm person who is not easily angered. Now your boss is humiliating you, but instead of feeling angry, the "natural" consequence of the situation, you are polite and conciliating and do not feel anger. A structure of your personality has suppressed certain possible interactions between other structures.

Let us now look at the case of smoother interaction between structures. We may, for instance, have two structures that interact readily and smoothly with one another to form a composite structure, a system whose properties may be additive properties of the individual structures, as well as gestalt properties unique to the combination. Or, two or more structures may interact with one another in such a way that the total system alters some of the properties of the individual structures to various degrees, and so we have a system formed that has gestalt properties but not necessarily the simple additive properties of the individual structures. Unstable interactions between two (or more) structures may take place when they in some sense compete for energy; here we have a kind of unstable, shifting relationship in the composite system.

All of these considerations about the interacting structures apply to both hardware and software structures. For example, two systems may not interact for a lack of connection in the sense that their basic neural paths, laid down in the hardware of the human being, cannot accommodate such interaction. Or, two software structures may not interact for lack of connection because in the enculturation, the programming of the person, the appropriate connections simply were not created.

One could look at all the classical psychological defense mechanisms in these system terms.

Remember that in the real human being many structures probably are interacting simultaneously, and all the factors for facilitating or inhibiting interaction to various degrees at various points in the total system formed are at work.

The basic point of this postulate, to summarize, is that although the interaction of structures is affected by the way attention/awareness energy is deployed, it is affected also by the properties of individual structures.

Developmental Construction of Ordinary Consciousness

I have postulated basic components of consciousness: attention/ awareness energy and structures. Let us look at how our ordinary, or so-called normal, state of consciousness is formed, how attention/awareness and structures form a *system*.

THE SPECTRUM OF HUMAN POTENTIALITIES

A helpful concept that I learned from anthropology is the idea of the *spectrum of human potentialities*. Figure 1 diagrams this idea. By virtue of being born a human being, having a certain kind of body and nervous system (the hardware), and functioning in the general environment of spaceship Earth, the individual has a very wide variety of behaviors and experiences *potentially* available. These may include running a four-minute mile, learning sophisticated mathematics, and enjoying various kinds of esthetic experiences.

But any individual human being will develop only a small fraction of his total human potentialities because he is born into a particular culture at a particular place and time, has certain parents, relatives, peers, and teachers, and has various "random" events happen to him. A culture can be looked at as a group of programmers who have (implicitly) agreed that certain human potentialities are beneficial and should be developed; they have set up a society, a system of interlocking relationships, to select these potentialities out of the total spectrum of human potentialities and to develop them, program them, to various degrees. These selections are shown by the pointed arrows in Figure 1. The same culture knows about certain other human potentialities but considers these undesirable or bad and actively blocks their development. Trance states, for instance, are a fundamental aspect of American Indian cultures but are at best highly suspect to Westerners (see Chapter 3 of this volume).

Figure 1 shows two cultures making different selections from the spectrum of human potentialities. Sometimes two cultures' potentials overlap. All cultures, for instance, teach people some kind of language. Note further that not only does a given culture selectively develop some potentials and actively inhibit others but also that the culture simply does not know about a very large variety of other potentials. Eskimos, for example, discriminate and have separate words for seven different kinds of snow. We do not make these fine distinctions in our culture, as it does not occur to us that we need to, or could, make them.

The human potentials that a given individual develops, the structures built and molded into a system, are in many ways severely limited by the culture he is born into. Within the cultural framework there will be further limitations depending on particular circumstances, and there are probably also genetic limitations on each person. At this point, however, cultural limitations and selections, the programming of the software, are much more easily identified than genetic ones.

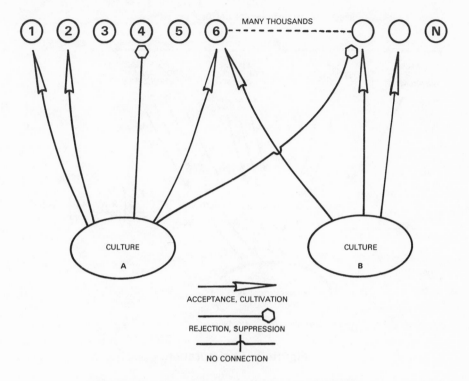

Figure 1. Spectrum of human potentialities.

Figure 2 summarizes the process of enculturation, of "maturation" (given culturally relative standards for "maturity"). We come into the world with a range of human potentialities that include (a) a basic capacity for awareness; (b) fixed structures (hardware) such as a skeleton, musculature, digestive organs that *must* develop if we are to be a functioning organism; (c) fixed structures that *may* develop, given the necessary conditions (which may not exist in a particular culture), such as Jung's archetypal experiences; and (d) a very wide range of highly programmable structures from which the culture will develop a number, such as the potential to speak English. The selective development and inhibition of potential structures by cultural, physical, and random factors, and the automatization of attention/awareness energy within the system built from these structures, produce a "normal" consciousness for a given culture, an individual who perceives reality and acts "appropriately" within the culturally sanctioned framework (consensus reality). Enculturation is an enormously complex process, discussed in more detail elsewhere (Tart, 1975a).

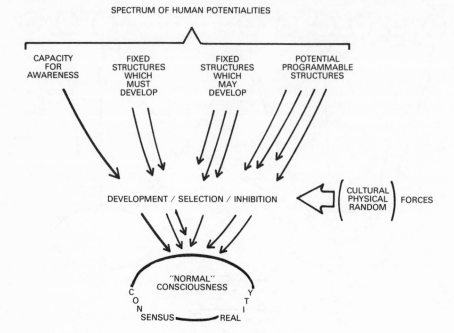

Figure 2. Enculturation.

THE SPECTRUM OF EXPERIENTIAL POTENTIALITIES

This same concept of the spectrum of human potentialities can be extended to a spectrum of consciousness potentialities, or experiential potentialities. Look again at Figure 1, but change the label "culture" to "state of consciousness." This illustrates how two different cultures have different systems comprising their ordinary states of consciousness, but let us view the figure as showing two possible organizations, systems, states of consciousness in one individual. In his ordinary state of consciousness, the culturally "normal" state, represented by the circle at the lower left, a given individual is able to have certain kinds of experiences, use certain kinds of psychological skills. Some other kinds of mental skills are actively inhibited in the ordinary state of consciousness. Many other experiential potentials that the individual was born with simply were never developed and so are not available in his ordinary state of consciousness. Some of these may be latent, waiting for the right stimulus to turn them into usable structures; others may no longer be developed due to disuse. An individual is simultaneously the beneficiary and the victim of his culture's choices from the spectrum of experiential potentialities.

Now, using the idea of the states of consciousness as implying an overall active organization of consciousness, an interacting system of structures activated by attention/awareness and other kinds of energy, it may be possible for this same individual to change into an *altered* state of consciousness, a new active organizational patterning of his consciousness, and in this second state he may be able to tap and use certain of these potentialities/structures that are unavailable in his ordinary state of consciousness. This is represented by the lower right-hand circle in Figure 1. The availability of new human potentials in altered states of consciousness is a prime reason for our interest in them, especially if you do not feel that your ordinary state of consciousness allows optimal functioning.

Just as two cultures may develop some common human potentialities, most of the altered states of consciousness that we know much about do share some psychological structures in common with our ordinary state of consciousness. For example, a person usually speaks his native language in both his ordinary state of consciousness and an altered state of consciousness.

Discrete States of Consciousness

TERMINOLOGICAL PROBLEMS

As we now start to focus on states of consciousness, terminological problems arise. The terms *states of consciousness* and *altered states of consciousness* have become very popular. As a consequence of their becoming popular, however, they are frequently used in such a loose fashion as to have little meaning. Many people use state of consciousness, for example, simply to mean whatever is on their mind. If I pick up a water tumbler and look at it, I am in "water tumbler state of consciousness"; if I touch a microphone, I am in "microphone state of consciousness"; and if I touch the top of my head, I am in "top of my head state of consciousness." Then an *altered* state of consciousness simply means that what you are thinking about or experiencing now is different from what it was a moment ago. To rescue the concepts of state of consciousness and altered state of consciousness for scientific use I propose the terms *discrete state of consciousness* (d-SoC) and *discrete altered state of consciousness* (d-ASC). I have already presented the basic theoretical postulates for defining these crucial terms. Here, I would like to look more closely, taking a slightly different route, at certain kinds of experiential data that lead up to the concepts.

MAPPING EXPERIENCE

Comprehensive and accurate description is the first business of science. It is commonly accepted that an individual's experience could be adequately described at any given moment if we knew all the important dimensions along which experience varies and could assess the exact point along each dimension that an individual occupied at a given moment. That is, if we have a multidimensional map of psychological space and know exactly where an individual is in that psychological space, we have adequately described his experiential reality for that time. This is a generally accepted theoretical idea, but it is very difficult to apply in practice because there may be many psychological dimensions important for an individual's experience at any given moment. We may be able to assess only a small number of them, and/or an individual's position on some of these dimensions may change even as we are busy assessing the value of others. Nevertheless, it is an ideal to be worked toward, and we shall assume that we can do this with some adequacy. Marsh advocates this kind of mapping in Chapter 5, although I do not believe her four dimensions are adequate.

To simplify further, let us assume that what is important about an individual's experiences can be mapped along only two dimensions. Figure 3 represents such a mapping. Ignore the illustrative labels on the two dimensions for a moment and simply consider the axes as two dimensions of psychological experience. Each small circle represents an observation, at a single point in time, of where a particular individual was in this two-dimensional psychological space. In this particular example, we have taken a total of twenty-two measures at various times.

The first thing that strikes us about this individual is that his experiences seem to fall into three distinct clusters and that there are large gaps between these three distinct clusters. Within each cluster this individual shows a certain amount of variability, but he has not had any experiences at points outside the defined clusters. This kind of clustering in the plot of an individual's location at various times in experiential space is precisely what I mean by a *discrete state of consciousness*. It means that you can be in a certain region of experiential space, and show some degree of variation within that space, but that to move out of that space you have to cross a "forbidden zone" where you either do

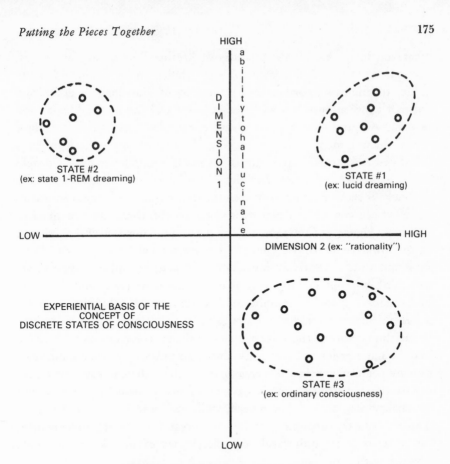

HIGH

DIMENSION 1

ability to hallucinate

STATE #2
(ex: state 1-REM dreaming)

STATE #1
(ex: lucid dreaming)

LOW ← → HIGH

DIMENSION 2 (ex: "rationality")

EXPERIENTIAL BASIS OF THE
CONCEPT OF
DISCRETE STATES OF CONSCIOUSNESS

STATE #3
(ex: ordinary consciousness)

LOW

Figure 3. Mapping experience.

not function and/or do not have reliable experiences and/or are not conscious of having experiences. (The term *forbidden zone* applies under ordinary circumstances to a stable personality and shall not be taken in an absolute way.) So you find yourself in a discretely different experiential space. It is the quantum principle of physics applied to psychology (Tart, 1975b): You can be either here or there, but there is no way for you to be in between. There are transitional periods between some d-SoCs, and we will deal with them in more detail later. For now, being in a d-SoC means that you are in one or another of these three distinct regions of psychological space shown in Figure 3.

Now let's concretize this example and refer to the labels I have put on the two axes of Figure 3. Let's call dimension 1 your ability to image or "hallucinate." At the low extreme is mere "imagining" that you see something outside yourself but you do not have anything corresponding to a sensory perception at all; at the high extreme of this continuum, what you image has all the qualities of "reality," of an actual sensory perception. Let's call dimension 2 your ability to be "rational," your ability to think in accordance with the rules of some logic or other. We will not concern ourselves with the cultural arbitrariness of "logic" for now but simply take logic as a given set of rules. You can vary from a low of making many mistakes in the application of this logic, as on days when you feel rather stupid and have a hard time following what people say, to a high of following the rules of the logic perfectly, feeling sharp as a tack, as they say, with your mind working like a precision computer.

Now we can give names of d-SoCs to the three clusters of data points in Figure 3. *Ordinary consciousness* (for our culture) is shown in the lower right-hand corner. It is characterized by a high degree of rationality and a relatively low degree of imaging ability. Usually, we can think without making very many mistakes of logic, and for most of us mental images have some mild sensory qualities but these are on a far less intense level than sensory perceptions. Notice again that there is variability within the state we call ordinary consciousness. My logic may be more or less accurate, my ability to image may vary somewhat, but my performance in these areas stays in the ordinary, habitual range.

At the opposite extreme is a region of psychological space in which rationality may be very low indeed, while ability to image is quite high. This is ordinary dreaming, where we create the entire dreamworld, image it. It seems quite real, yet therein we often take considerable liberties with rationality.

The third cluster of data points defines a particularly interesting d-SoC, *lucid dreaming*. This is the special kind of dream named by the Dutch physician Frederick Van Eeden (1913/1969), in which you feel as if you "wake up" in terms of mental functioning *within* the dreamworld; that is, you feel as rational and as in control of your mental state as you do in your ordinary state of consciousness but you are still *experientially located within the dreamworld*. Here we have a range of rationality at a very high level and a range of ability to image at a very high level, too.

A d-SoC, then, refers to a particular region of experiential space as we have shown here; adding the adjective *altered* simply means that with respect to some state of consciousness (usually our ordinary state) that we use as a baseline, we have made the "quantum jump" to another region of experiential space, another d-SoC. The quantum jump may be both *quantitative* in the sense of structures functioning at higher or lower levels of intensity and *qualitative* in that structures in the baseline state may cease to function, previously latent structures may begin to function, and the system pattern may change. The graphical presentation of Figure 3 does not lend itself to expressing qualitative changes, but they are more important than the quantitative ones.

To emphasize the qualitative pattern difference between two discrete states of consciousness, I have drawn Figures 4 and 5. Here various structures are shown connected into a pattern in different ways. A latent pattern, a discrete altered state of consciousness, is shown in lighter lines on each figure. The two states share many structures/functions in common, yet the organization is distinctly different in each.

Let us go into greater detail. I shall now define a d-SoC for a given individual as a unique *configuration* or *system* of psychological struc-

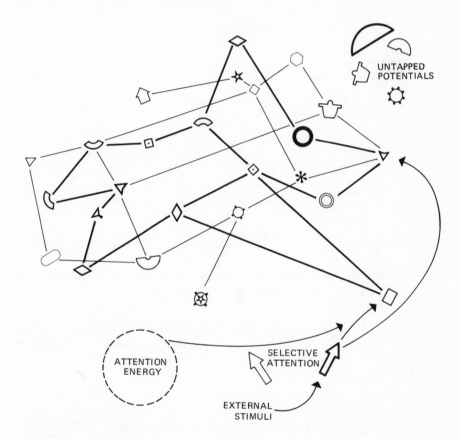

Figure 4. Representation of a d-SoC as a configuration of structures/ subsystems forming a recognizable pattern.*

*Light lines and circles represent *potential* interaction and potentialities/structures/ subsystems not used in the baseline d-SoC.

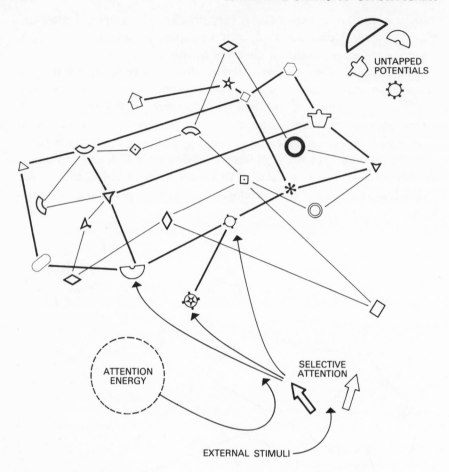

Figure 5. Representation of a d-ASC as a new configuration of structures/subsystems, a new gestalt.*

*The configuration of the baseline d-SoC (Figure 4) is shown in light lines and circles. Although there is some overlap of connections and structures/subsystems, a distinctly new pattern has emerged, and different human potentials are used in different ways to form a new system, the d-ASC.

tures or subsystems. The structures show some variation in the way in which they process information, or cope, or have experiences within one or more varying environments. The structures operative within a d-SoC comprise a *system* in which the parts, the psychological structures, interact with each other and stabilize each other's functioning by means of feedback control; in this way the *system*, the d-SoC maintains its overall pattern of functioning within a varying environment. That is, the parts of the system that comprise a state of consciousness may vary over different ranges individually, but the overall, general configuration, the overall pattern of the system, remains recognizably the same. Attention/awareness and other kinds of energies are the "fuel" that operates the system, the d-SoC.

In order to understand a d-SoC, then, we must understand the nature of the parts, the psychological structures/subsystems that comprise it, the information and energy flows, and, on taking into account the gestalt, the pattern properties that arise from the overall system that are not an obvious result of the functioning of the parts. For example, the parts of a car laid out singly on a bench may tell me little about the nature of the functioning system we call an automobile; a list of an individual's traits and skills may tell me little about the pattern that emerges from their organization into a personality, into a normal state of consciousness.

To concretize this, let's go back to the question I discussed at the start of this chapter—whether one thinks one's current experience might be a dream rather than one's ordinary state of consciousness. To conclude that what is happening to you is real, you may look at the functioning of your component structures—my reasoning seems sound, sensory qualities are in the usual range, body image seems right, criticalness is here, etc.—and conclude that since these component structures are in the range you associate with your ordinary state of consciousness you are in that state. Possibly, you simply "feel" the gestalt pattern of your functioning, without bothering to check component functions, and instantly recognize it as your ordinary pattern. Either way, you scan data on the functioning of yourself as a system and categorize the system's state of functioning as its ordinary one.

Let me make a few further comments about the discreteness of different states of consciousness, the quantum leap between them.

DISCRETENESS OF STATES OF CONSCIOUSNESS

First, it should be realized that the concept of d-SoCs, in its commonsense form, did not come from the kind of precise mapping along psychological dimensions that I have done in Figure 3. Rather, the immediate experiential basis of the state usually is gestalt pattern recognition, the feeling that "this condition of my mind feels *radically different* from some other condition rather than just an extension of it." The experiential mapping is a more precise way of saying this.

Second, for most of the d-SoCs that we know something about, there has been very little or no mapping of the relation of the baseline state of consciousness to the altered state. Little has been done, for example, in examining the process whereby one passes from an ordinary state of consciousness into the hypnotic state, although preliminary psychoanalytic investigations by Gill and Brenman (1959) are of interest here. Nevertheless, for most subjects the distinction between the well-developed hypnotic state and their ordinary state is very marked. Similarly, when one begins to smoke marijuana, there is a period of time during which one is in an ordinary state of consciousness and smoking marijuana; later, one is clearly "stoned," or in a d-SoC we call marijuana intoxication. The only study of this phenomenon is a preliminary survey that I and Joseph Fridgen carried out (Tart & Fridgen, 1976), asking experienced marijuana users about the transition from one state to the other. Our main finding was that users almost never bothered to look at the transition, either being in a hurry to enter the intoxicated state or being in social situations that did not encourage them to observe what was going on in their minds.

So, in general for d-SoCs, we do not really know what the size and the exact nature of the quantum jump are or, indeed, whether it might in some cases be possible to effect a continuous transition between two regions, thus making them extremes of one state of consciousness rather than two discrete states. Since that survey, I have asked many users of marijuana and other psychedelic drugs to look deliberately for the transition period and to try to characterize it; I have found that it is extremely difficult to observe the transition period between two d-SoCs. Weil (1975), too, has found the transition between states difficult to observe, although it is clearly there, in spite of his characterization of altered states as being on a continuum (see Chapter 2). We shall consider transitions later in discussing the induction of a d-ASC. The ability to understand transitions is crucial to ultimately understanding consciousness and toward finding Deikman's missing center (see Chapter 9).

Stabilization of a Discrete State of Consciousness

The basic function of a d-SoC is to cope successfully with a world, or external environment. It is a tool, a sensing tool, that interprets what the world is and plans and executes strategies for dealing with that changing world. A good tool should not break easily when applied to the job: The system of structures and (attention/awareness) energies that constitutes our state of consciousness should maintain its integrity in coping with the changing world for which it was designed. So a d-SoC is a dynamic system—parts of it are changing all the time—maintaining the overall pattern/organization that is its nature. Let us look at the stabilization process.

There are at least four major ways of stabilizing a system that constitutes a d-SoC. They are analogous to the ways in which people control one another. If you want someone to be a "good citizen" (a) you keep him busy with the activities that constitute being a good citizen, so he has no time or energy for anything else; (b) you reward him and make him feel good for carrying out these activities; (c) you punish him if he engages in undesirable activities; and (d) you try to limit opportunities for engaging in undesirable activities. Similarly, there are four ways in which to stabilize a d-SoC. The following discussion can apply both to the d-SoC as a whole and to the stabilization of the individual structures/subsystems within that d-SoC.

LOADING STABILIZATION

The first major type of stabilization is what we might call ballasting, or *loading*, to use an electrical analogy. In electrical ballasting, you impose a large electrical load on an output circuit that draws on the power resources sufficiently so that very high voltages cannot occur, the power supply lacks the capacity to produce them, given the load. Loading in general refers to any kind of activity that draws most of the energy of the system so that the system cannot swing into undesirable excesses of energy. A load may also store energy, giving the system inertia that prevents sudden slowdowns. Psychologically, loading means keeping a person's consciousness busy with the desired types of things, involving such a large proportion of the attention/awareness energy normally produced in the desired activities that not enough is left over to constitute the potential for disrupting the system operation. As don Juan told Carlos Castaneda, the ordinary, repeated, day-to-day activities of people keep their energy so bound within a certain pattern that they are kept from becoming aware of nonordinary realities (Castaneda, 1971).

For example, right now in your ordinary state of consciousness a number of things act as loading stabilization processes. The stable physical world around you, the invariant relationships in it, give you a pattern of input that constantly stimulates you in expected, familiar patterns. If you push your hand against the chair you're sitting in, it feels solid, just as it always has felt. If you push again, the chair will still feel solid. You can depend on the lawfulness of the spectrum of experience we call "physical reality." But, if the next time you pushed on the chair, your hand started passing *through* it, I expect most of you would be rather surprised or alarmed and immediately begin to suspect that you were not in your ordinary state of consciousness!

As a second example, your body (and your internalized body image) is another source of stabilization via loading. Every morning when you wake up you have one head, two arms, and two legs. Although the exact relationship of the parts of your body to one another changes, as do internal feelings within the body, all shifts fall within a well-learned range. If you suddenly felt half your body starting to disappear, you would wonder whether you were outside your ordinary state of consciousness.

As a third example, if you move your body, it has a certain feel to it; kinesthetic feedback information on the relation of parts of your body and muscle tensions as you move also is of a certain anticipated sort. We move around considerably, which furnishes us with extensive, familiar input. If your arm suddenly felt three times as heavy to lift, this would tend to disrupt your ordinary state of consciousness.

As a fourth example, consider your constant internal thinking process, your constant internal chatter, which runs through familiar and habitual associative pathways and keeps you within your ordinary state of consciousness. We think the kinds of things that please us; we feel clever as a result of thinking them; feeling clever makes us relax; feeling relaxed makes us feel good; feeling good reminds us that we are clever; and so on. This constant thinking, thinking, thinking, thinking, thinking also loads our system and is very important in maintaining our ordinary baseline state of consciousness.

NEGATIVE FEEDBACK STABILIZATION

The second major type of stabilization is what we might call *negative feedback*. Particular structures or subsystems sense when the rate or quality of operation of other subsystems goes beyond certain preset limits and then begin an active correction process. This correction signal might be conscious as, for example, the anxiety that results when thoughts stray into certain areas that are taboo for the thinker. The anxiety then functions to alter subsystems to restabilize them within the acceptable range.

You may not be conscious of a particular feedback correction process. For example, you may be lost in thought and suddenly find yourself very alert and listening to your environment although not knowing why. A sound signal that indicated a potentially threatening event may have occurred very briefly; although not intense enough to be consciously perceived the signal was sufficient to activate a monitoring mechanism that accordingly sent out correction signals to bring the system of consciousness back within optimal (for dealing with the threat) limits. This kind of negative feedback stabilization essentially measures when a system's or structure's operation is going beyond acceptable limits and initiates activity to reduce the deviation.

POSITIVE FEEDBACK STABILIZATION

The third kind of stabilization process is what we might call *positive feedback*; it consists of structures or subsystems that detect the occurrence of acceptable activity and further enhance such activity. We may or may not be particularly conscious of a "feeling good" quality when there is emotional enhancement. We like to maintain and repeat the rewarded activity. In terms of the formation of our ordinary state of consciousness during childhood, we are greatly rewarded by parents, peers, and teachers for doing various socially approved things and, insofar as most of our socially approved actions are initiated by socially approved thoughts, we internalize this reward system and feel good simply by engaging in the thoughts or actions that have been rewarded earlier.

LIMITING STABILIZATION

A fourth way of stabilizing a d-SoC can be called *limiting* stabilization. Here we interfere with the ability of some subsystems or structures to function in a way that might destabilize the ongoing state of consciousness.

An example of limiting stabilization would be one of the effects of tranquilizing drugs: Many of them seem to blunt emotional responses of any sort; they limit the ability of certain subsystems to produce strong emotions. Insofar as strong emotions can be important disrupting forces in destabilizing an ongoing state of consciousness, this limiting thus stabilizes the ongoing state. Sufficient limiting of crucial subsystems could thus make it impossible to enter a d-ASC that required the functioning of the spoiled subsystems.

Note that when dealing with a system as multifaceted and complex as a d-SoC, at any given instant there may be several of each of the four types of stabilization activities going on. Furthermore, any particular action may be complex enough actually to constitute more than one of these kinds of stabilization simultaneously. For example, suppose I have taken a drug and for some reason decide I don't want it to affect my consciousness. I may begin thinking *intensely* about personal triumphs. This process can stabilize my ordinary state of consciousness by loading it, focusing most of my attention/awareness energy on that activity so that it cannot shift to areas that would help the transition to an altered state. Also, it would act as positive feedback, making me feel good, and so increase my desire to keep up this kind of activity.

Note that the terms *positive feedback* and *negative feedback*, as used here, do not necessarily refer to consciously experienced good or bad feelings. Negative feedback refers to a correction process initiated when a structure or system starts to go, or has gone, beyond acceptable limits, a process of decreasing deviation. Positive feedback is an active reward process that occurs when a structure or subsystem is functioning within acceptable limits, enhancing functioning within those limits.

Subsystems Comprising Discrete States of Consciousness

The general picture of a particular d-SoC being made up of a certain number of psychological structures or subsystems, each with its own characteristics, interacting with each other in a certain pattern, can be made more detailed in many ways. The subsystems are structures or groups of related structures that are activated by attention/awareness and/or other sorts of energy. The particular number and kind of subsystems necessary for an adequate system description will vary greatly over particular problem focuses and theorists, and what might look like a *basic* psychological structure or subsystem to one theorist would be seen as capable of being further broken down by another. My own theorizing at this time calls for ten major subsystems plus an undetermined number of latent psychological functions that may come into operation in a d-SoC. My current choice of subsystems is based on what I know about the general kinds of variations one sees in many d-SoCs, as conceptualized by the kind of psychological knowledge currently available. I want to mention them briefly just to put a little flesh on the skeleton I have been building. Fuller descriptions can be found in Tart (1975b). Each of the subsystems I shall talk about is a *convenient* subsystem in terms of summarizing present knowledge, but certainly all are susceptible to finer analysis when we have the data to do so. Eventually, each of these subsystems will be treated as a system itself and analyzed into component subsystems.

Figure 6 shows ten major subsystems: *exteroceptors, interoceptors, input processing, memory, sense of identity, evaluation and decision making, subconscious, emotion, space/time sense,* and *motor output.* The heavy arrows represent major information and energy flow pathways within the system. The extra large arrows represent input from the external world or body or output to the external world or body. The dashed, heavy arrows represent important information flow routes that are only inferential rather than directly experiential in our ordinary state of consciousness. The lighter, hatched arrows represent feedback control pathways between various psychological systems; that is, information flow routes that do not necessarily represent consciously experienced information but the influences of one subsystem on another that keep the subsystems operating within a range appropriate for maintaining the overall d-SoC.

I have not attempted to show all major information flow routes—to do so would produce much too messy a diagram. Thus, Figure 6 dis-

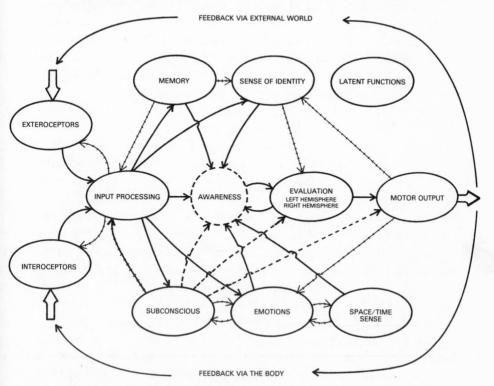

Figure 6. Subsystems comprising states of consciousness.

plays only some of the major and more obvious information and feedback flow routes. An oval for latent functions is shown as not connected to other psychological subsystems; this oval illustrates the latent structures that may be activated or constructed as we enter a d-ASC. The dotted circle labeled "awareness" is the ghost in the machine, the psychological function of basic attention/awareness, the function that extends into or activates structures/subsystems.

I shall very briefly say something about the nature of each subsystem and the range of variations it may show in various d-ASCs.

"Exteroceptors" refer to our sensory organs for perceiving energies in the external world; "interoceptors" refer to those senses whereby we perceive the conditions of our own body. Deliberately altering input to exteroceptors and interoceptors is used in most techniques for inducing d-ASCs. There may be changes in the functioning of interoceptors or exteroceptors resulting from the induction of an altered state although these changes are usually insignificant compared to other subsystem changes.

We know very little about the functioning of exteroceptors and interoceptors in isolation, psychologically speaking, because they each feed their information into one of our most important psychological subsystems, "input processing." This is the vast collection of perceptual learnings that makes our perception highly selective. It is the process that throws away 99 percent of the sensory data actually reaching us and passes on to awareness only instantaneous abstractions of what's "important" in the stimuli reaching us at any time. Changes in input processing, such as the de-automatization (Deikman, 1966) of this abstracting process, occur in many altered states and account for the reports of enhanced vividness and beauty of perception. Information flow can be cut to almost nothing, producing phenomena like analgesia.

All of these psychological subsystems are here being given convenient names for what are related collections of structures and functions, as is obvious in the case of "memory." It is a great oversimplification to speak as if we have one unitary memory. We have a large number of specialized memories for handling different kinds of information. In various altered states, memory function may be reduced or enhanced, or it may shift in its style of functioning, as when memories start being recalled as vivid visual images rather than verbal abstractions about stored data or when state-specific memory functions.

The psychological subsystem labeled "sense of identity" is that collection of psychological functions that we might call the ego or the sense of my-ness. It is a *quality* that gets added to other information within our state of consciousness, rather than necessarily being information itself, a quality that, because we value our egos, calls for the special handling of the information to which it is attached. For example, if looking out the window of my New York City apartment I see some kids smashing a parked car, I might feel indignant about the lawlessness of our times but be disinclined to intervene. If, with further information coming out of input processing and memory, I notice that it is *my* car they are messing up, the same information that a car is being smashed up now acquires an entirely new priority and emotional tone. The sense of my-ness or ego-ness is highly variable in d-ASCs; it may go from a low of zero—everything is perceived simply as information and there is no ego on the scene—to a high where the self becomes extended to include other people, other events, or even the universe. The construction of the ego sense is examined in detail by Deikman in Chapter 9.

The subsystem labeled "evaluation and decision making" refers to our cognitive processes, the various learned (and perhaps partially innate) rules and procedures we have learned for analyzing and working with information according to one or more kinds of logic. Not only can this subsystem work more or less efficiently in d-ASCs, but also the particular logic with which it works can be deliberately altered. For example, in hypnosis a subject can be given an axiom that there is no such thing as the number five; he then evolves a new arithemetic taking this axiom into account. Or gestalt qualities may become more important than verbal components in deciding whether two things are "equivalent" in reasoning. Often, shifts in balance between the styles of thinking associated with right- and left-hemisphere functioning are prominent.

The subsystem labeled "subconscious" includes the classical Freudian and Jungian unconscious as well as many of the things that Frederick Myers, for example, would have included as the subliminal self. It refers to all those psychological functions that are not directly available to consciousness in an ordinary state of consciousness but that we hypothesize as being active in order to account for observable conscious behavior and experience. In some d-ASCs, processes that were subconscious in the ordinary state, i.e., that we only *hypothesized* to exist, may become capable of being directly experienced.

The subsystem labeled "emotion" refers to all of our various emotional feelings. In d-ASCs a variety of changes may take place, such as stimuli triggering atypical emotions or emotional intensity being much heightened or reduced. *Extreme* values of emotion can disrupt our ordinary state of consciousness and induce altered states of consciousness (d-ESoCs).

The psychological function labeled "space/time sense" refers to the general feeling we have for the rate of flow of time and the structuring of experience in terms of psychological space/time. It may be based at least partially on internal biological rhythms, as well as upon cues from external events and cultural learnings. In various d-ASCs, time sense may speed up, slow down, seem to stop, or events may even seem to happen totally out of their normal order, with the future preceding the past. Distances and spatial relations may alter radically. I stress that this is a *psychological* space and time sense, a construction, rather than some kind of physiological or psychological process that merely mirrors clock time (Ornstein, 1969) or meter sticks. Whether we want to consider clock time and metered space more "real" is an interesting question.

The final subsystem in Figure 6 is "motor output," which refers to the voluntarily controlled skeletal muscles and to the various internal effects different actions have on our body (e.g., glandular secretions). Motor output may be inhibited, unaffected, or enhanced in various altered states.

Predictive Capabilities of the Theory

Having given our abstract structures more definite shape in terms of current knowledge, we can now see how the theoretical system may be used to make testable predictions about d-SoCs, in addition to being a convenient descriptive system. The basic predictive operation is a cyclical one. The first step is to observe the properties of structures/subsystems and their interactions as well as the current state of knowledge permits. The second step is to organize the observations to make better theoretical models of the nature of the various structures/subsystems observed; from these models, the third step is to predict how the structures/subsystems can and cannot interact with each other under different conditions. Fourth, we test these predictions by looking for, or attempting to create, d-SoCs that fit or do not fit these improved structure/subsystem models and determine how well the models work. This procedure takes us back to the first step, further altering or refining our models, etc.

Basically what the conceptual system herein proposed does is provide a framework for organizing knowledge about states of consciousness and a process for continually improving our knowledge about the structures/subsystems. The ten subsystems sketched in the preceding section are crude; eventually they should be refined by more precise knowledge about the exact nature of a larger number of more basic subsystems and their possibilities for interaction to form systems.

I have given little thought to date to making predictions based on the current state of the theory. The far more urgent need at this chaotic stage of the new science of consciousness is to organize the mass of unrelated data at hand. I believe that most of the data now available can be usefully organized in the conceptual framework I am presenting and that this framework represents a clear step forward in the study of consciousness. The precise fitting of the data into this theoretical framework will be a work of years, however.

One obvious prediction of the theory is that because of the differing properties of structure, restrictions, their interaction, there is a definite limit to the number of stable d-SoCs. Ignoring enculturation, we can say that the number is large but limited by the neurobiological endowment of man. The possible states available to any individual are further limited by enculturation.

Individual Differences

Let us turn our attention to a methodological problem that has seriously slowed psychological research in general, as well as research on states of consciousness. This is the lack of adequate recognition of individual differences.

Lip service is paid to individual differences all the time in psychology courses but in reality individuals are somethings relegated to the clinical psychologists' domain, and "everyone knows" clinical psychologists practice more of an art than a science. As scientists who have been caught up in the all too human struggle for prestige, we ape the physical sciences, in which individual differences are not of great significance and the search is for general, "fundamental" laws. This lack of real recognition of individual differences was the rock on which psychology's early attempts to establish itself as an introspective discipline foundered. Following the lead of their more successful physicist and chemist colleagues, the early psychologists immediately began to look for the general laws of the mind; when they found their data were not agreeing, they took to quarreling and wasted their energies. They tried to abstract too much before coming to adequate terms with the prescribed subject matter.

All too often we do the same thing today, albeit in a more "sophisticated" form. Suppose that in the course of an experiment we take a couple of measures on a group of subjects. Let measure x be the degree of analgesia the subject can show and let measure y be the intensity of the subject's imagery. Tempted by the convenience and "scientificness" of a nearby computer, we dump our group data into a prepackaged analysis program and get a printout like that displayed in the lower right-hand corner of Figure 7, showing a nice straight line fitted to the data and a highly significant (thus publishable) correlation coefficient between variables x and y. It looks as if ability to experience analgesia is linearly related to intensity of imagery.

If we distrust this much abstraction of the data, we might ask the computer to print out a scatter plot of the raw data. Then we might see something like the plot in the lower left-hand corner of Figure 7, which reassures us that our fitted curve and correlation coefficient are quite adequate ways of presenting and understanding our results.

Suppose, however, that we go back to our subjects and test some of them repeatedly, doing a time sample of their simultaneous abilities to experience analgesia and image. Suppose we find that our subjects actually fall into three clear types, shown in the upper half of Figure 7.

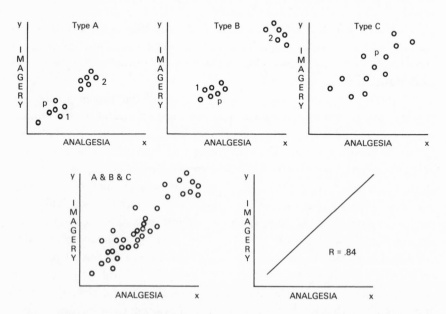

Figure 7. Methodological problems in using group data.

Type A shows either a low degree of both analgesia and imagery or a fair degree of analgesia and imagery, but nothing else. Type B shows a low-to-fair degree of analgesia and imagery or a very high degree of analgesia and imagery, but nothing else. Type C shows a high variability of degree of analgesia and imagery.

For type C subjects, the conclusion drawn from the group data of a linear relationship between intensity of imagery and intensity of analgesia is valid. But how many type C subjects were included in our group? Subjects of types A and B, on the other hand, do *not* show a linear relationship between x and y, analgesia and imagery. For type A subjects, x and y cluster together at low levels of functioning or at moderate levels of functioning but show no clear linear relationship within either cluster. For type B subjects, x and y cluster at low-to-moderate or at very high levels; again, no clear linear relationship appears within either clustering. Indeed, subjects of types A and B show the clustering we used to define the concept of d-SoCs; whereas, subjects of type C seem to function in a single d-SoC only.

Note, too, that if we had a distribution of mostly subject types A and B, and only a few Cs, in our experimental group, and if we average a single data point from each subject, and if some of the As and Bs are in one or another of the d-SoCs they can be in, then we will get pseudo-continuity in our group data and not even suspect the existence of different d-SoCs in our experiment. We shall think all subjects are type C. There may even be more d-SoCs than is apparent at first glance, for while the lower clusters for type A and type B subjects might be the same d-SoC, the moderate and high ones might not be.

A variety of misinterpretations of experimental data can result from these types of errors.

I think it is hard to realize the full impact of individual differences because of the deep (emotional) ingrainedness of the assumption that we all share a common state of consciousness to begin with, our ordinary or so-called normal state of consciousness. Insofar as we are members of a common culture this claim is generally true, but the more I have really come to know other individuals and started to get a feeling for the way their minds work, the more I have become convinced that this general truth, the label *ordinary state of consciousness*, collapses enormous individual differences.

Psychologically, we each tend to assume that our own mind is an example of a "normal" mind; we then project our own experiences onto other people without being aware of how much projecting we are doing. This tendency can have interesting results scientifically. For example, there is a raging controversy in the hypnosis literature over whether the concept of a d-SoC is necessary to explain hypnosis or whether the hypnotic state is in fact continuous with the ordinary state; in the hypnotic state, this view holds, certain psychological functions such as suggestibility and role-playing involvement are pushed to levels of activity somewhat higher than the ordinary. One of the chief proponents of this view, Theodore X. Barber, can produce most of the classical hypnotic phenomena in himself without doing anything "special"; for instance, he can sit down and anesthetize his hand or produce mild hallucinations without experiencing a breakdown of his ordinary consciousness, a transitional period, or anything else "special" (Barber, 1972). That is, included in Barber's ordinary state of consciousness is a range of phenomena that, for another person, must be attained by unusual means. How much does this affect Barber's theorizing? To go back to Figure 7, whereas A and B type people might have one state of consciousness that we call their ordinary state and a second called their hypnotic state, type C's ordinary range of consciousness includes both these regions. So it is more accurate to say that what has been called hypnosis, to stick with this example, is indeed "merely" an extension of the ordinary range of functioning for *some* people, but for other people it is a d-ASC.

I cannot emphasize too strongly that the mapping of experience and the use of the concept of d-SoCs *must first be done on an individual basis. Only* after that, *if* we find regions of great similarity across individuals, does it become legitimate to coin common names that apply across individuals.

Induction of a Discrete Altered State of Consciousness

Let us look at the process of inducing a d-ASC.

Our starting point is the baseline state of consciousness (b-SoC), usually our ordinary state of consciousness. The b-SoC is an active, stable, overall patterning of psychological functions that, via multiple (feedback) stabilization relationships among the parts making it up, maintains its identity in spite of environmental changes. I emphasize *multiple* stabilization because there are many processes maintaining a state of consciousness: the state would be too vulnerable to unadaptive disruption if there were only one or two processes at work.

Given this starting point, inducing the transition to a d-ASC is a three-step process based on two psychological (and/or physiological) operations. I will describe the steps of the process sequentially and the operation sequentially; however, in reality the same action may function for both induction operations.

INDUCTION OPERATIONS

The first induction operation is to *disrupt* the stabilization of the b-SoC, to interfere with the loading, positive and negative feedback, and limiting processes/structures that keep one's psychological structures operating within their ordinary range. We must disrupt several stabilization processes. For example, if a sudden, sharp noise occurred right now it would increase your level of activation and might even make you jump. I doubt very much, however, that you would enter a d-ASC even though your level of activation momentarily peaked up rather high. With such a totally unexpected and intense stimulus, there would be a momentary shift *within* the pattern of your ordinary state of consciousness but not a shift to an altered state. In the mapping analogy of Figure 3, you would move within a cluster but not out of it. (This particular example works for your ordinary state of consciousness, but if you had been asleep when the noise occurred, you might have been awakened as a result of the stimulus. It might be sufficient in a sleep state to disrupt stabilization enough to allow a transition back to ordinary waking consciousness.)

So the first operation in inducing a d-ASC is to disrupt enough of the multiple stabilization processes to a sufficient extent so that the baseline pattern of consciousness can no longer hold together. You may try to disrupt stabilization processes directly when they can be identified, or indirectly by pushing some psychological functions to and beyond their limits of functioning. You may disrupt particular subsystems, for example, by overloading them with stimuli, depriving them of stimuli, or giving them anomalous stimuli that cannot be processed in habitual ways. Or you may disrupt the functioning of a subsystem by withdrawing attention/awareness energy from it, a gentle kind of disruption. If the operation of one subsystem is disrupted, the operation of a second subsystem may be altered via feedback paths.

The second induction operation is to apply what I call *patterning forces,* stimuli that push disrupted psychological functioning toward the new pattern of the desired d-ASC. These patterning stimuli may serve also to disrupt the ordinary functioning of the b-SoC insofar as they are incongruent with the functioning of the b-SoC. Thus, the same stimuli may serve as both disruptive and patterning stimuli. One might, e.g., show someone a diagram that makes no sense or is unesthetic in the baseline state, a mild disrupting force, but that makes sense or is esthetically pleasing in the desired altered state, a patterning force.

INDUCTION STEPS

Figure 8 sketches the steps of the induction process, using the analogy of d-SoCs being like variously shaped and sized blocks (representing particular psychological structures) forming a system/construction (the state of consciousness) in a gravitational field (the environment). At the extreme left, we see a number of psychological structures assembled into a stable construction, our b-SoC. The detached figures below the construction represent some psychological potentials that are not available in the b-SoC.

The most left-hand figure is our starting point, a stable state of consciousness. We apply disrupting (and patterning) forces to begin induction. The second figure from the left is this beginning and represents *quantitative* change within the b-SoC; that is, the disruptive (and patterning) forces are being applied, and while the overall construction remains the same, some of the relationships within it have changed. Quantitative change has about reached its limit, as, for example, at the right and left ends of the construction, where organization is severely disrupted. Particular psychological structures/subsystems have varied as far as they can while still maintaining the overall system. (There is a *depth* or intensity dimension within some d-SoCs, which I have discussed elsewhere, Tart, 1972b, 1975b). I have indicated some of the latent potentials outside consciousness changing their relationship, something we must postulate from this theory and our knowledge of the dynamic unconscious but about which we have very little empirical data at present. (Psychoanalytic studies by Gill and Brenman, 1959, of hypnotic induction, for example, give us inferential information on such activities.)

If the disrupting forces are successful in finally breaking down the organization of the b-SoC, the second step of the induction process occurs, the construction/state of consciousness comes apart, and a transitional period occurs. In Figure 8 this is drawn as the parts of the construction being scattered about, with no clear-cut relationship to one another, or perhaps momentary relationships forming, as with the small square, the circle, and the hexagon on the left side of the figure. The disrupting forces are now represented by the light arrow, as they are

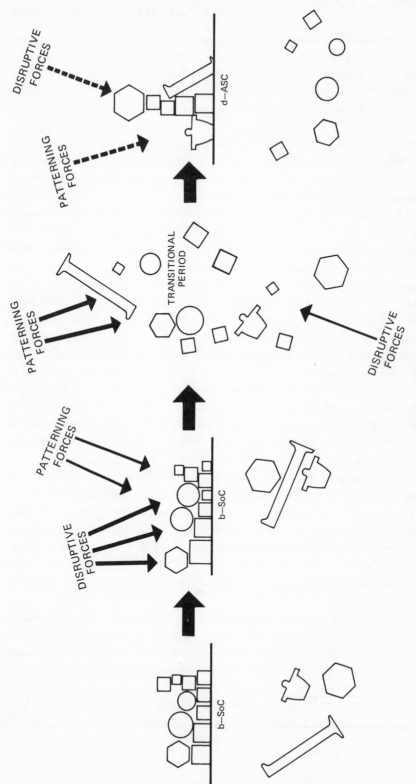

Figure 8. Induction of a discrete altered state of consciousness.

not as important since the disruption actually occurred; the patterning forces are represented by the heavy arrows. The patterning stimuli must now push the isolated psychological structures into a new construction, the third and final step of the process: A new, self-stabilized structure, the d-ASC, forms. Some of the psychological structures/ functions present in the b-SoC, such as those represented by the circles, may not be available in this new state of consciousness, while other psychological functions not available in the b-SoC have now become available. Some functions available in the b-SoC may be available at the same or an altered level in the d-ASC.

I have indicated also that the patterning forces and disrupting forces may have to continue to be present, perhaps in attenuated form, in order for this new state to be stable; that is, the d-ASC may not have enough internal stabilization at first to hold up against internal or environmental change, and so artificial "props" may be necessary for some time. A person, for example, may at first have to be hypnotized in a very quiet, supportive environment in order to make the transition into hypnosis; after being hypnotized a few times, he can be hypnotized under very noisy, chaotic conditions because the d-ASC is now well enough established.

In following this example you probably thought of going from your ordinary state to some more exotic altered state of consciousness, but this theoretical sequence applies for transition from any d-SoC to any other d-SoC. Indeed, this is also the *de*-induction process, the process of going from a d-ASC back to the b-SoC. You apply forces to disrupt the altered state and patterning forces to reinstate the baseline state; a transitional period ensues; and the baseline state re-forms. Since it is generally much easier to get back into our ordinary state, because it is so overlearned, than to enter an altered state, we usually pay little attention to the de-induction process although it is just as complex in principle as the induction process.

Later we shall consider the question of what can be self-observed during the transitional period.

It may be that some d-SoCs cannot be reached directly from other d-SoCs: An intermediary d-SoC has to be gone through. It is like crossing a stream that is too wide to leap over directly, so you have to leap onto one or more stepping-stones in sequence to reach the other side. Each stepping-stone is a stable place in itself, but they are transitional with respect to the beginning and end points of the process. Some of the *jnana* states of Buddhist meditation (Goleman, 1972) may be of this nature. This kind of stable transitional *state* should not be confused with the inherently unstable transitional *periods* we have been discussing.

FALLING ASLEEP

To illustrate induction briefly, consider the highlights of the process of going to sleep. You lie down in a dark, quiet room, closing your eyes. Most of the loading stabilization of the external environment is thus removed. By lying still, your kinesthetic receptors adapt out, removing the loading stabilization input from your body. You adopt an attitude of nothing being particularly important; there is nothing to accomplish, so attention/awareness is withdrawn from both positive and negative feedback stabilization systems; there is no "norm" to which to hold the system. These are all gentle disrupting forces. Tiredness, the physiological need for sleep, is both a further disrupting force and a preprogrammed, "hardware" patterning force. As data from Vogel and his associates (1969) illustrate, the intact ego state, the ordinary state of consciousness, persists for a time after lying down. Then, as reality contact and plausibility of thought are lost, the destructuralized ego state appears. We will take the destructuralized state as the transitional period although future research may require us to make finer distinctions if there turns out to be a stable pattern to this seemingly destructuralized state. The transitional period ends with the restructuralized ego state, with plausibility of content returning even though reality contact remains lost. Vogel and his collaborators accept a psychoanalytical interpretation of this process, viewing the restructuring as due to defenses against the anxiety the destructuralized state could engender. As defense mechanisms have temporarily broken down in the destructuralized state, we would say further patterning forces operate to form the restructuralized state, the d-ASC.

Methodological Hazards of Operationalism

In our consideration of induction, we come to another major methodological problem that has greatly plagued psychological research on altered states: operationalism carried out "rigorously," to the point of absurdity. That is, in our search for "objectivity" we start emphasizing things that can be physically measured, to the point of making our experiments useless.

A good example in psychological research is the equating of the hypnotic *state* with the *performance* of the hypnotic induction *pro-*

cedure by the hypnotist. The hypnotic *state* is a purely psychological construct (or experience if you have ever achieved it), not at all defined by measurement with a voltmeter or a camera. The hypnotic induction *procedure*, on the other hand, the "magic" words the hypnotist says aloud, is susceptible to physical measurement. One can photograph it, videotape it, record it, measure the intensity of the hypnotist's voice, and come up with all sorts of precise data. If we talk about the responses of the "hypnotized" subjects, as some experimenters do, when we mean that these are subjects who sat in the same room in which the hypnotist pronounced the magic words (an objective measurement), we err seriously: The fact that the *hypnotist* goes through the procedure does not mean that *subjects* will enter the d-SoC we call the hypnotic trance.

I stress that the concept of a d-ASC is a *psychological, experiential construct*, and so the ultimate criterion for whether a subject is in an altered state is a mapping of his experiences actually to determine at a given time whether he is in a region of psychological space we call a d-ASC. (Practically, once we have an adequate overall map for a particular d-SoC for a given subject, we may just sample a few uniquely characteristic points to decide whether the subject is in that d-SoC at a given time.) We must not equate a d-SoC with the performance of the induction technique. Going through a hypnotic induction does not necessarily induce hypnosis; lying down in bed does not necessarily mean you are sleeping or dreaming; performing a meditation exercise does not necessarily mean that you enter into some kind of meditative state of consciousness.

When the induction technique is apparently physiological, as, for example, when drugs are used, it is very tempting to think that that is a complete or sufficient definition of the altered state, but this position is incorrect. Smoking marijuana, e.g., does not necessarily mean that the smoker gets "stoned," enters into a discrete altered state. Subsequently, I elaborate on this problem.

Nevertheless, we do need to describe techniques in detail in reporting experiments. We need also to have measures of the *effectiveness* of these techniques in actually altering a subject's state of consciousness *for each individual subject*.

Space does not permit discussion of how these assessments can be carried out. I refer the reader to Tart (1972b) and Tart and Kvetensky (1973), which show some of the ways we can make such assessments.[3]

---

[3] We do not have space to treat physiological correlates of discrete states of consciousness, so I shall just say that where we have such correlates (stage 1 REM

In discussing operationalism in this section, I have been referring to a *physical* operationalism, a definition of terms based on the manipulation of external, physical objects. Ultimately we need an *internal* operationalism to define crucial terms and processes in experience. Our present language is ill equipped for this task, so we are a long way from the precision of an internal operationalism.

The Use of Drugs to Induce Discrete Altered States of Consciousness

I spoke of the methodological problem that comes from equating a *technique* that might *induce* a d-SoC with the altered state itself. This error is particularly seductive when one is talking about psychoactive or psychedelic drugs, for we tend to accept the pharmacological paradigm, the essence of which is that the specific chemical properties of the drug affect the chemical and physical structure of the nervous system in a lawfully determined way, invariably producing certain kinds of results. This view may be mostly true at neurological levels but can be more misleading than helpful in regard to consciousness. Observed variability in human reactions tends to be seen as the result of psychological idiosyncrasies interfering with basic physiological reactions and is averaged out by being treated as "error variance." Although this pharmacological paradigm seems useful and valid for a number of simple drugs, such as barbiturates, it is quite inadequate and misleading for psychedelic drugs like marijuana or LSD.

NON-DRUG FACTORS

Figure 9 shows a complete model of drug effects on consciousness that I developed when I was beginning to study marijuana intoxication (Tart, 1970, 1971). In addition to the physiological stimuli, constituting disrupting and patterning forces impinging on the subject, shown in the upper right side of the figure, numerous psychological disrupting and patterning forces exist; in many cases, these forces are far more important than the former for determining whether a d-ASC will occur and what the exact nature of the state will be. Thus, although it is

---

dreaming, for example), we can use them with the convergent operations strategy advocated by Stoyva and Kamiya (1968). Remember, however, that *state of consciousness* is a psychological concept, and psychology does not need a physiological basis to be scientific and useful. Indeed, premature "physiologizing" has hampered the development of psychology.

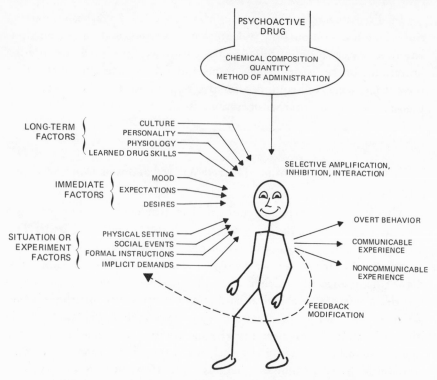

Figure 9. Drug-induced effects on consciousness.

useful to know what drug a subject has taken, the quantity of the drug, and the method of administration, in some ways this information is least important to the researcher. Without having some knowledge of psychological factors, we can ill predict the subject's behavioral and experiential reactions.

Non-drug factors include the culture in which the subject was raised and all the effects that culture has had in terms of structuring his b-SoC and providing specific expectations about the drug taken; the personality of the subject; possible specific physiological vulnerabilities he might have to the drug; and particularly his learned drug skills—has he taken this drug many times before and learned to enhance desired reactions and inhibit undesired reactions or is he naive with respect to this drug, so that most of his energy will go into coping with the (often stressful) effects of novelty?

Then we come to a class of more immediate factors. What is the subject's mood when he takes the drug? (This mood may be amplified or inhibited.) What does he expect to experience in the drugged state? Are these expectations the same as what he *desires* to experience?

There are non-drug factors dealing with the situation or experimental setting in which the drug is taken. What is the physical setting and how does it affect the subject? And the social setting? What kind of people are with the subject and how do they interact with him? A frightened person present, for example, may communicate his fear sufficiently to the subject to make the effect of the drug quite anxiety provoking. If this is an experiment, what are the formal instructions given to the subject? How does he react to and interpret them? Perhaps even more important, what are the demand characteristics (Orne, 1962; Rosenthal, 1966), the *implicit* instructions, and how do they affect the subject? If, for example, the experimenter tells the subject that the drug is relatively harmless but has him sign a comprehensive medical release form, the total message communicated belies the statement that the drug is relatively harmless.

Furthermore, the subject is not a passive recipient of all these forces impinging on him; he may selectively facilitate the action of some of them and inhibit others. Again, space prevents me from going into detail on these many non-drug factors, but they are vitally important in determining how a drug will affect a person; whether or not a d-ASC will result from the drug's action; and the specific nature of events within the altered state.

PHYSIOLOGICAL AND PSYCHOLOGICAL EFFECTS OF DRUGS ON CONSCIOUSNESS

Given this cautionary note on the complexity of using drugs to induce altered states of consciousness, there are nevertheless a few general things we can say about drug-induced states in terms of our theoretical model. Particular drugs may have specific effects on the neurological basis of various psychological structures/subsystems, possibly exciting or activating some of these structures/subsystems, suppressing or slowing the activity of others of these structures/subsystems, or altering or distorting the mode of information processing within some structures/subsystems. Psychological processes in relatively unaffected structures/subsystems may compensate for changes in affected subsystems and/or maintain sufficient stabilization processes so that the b-SoC does not break down. That is, the drug may both disrupt and pattern on a *physiological* level. How does this action translate to a psychological level?

Given physiological factors that may affect various structures/subsystems, we must remember that it is partly how one *interprets* a particular physiological effect that determines much of one's reaction to it and whether or not a d-ASC results. To take one of the most common examples, most marijuana smokers have to *learn* how to achieve the d-ASC we refer to as marijuana *intoxication*, or being "stoned." Typically the first few times a person smokes marijuana, he may feel an occasional isolated effect, but the overall pattern of his consciousness remains that of his ordinary state. Usually, he wonders why people make so much fuss about taking a drug that does not seem to do much of anything interesting. With the assistance of practiced drug users, who suggest he focus his attention on certain kinds of happenings or try to have various specified kinds of experiences, additional psychological factors, patterning and disrupting forces, are brought to bear to disrupt the ordinary state of consciousness and pattern the d-ASC. Often quite suddenly the transition takes place and the person finds that he is now stoned. This example is a good illustration of how the physiological action of the marijuana may disrupt many of the feedback stabilization processes of our ordinary state of consciousness, but not enough of them, so the state of consciousness does not change.

The fact that naive users may smoke enormous amounts of marijuana the first several times without getting stoned yet easily get stoned with a tenth as much drug for the rest of their use careers is paradoxical to pharmacologists. They have called this the "reverse tolerance effect." This effect is not at all puzzling in terms of our theoretical framework. Quite simply, the disrupting and patterning effect of the drug per se is generally not sufficient to destabilize the baseline state of consciousness. Once the user knows how to deploy his attention/awareness energy properly, however, he needs only a small amount of boost from the physiological effects of the drug to destabilize the baseline state and pattern the altered state of being stoned. Indeed, the "placebo" response of getting stoned on marijuana that has had the THC extracted from it may not indicate that some people are fools so much as illustrate that psychological factors may be the main component of the altered state associated with marijuana use.

We should note also that it is common for marijuana users (Tart, 1971) to say they can "come down" at will; that is, if they find themselves in a situation in which they do not feel able to cope adequately while stoned, they can deliberately suppress all the drug's effects and temporarily return almost instantly to their ordinary state of consciousness. By psychological methods they can disrupt the altered state and pattern their ordinary state into existence.

A third and quite striking example of the importance of psychological factors in deciding whether a drug produces a d-ASC or not comes from a review by Snyder (1971) of the attempts to use marijuana in medicine in the nineteenth century. Snyder says:

> It is striking that so many of these medical reports fail to mention any intoxicating properties of the drug. Rarely, if ever, is there any indication that patients—hundreds of thousands must have received cannabis in Europe in the nineteenth century—were "stoned," or changed their attitudes toward work, love, their fellow men, or their homelands. . . . When people see their doctor about a specific malady, they expect a specific treatment and do not anticipate being "turned on." (p. 13)

Apparently, then, unless you have the right kind of expectations and a "little help from your friends," it is unlikely that marijuana will produce a d-ASC. Hence, equating the smoking of marijuana with the existence of a d-ASC is a very tricky business.

One might think that this phenomenon shows that marijuana is a weak drug, but it is also the case that some people do not respond to large doses of far more powerful drugs like LSD.

Major Psychedelic Drugs

In dealing with very powerful drugs like LSD, mescaline, or psilocybin, we come into an area of extreme variability of outcomes that requires great caution. It is clear that for almost everyone who takes these psychedelic drugs, their ordinary state of consciousness is disrupted. In a sense we may say that the *primary effect* of the powerful psychedelic drugs is to disrupt the stabilization processes of the ordinary state of consciousness sufficiently to break down that state. But, while there is a great deal of commonality of experience among marijuana users—at least in our cultural setting (Tart, 1971)—so that it is useful to speak of the "marijuana state" as a distinctive state of consciousness across subjects, variability with the powerful psychedelics is so great that I interpret evidence as showing that there is no particular d-SoC necessarily produced by the major psychedelic drugs. Rather, we see a highly unstable state in which there are only very transient formations of patterns that constitute d-ASCs. The temporary association of scattered functions in the third part of Figure 8 illustrates this point. We see continuous transition between various kinds of unstable states. The colloquial expression *tripping* is very apropos; one is continually going somewhere but never arriving—at least in American culture.

However, in Carlos Castaneda's fascinating accounts of his work with don Juan (Castaneda, 1968, 1971, 1972) it is clear that although Castaneda's initial reactions to psychedelic drugs followed the preceding description, don Juan was not interested in having Castaneda "trip." Instead, he tried to train Castaneda to *stabilize* the effects of psychedelic drugs so that he could get into a particular d-SoC suited for a particular kind of task at various times. Thus, with the addition of further psychological patterning forces to the primarily disruptive forces caused by psychedelic drugs, it is impossible that stable states of consciousness can be developed that will have particularly interesting properties.

Meanwhile, we should not talk about "the LSD state" or believe that the statement "X took LSD" tells us much of anything about what happens to X's consciousness.

Observation of Internal States

Ordinarily when we think of observation in science we think of observing the external environment, and the observer is taken for granted. Or, if we recognize that the observer has inherent characteristics that limit his ability to observe, we attempt to compensate for these specific characteristics, as by instrumentally aiding the senses; again we largely take the observer for granted, our interest being in the external phenomena to be observed. When we use experiential data in trying to understand states of consciousness, taking the observer for granted becomes suspect. Let us look at the process of observation in more detail.

Given what has been said earlier about the construction of ordinary consciousnes or of any d-SoC, making experiential observations about one's own state of consciousness requires that the system observe itself. Attention/awareness must activate structures that are capable of observing processes going on in other structures. There seem to be two ways of doing this. We shall discuss them as pure cases even though in many instances they may be mixed. The first way is to see the d-SoC, the system, breaking down into two subsystems, one of which constitutes the observer and the other of which constitutes the system to be observed. I notice, for example, that I am rubbing my left foot as I write and that this action does not seem to be relevant to the points I want to make. A moment ago I was absorbed in the thinking involved in my writing and in rubbing my foot, but some part of me then stepped back for a moment, under the impetus to find an example to illustrate the current point, and noticed that I was rubbing my foot. The "I" that observed that I was rubbing my foot is very much my ordinary I, my personality, my ordinary state of consciousness. The observation is that the major part of my system, my personality, my ordinary state of consciousness held together but temporarily singled out a small, connected part of itself to be observed. Insofar as I am still my ordinary "I," all the characteristics of that particular observation are my characteristics. Thus, there is "objectivity" to my own observation of myself. My ordinary "I," for example, is always concerned with whether what I am doing is useful toward attaining my short-term and long-term goals, and the judgment was automatically made that rubbing my foot was a useless waste of energy. Having immediately classified foot rubbing as useless, I had no further interest in observing it more clearly, seeing what it was like.

By contrast, many meditative disciplines take the view that attention/awareness can achieve a very high degree of independence from the particular structures that constitute the ordinary state of consciousness and the personality; that is, one possesses (or can develop) an Observer that is highly objective with respect to the ordinary personality because it is an Observer that is essentially pure attention/awareness, it has no characteristics of its own. If the Observer had been active, I might have observed that I was rubbing my foot but there would have been no structure immediately activated that passed judgment on this action. Judgment, after all, means relatively permanent characteristics coded in structure against which to make comparisons. The Observer simply would have noted whatever was happening without judging it. The Observer is an experiential reality to many people, especially those who have attempted to develop such an Observer by practicing meditative disciplines. We shall treat the Observer as an experiential reality but not pursue the question of its ultimate degree of separation from any kind of structure.

In many cases it would not be easy to make this clear-cut distinction between the observer and the Observer. Many times, for example, when I am attempting to function as an Observer, I will Observe myself doing certain things, but this Observation immediately activates some aspect of the structure of my ordinary personality, which then acts as an observer connected with various value judgments that are immediately activated. That is, I pass from the function of Observing from "outside" the system to observing from "inside" the system, from relatively objective observation to judgmental observation by my conscience or superego. There are meditative disciplines that supposedly make one able to maintain the Observer for very long periods of time, with this Observer able also to Observe the judgments consequent upon observation by the ordinary observer.

The distinction between these two kinds of observers is important in considering the transition period between two d-SoCs. If we ask questions about what kinds of phenomena are experienced during the transition period, we must consider who is going to make these experiential observations for us. Insofar as our ordinary observer *is* the structure, the b-SoC, then the radical destructuring necessary for a transition into a d-ASC eliminates the ability to observe. At worst, if there is total destructuring, we can expect no direct experiential observation of the transitional period at all, perhaps only a feeling of blankness. Some people do report this feeling. The case is often not that bad, however. Destructuring of the b-SoC may not be total; certain parts of it may hold together as subsystems through the transition period; and partial observations may be made by these subsystems, which observations are recoverable on return to the baseline state or in the d-ASC. But the observations are necessarily limited and incomplete: They come from a partially incapacitated observer.

Now consider the case of the Observer, *if* it is well developed in a particular person, during the transition from one d-SoC to another. Because the Observer is not at all based in particular structures, or based only partially in particular structures, or based in structures that are not part of the b-SoC undergoing destructuring, it should have a much greater capacity to observe transitional phenomena. (E. R. Hilgard, 1973, found the concept of an at least partially dissociated observer useful in understanding hypnotic analgesia.) We have exactly this sort of phenomenal report from some persons who feel that they have a fairly well-developed Observer. They feel that this Observer can make essentially continuous observations not only within a particular d-SoC but also during the transition between two or more discrete states.

I shall say no more about the nature of the Observer at this time because we know so little about it in our Western scientific tradition. Clearly, it is extremely important to find out to what extent the Observer's apparent objectivity is a reality and to what extent a fiction. Insofar as it is a reality, it offers a kind of objectivity and a possible escape from cultural consensus reality conditionings that is highly important.

Discrete States of Consciousness and Identity States

The concept of d-SoCs comes to us in commonsense form, as well as in terms of my initial research interests, from the experience of *radically* altered states of consciousness—drunkenness, dreaming, marijuana intoxication, and certain meditative states, for instance. These represent such radical shifts in patterning, the system properties of consciousness, that most observers experiencing them are *forced* to notice that the state of their consciousness is quite different. (I say *most* observers to allow again for individual differences: Some people are extremely poor observers of their state of consciousness.) That is, people need not have developed an Observer in order to notice such a change in their state of consciousness, a number of things are so clearly different that the observation is forced on them. The lack of full automatization of many functions in altered states also serves to make their differentness more noticeable. If an individual has considerable experience with an altered state, automatization may rob the state of its glamor and freshness. Chronic marijuana users, for example, report fewer clear qualities of the state—this effect may be due to automatization in addition to, or instead of, any chemical tolerance buildup.

The theoretical approach we have discussed here in relation to the concept of d-SoCs is applicable to many variations occurring within the overall pattern that we call our ordinary state of consciousness, variations that can be called ego states or *identity states*. Both my own self-observation and large amounts of psychological data, particularly data gathered in the course of psychoanalytic investigations, indicate that as different situations impinge on us and activate different emotional drives, quite distinct changes in the organization of our egos can take place. Certain drives become inhibited or activated and the whole constellation of psychological functioning alters its configuration around them. These alterations in functioning, which I call identity states, are also d-SoCs within the concepts put forward by this theory. Yet, they are almost never noticed as d-SoCs for several reasons.

First, because each of us has a large repertoire of these identity states, and we move between one and another of them extremely readily, virtually instantly, there are practically no lapses or transitional phenomena that would make us likely to notice the transition.

Second, all of these various identity states have in common very large amounts of psychological functioning (for example, speaking English, responding to the same proper name, wearing the same sets of clothes, etc.); these shared features make it difficult to notice differences through ordinary observational activities.

Third, all of our ordinary range of identity states shares in our culturally defined reality. That is, although certain aspects of reality are emphasized by particular identity states, the culture as a whole has allowed a very wide variety of identity states in its definitions of normal consciousness and consensus reality. Within our cultural consensus reality, for example, there are well-understood concepts, perceptions, and allowed behaviors about being angry or sad, feeling sexual desire, being afraid, etc.

Fourth, our *identification* is ordinarily very high, complete with each of these identity states. That is, we project the feeling of "I" onto it (the sense of identity subsystem functions). Coupled with the culturally instilled need to believe that we are a single personality, we thus tend to gloss over distinctions. Thus, we say *I* am angry, *I* am sad, etc., rather than say that a state of sadness has organized mental functioning differently from a state of anger.

Fifth, identity states in a very real sense are *driven* by needs, fears, attachments, defensive maneuvers, coping mechanisms, and so forth. This highly involved quality of identity states makes it unlikely that the person involved will be engaged in much self-observation.

Sixth, because many identity states have as their focus emotional needs and drives that are socially acceptable only partially or are socially unacceptable, and given that people need to feel accepted, an individual may have many important reasons *not* to notice that he has discrete identity states. Thus, when he is in an identity state that is socially normal, he may not be able to be aware of a different identity state that sometimes occurs when he hates his best friend. The two states do not go together, so automatized defense mechanisms prevent the person from being aware of the one identity state while in the other identity state. Ordinarily it takes special psychotherapeutic techniques to make people aware of these contradictory feelings and identity states within themselves. Meditative practices designed to create the Observer also facilitate this sort of knowledge.

The development of an Observer can allow a person considerable access to observing different identity states, and an outside observer may often clearly infer different identity states, but a person himself who has not developed the Observer function very well may never notice the many transitions from one identity state to another. Indeed, what we call ordinary consciousness, or what a society values as normal consciousness, may actually consist of a large number of d-SoCs that I call identity states: The overall similarities between these identity states and the difficulties in observing them, for reasons discussed, lead us to think of ordinary consciousness as a relatively unitary state.

Insofar as our interest is in *radically* altered discrete states like hypnosis or drunkenness, the concept of the ordinary state of consciousness as relatively unitary is useful. As the present theoretical scheme becomes more articulated, however, we shall need to begin dealing with these identity states, which exist within the boundaries of the ordinary state of consciousness and which probably also function within the boundaries of various d-ASCs.

In terms of the use of language within this chapter, then, I shall continue to use the terms *discrete state of consciousness* and *discrete altered state of consciousness* to refer to the rather radical alterations that gave rise to the concept in the first place and to use the term *identity state* to indicate this finer division.

Stability and Growth

Implicit in the very act of mapping an individual's psychological experiences is the assumption of a reasonable degree of stability of the individual's structure and functioning over time. There would be no point in putting in a lot of effort into obtaining a map if the map were going to be changed before we had time to make much use of it.

Ordinarily we assume that the personality of an individual or his or her ordinary state of consciousness is reasonably stable over quite long periods of time, generally over a lifetime once his basic personality has been formed (by late adolescence). The major exceptions to this assumption are individuals exposed to severe, abnormal conditions, such as disasters, that may radically alter parts of their personality structure or to psychotherapy and related psychological growth techniques. Although the personality change from much psychotherapy is often considered rather small, leaving our former map of the individual's personality relatively useful, it can be quite large in some cases.

Applying this possibility of large change to the concept of d-SoCs, perhaps individuals eventually may learn to merge two d-SoCs into one. Perhaps it may be a matter of transferring some state-specific experiences and potentialities back into the ordinary state, so that eventually most or many state-specific experiences become available in the ordinary state. The ordinary state, in turn, will undergo certain changes in its configuration. Or, by growth or therapeutic work at the extremes of functioning of two d-SoCs, they may gradually be brought closer together until experiences become possible all through the former "forbidden region."

We might also get a sort of pseudo-merging of two d-SoCs. As an individual more and more frequently makes the transition between the two states, he may automate the transition process to the point that he no longer has any awareness of transition, and/or efficient routes through the transition process become so thoroughly learned that the process takes almost no time or effort. Then, unless the individual were observing his whole patterning of functioning or an observer were assessing the whole pattern of functioning, we might have the appearance of a single state of consciousness simply because transitions were not noticed. This latter case would be like the rapid, automated transitions between identity states within our ordinary state of consciousness.

Insofar as a greater number of human potentials are available in two states compared to one, we can see such merging or the learning of rapid transitions as growth. Whether the individual or his culture would see growth in these processes would depend on cultural valuations of the added potentials and the individual's own intelligence in the actual utilization of the two states. Having more potentials available is no guarantee that they will be used wisely.

Strategies in Studying Discrete States of Consciousness

Let us briefly overview the strategies to be followed in investigating various d-SoCs that follow from our conceptual model. These strategies are idealistic and subject to modification in practice, especially as we already have a lot of (poorly organized) data collected without this framework.

First, I reemphasize starting with the study of *individuals*, the first task being a mapping of the experiential space of various individuals to see whether their experiences do show the distinctive clusterings and patternings that constitute d-SoCs. For individuals thus characterized, we go on to the second step of more detailed individual investigation. For those not in this category, we begin to carry out studies across individuals to ascertain why some individuals show various discrete states but others do not: In addition to recognizing the importance of individual differences, we must find out why they exist and what function they serve.

Second, we map the various d-SoCs of particular individuals *in detail*. What are the main features of each state? What induction procedures produce the states? What de-induction procedures cause an individual to move out of a given state? What are the limits of stability of each state? What uses, advantages does each state have? What disadvantages or hazards? Are there depth dimensions to the states? How do we measure the depth? What are the convenient marker phenomena of each state that rapidly reveal when someone is in it?

With this background, we can then profitably ask questions about inter-individual similarities among the various discrete states. Are the states enough alike across individuals to warrant common names? If so, does this convergence tell us mainly about cultural similarities among the individuals studied or something more fundamental about the nature of the human mind?

Finally, we can do more microscopic studies of the nature of particular discrete states, the various structures/subsystems comprising them, etc. I put this sort of investigation at a late stage in order to avoid *premature reductionism.*

In the latter stages of this plan of investigation we shall have gone beyond a mainly descriptive and classificatory level into a predictive level, with considerable sharpening of our approach.

Methodological Consequences of the Theory

Many methodological points have been discussed in the course of outlining the theory. I shall briefly summarize some of the major ones here to bring them together.

First, the emphasis on the (semi-)arbitrary, constructed nature of our ordinary state of consciousness points up the cultural biases built into it, and our need continually to search for, and be aware of, these limiting biases in order to make scientific progress.

Second, the importance of basic awareness, attention-directed awareness, and self-awareness, particularly as they act as a kind of energy for activating psychological structures, focuses the need for a better understanding of these relatively neglected topics in psychology.

Third, the importance of system qualities, gestalt qualities arising out of the interaction of basic structures activated by attention/awareness energy, points out the importance of comprehensive, overall mapping of d-SoCs, lest premature reductionism waste too much of our investigative energies on trivial details.

Fourth, the possibilities of tapping and developing latent human potentials for our personal and cultural development are inherent in this theoretical framework, for fuller understanding and control of d-ASCs are the key to such development in many cases.

Fifth, although the theory is primarily at a descriptive and organizing stage to fit our current needs, the predictive possibilities within it will allow sharpening of our knowledge about the fundamental structures/subsystems comprising the human mind.

Sixth, the great importance of individual differences is stressed since ignoring human variation can lead to erroneous experimental procedures and interpretations about d-SoCs, such as obscuring the existence of particular discrete states.

Seventh, the recognition of multiple stabilization processes maintaining the functional integrity of d-SoCs points up the limited value of studies that investigate only single variables when we are dealing with complex patterns or that mistakenly equate the performance of experimental operations with the actual attainment of d-ASCs.

Eighth, the theory shows how too much dependence on the "pharmacological paradigm," the belief that the chemical nature of an ingested drug causes relatively invariant results due to physiological specificity, leads to misleading results when consciousness is studied. The apparent paradox of reverse tolerance to marijuana, for example, is not at all paradoxical within our conceptual framework as it follows naturally from the existence of multiple stabilization processes.

The final major methodological consequence, the need for state-specific sciences, deserves fuller discussion as it has been barely touched on in the preceding parts of this chapter.

State-Specific Sciences

The theory of d-SoCs I have presented here is the background for a proposal I made some years ago (Tart, 1972c, 1972d, 1975c) for the establishment of *state-specific sciences*. Earlier, I pointed out that in many ways the ordinary state of consciousness is an *arbitrarily* constructed state, containing large numbers of structures shaped by a particular culture's value judgments. Structuring might well have taken in a different form. Similarly, any d-ASC is a structure that is (at least partially) quite arbitrary in its construction.

Let me qualify the word *arbitrary*. Given that we have a real, physical world around us in which we, as biological entities, have to survive, there are limits to arbitrariness in constructing a state of consciousness. If we walk off the edge of a cliff, we shall fall and be severely injured or perhaps killed. Any state of consciousness a culture can construct will be *effective* in insuring biological survival from this particular peril if it provides some kind of structure/rationale to prevent its members from walking off cliffs. We could construct a rationale based on a potent and invisible force called "gravity," which will throw one to the bottom of the cliff, causing physical pain. Or we could construct a rationale based on the idea that demons lurk at the bottom of every cliff and smash up people who fall over the edge. Or we could form a rationale around the belief that the rapid acceleration in falling makes the soul leave the body, thereby rendering the body vulnerable to physical hurt. Any of these rationales encourage one not to step off the edge of cliffs.

It is very easy to protest, "But *our* reason is scientific!" There we commit the all too common human fallacy of getting into shouting, "*My* culture is better than *your* culture!"—which tends to lead to: "Well, if you don't believe my culture is better than yours, you pick up your spear and I'll pick up my hydrogen bomb and we'll see whose is better." We live in a very big world, and although Westerners have some sciences that are very successful in *some* areas, we have not been terribly successful in others, especially psychological areas. The sheer size and complexity of the world allows us to conceptualize it in a vast variety of ways; thus the diversity of cultures. Most of these ways are much too complex to be subjected to simple tests like whether or not one falls when one steps over the edge of a cliff.

The science we have developed is an ordinary state of consciousness science; it is observation and conceptualization carried out within the highly selective framework provided by our culturally determined ordinary state of consciousness. Thus, our science is culture-bound in many ways. We seem to have overcome a good deal of this limitation in the physical sciences: Physical bodies fall at the same real rate (we firmly believe) regardless of the language of the observer who is measuring them. But in the psychological sciences, our observations and theories are very much culture-bound, very much affected by our ordinary state of consciousness.

The methodological promise of d-ASCs is intriguing: Because they represent radically different ways of organizing our observations and re-working our conceptualizations of the universe, including ourselves, if we developed various *sciences within* a particular d-ASC, we would have a quite different view of the universe. Insofar as we were careful to preserve the essence of the scientific method, as I have argued elsewhere (Tart, 1972c, 1972d, 1975c), then the science developed in a particular discrete altered state would be just as scientific as ordinary state of consciousness science. In some ways it would have the same kind of blinders built in that ordinary state of consciousness science does because a d-ASC is still a partially arbitrary way of organizing consciousness. But by giving us a *different* look at things, a different perspective, a d-ASC science might greatly supplement or complement our ordinary consciousness science (see Tart, 1972c).

Because I am a scientist my concern is with developing sciences operating within d-ASCs, but the hope that this sort of endeavor might be advantageous is hardly confined to scientists. One of the reasons so many of our children and students are using psychedelic drugs or meditating or practicing yoga and various other spiritual disciplines is that they have accepted the idea that our ordinary state of consciousness imposes certain dangerous limitations on us, and they believe that learning to function in various d-ASCs may organize their minds in ways that will at least partially bypass some of those limits. It is easy to feel frustrated at the limits of our ordinary state of consciousness—and easy to become very enthusiastic about some of the obvious benefits of the perspective gained through d-ASCs—but most of our enthusiasts have not yet learned that the partially arbitrary nature of altered states also gives *them* limitations. Everything has its price. I hope that the eventual development of state-specific sciences will make both the advantages and the limitations of various d-ASCs clear to us soon, so we may choose states appropriate to problems before we, as a culture or as individuals, enthusiastically exchange one set of limits for another while shouting, "Freedom!"

Summary

This chapter presents a theoretical framework for understanding some.aspects of human consciousness, particularly the areas called *states of consciousness* and *altered states of consciousness*. The theory casts light on a range of issues, such as psychedelic drug use, that are not being treated well by conventional approaches.

We begin by noting that our ordinary state of consciousness is not something natural or just given but a highly complex *construction*, a specialized tool for coping with the environment, a tool useful for some things but not very useful for others. Sixteen basic theoretical postulates, based on human experience, cover the materials from which a state of consciousness is constructed.

The basic postulates start our theorizing with the existence of a basic *awareness,* and a more refined awareness of being aware, *self-awareness.* Because some volitional control of the focus of awareness is possible, this aspect of human beings is referred to as *attention/awareness.*

Further basic postulates deal with *structures,* those relatively permanent structures/functions/subsystems of the mind/brain that act on information to transform it in various ways. Arithmetical skills, for example, constitute a (set of related) structure(s). The structures of particular interest to us are those that require some amount of attention/awareness to activate them. Attention/awareness acts like a *psychological energy* in this sense. Most systems for controlling the mind come down to ways of deploying attention/awareness energy so as to activate desirable structures (traits, skills, and attitudes), and to deactivate undesirable structures.

Psychological structures have individual characteristics that limit and shape the ways in which they can interact with one another. Thus, in considering systems built of psychological structures, we noted that the possibilities of the system are shaped and limited by both the deployment of attention/awareness energy and the characteristics of the structures comprising the system. The human computer, in other words, has a large, but limited number of possible modes of functioning.

Because we are born human beings, creatures with a certain kind of body and nervous system operating on spaceship Earth, a very large number of human potentialities are in principle available to us. But we are born into a particular culture that selects and develops a small number of these potentialities, actively rejects others, and is ignorant of most. The small number of experiential potentialities selected by our culture, plus some random factors, constitute the structural elements from which our ordinary state of consciousness is constructed. We are at once the beneficiaries and the victims of our culture's selectivity. The possibility of tapping and developing latent potentials outside the cultural norm by going into an altered state of consciousness, by temporarily restructuring our consciousness, is the basis of the great interest in this area.

The terms *state of consciousness* and *altered state of consciousness* have been used, too loosely, to mean whatever is on one's mind at the moment. I propose *discrete state of consciousness* (d-SoC) for scientific use. *A d-SoC is a unique, dynamic pattern or configuration of psychological structures; a d-SoC is an active system of psychological subsystems.* Although the component structures/subsystems shows variation within a d-SoC, the overall pattern, the overall *system properties,* remains recognizably the same. In spite of subsystem environmental variation, a d-SoC is stabilized by a number of processes so it retains its identity and function. By analogy, an automobile remains an automobile whether on the road or in the garage (environment change); whether spark plug brand or seat cover color (internal variation) is changed.

Examples of d-SoCs are our ordinary waking state, non-dreaming sleep, dreaming sleep, hypnosis, alcohol intoxication, marijuana intoxication, and some meditative states.

A *discrete altered state of consciousness* (d-ASC) refers to a d-SoC different from some baseline state of consciousness. Usually our ordinary state is taken as the baseline state.

A d-SoC is stabilized by four kinds of processes: (1) *loading stabilization,* keeping attention/awareness energy deployed in habitual, desired structures by loading the person's system heavily with appropriate tasks; (2) *negative feedback stabilization,* actively correcting the functioning of erring structures/subsystems when they deviate too far from the normative range that insures stability; (3) *positive feedback stabilization,* providing rewarding experiences when structures/subsystems are functioning within desired limits; and (4) *limiting stabilization,* limiting the ability to function of structures/subsystems whose operation would destabilize the system.

In terms of current psychological knowledge, ten major subsystems (collections of related structures) that show important variations over known d-ASCs need to be distinguished: (1) *exteroceptors* (sense organs for sensing the external environment); (2) *interoceptors* (senses for knowing what our bodies are feeling and doing); (3) *input processing* (automated selecting and abstracting of sensory input so we perceive only what is "important" by personal and cultural reality standards); (4) *memory;* (5) *subconscious* (the classical Freudian unconscious plus many other psychological processes going on outside our ordinary d-SoC that may become directly conscious in various d-ASCs); (6) *emotions;* (7) *evaluation and decision making* (our cognitive evaluating skills and habits); (8) *time sense* (the construction of *psychological* time and the placing of events within it); (9) *sense of identity* (the quality added to experience that makes it *my* experience instead of *just* information); and (10) *motor output* (muscular and glandular outputs to the external world and the body). These named subsystems are not any sort of ultimates but only convenient categories for organizing the available data.

Our current knowledge of human consciousness and d-SoCs is highly fragmented and chaotic. The main purpose of the proposed theory is organizational: It collects and relates many formerly disparate bits of data and has numerous methodological implications for guiding future research. It makes the general prediction that the number of stable d-SoCs available to human beings is definitely limited (although we have not come anywhere near to understanding these limits). The theory further provides a paradigm for making more specific predictions that will sharpen our knowledge about the structures and subsystems that make up human consciousness.

The theory stresses the importance of studying d-SoCs in individuals because of enormously important *individual differences*. If we map the experiential space two people function in, one may show two discrete clusters of experiential functioning, two d-SoCs; the other may show continuous functioning across both regions as well as the connecting regions of experiential space. The first person must make a special effort to move from one region of experiential space, one d-SoC, to the other; the second makes no such effort and does not experience the contrast of pattern and structure differences associated with the two regions, the two d-SoCs. Thus, what is a "special" state of consciousness for one person may be an everyday experience for another. Great experimental confusion results if we do not watch for these differences. Unfortunately, many widely used experimental procedures are not sensitive to this phenomenon.

Induction of a d-ASC involves two basic operations that will lead, if successful, to the d-ASC from the baseline state. First we apply *disrupting forces* to the baseline state, psychological or physiological or drug actions that disrupt the stabilization processes either by interfering with them or by withdrawing attention/awareness energy from them. Because a d-SoC is a very complex system, with *multiple* stabilization processes operating simultaneously, induction may not work. A psychedelic drug, for instance, may not make a person enter a d-ASC because psychological stabilization processes hold the baseline state stable in spite of the disrupting action of the drug on a physiological level.

If induction is proceeding successfully, the disrupting forces push various structures/subsystems to their limits of stable functioning and then beyond, destroying the integrity of the system, disrupting the baseline d-SoC. *Patterning forces* are applied during this transitional, disorganized period, psychological or physiological or drug actions that pattern structures/subsystems into a new system, the desired d-ASC. The new system, the d-ASC, must develop its own stabilization processes if it is to last.

De-induction, return to the baseline d-SoC, is the same process as induction. The d-ASC is disrupted; a transitional period occurs; and the baseline d-SoC is reconstructed by patterning forces.

Psychedelic drugs like marijuana or LSD do not have invariant psychological effects even though much misguided research assumes they do. Within the context of the present theory, such drugs are seen as disrupting and patterning forces that act in addition to other psychological factors, all mediated by the operating d-SoC. Consider the so-called reverse tolerance effect with marijuana: New users consume very large quantities of the drug yet do not get "stoned," enter a d-ASC; experienced users require much smaller quantities to get into the d-ASC of being stoned. This phenomenon is paradoxical only with the standard pharmacological approach. According to our framework, the physiological action of the marijuana is not sufficient to disrupt the ordinary d-SoC; additional psychological factors must act to disrupt enough of the stabilization processes of the baseline d-SoC to allow transition to the d-ASC. Usually, these additional psychological forces are "a little help from my friends," the instructions for deployment of attention/awareness energy given by experienced users who know what functioning in the d-ASC of marijuana intoxication is like. These instructions serve also as patterning forces to shape the organization of the d-ASC, to teach the new user how to *use* the physiological effects of the drug to form a new system of consciousness.

Methodological research problems are discussed from the point of view of this theory, such as the way in which experiential observations of consciousness and transitions from one d-SoC to another are made, and I suggest shifts in research strategies that the theory demands. The theoretical framework can be applied within our ordinary d-SoC to deal with *identity states*, those rapid shifts in the central core of our identity and concerns that we overlook for many reasons (for example, the unacceptability of contradictions in ourselves) but that negatively influence so much of our daily life. Similarly, the theoretical framework indicates that latent human potentialities may be developable and usable in various d-ASCs, so that learning to shift into the d-ASC *appropriate* for dealing with a particular problem may be seen as psychological growth. At the opposite extreme, certain kinds of psychopathology, such as multiple personality, can be treated as d-ASCs.

One of the most important consequences of the theory is the deduction that we need to develop *state-specific sciences*. Insofar as any particular d-SoC, whether a culture calls it normal or not, is a semi-arbitrary way of structuring consciousness, a way that represses some human potentials while developing others, then the sciences we have developed belong to one state of consciousness. They are limited in some important ways. Our sciences have been very successful in dealing with the physical world but not very successful in dealing with particularly *human* problems, psychological problems. If we applied scientific method to developing sciences *within* various d-ASCs, we would have sciences based on radically different perceptions, logics, communications, and so gain new perspectives complementary to our current ones.

The search for new views, new ways of coping, through the experience of d-ASCs is hardly limited to science: It is a major basis for our culture's romance with drugs, meditation, Eastern religions, and the like. But infatuation with a new perspective, a new d-SoC, tends to make us forget that *any* d-SoC is a *limited* construction. It is vital for us to develop *sciences* of this powerful, life-changing area of d-ASCs if we are to optimize benefits from people's growing use of alternate states and avoid the dangers of ignorant or superstitious tampering with the basic structures of our consciousness.

8

Some Observations on the Organization
of Studies of Mind, Brain, and Behavior

Karl H. Pribram

THE ASSIGNED TOPIC OF alternate states of consciousness intrigues me because it reflects on another that I believe to be fundamental to our understanding of the organization of mind and brain. Psychology has made great strides over the past century and a half in making experimental observations in an area of inquiry that had hitherto been the exclusive domain of philosophical analysis. However, the science of psychology is now beset by the problem of organizing its data into a coherent body of knowledge. The lack of organization becomes a critical factor when the results of neurobehavioral experiments are to be reported: The relationship of brain organization to mind as adduced from the effects of brain lesions and excitations must be framed coherently in order to be communicated. Yet, for example, I have completed some thirty experiments—in as many years—on the functions of the frontal cortex in order to obtain some idea of what might have been the effects of the human lobotomy procedures only to find that these effects can be couched in the language of motivation and emotion, or decision theory, or operant reinforcement theory, or in the paradigms used by experimentalists interested in attention or in cognitive learning or in memory, or even in perception. Now, it is certainly possible that all psychological

The research involved was supported by Grant MH-12970-09, National Institute of Mental Health, and Career Award MH-15214-13, National Institute of Mental Health, to the author.

processes are influenced by the frontal lobe of the brain, but if this is so, there should still be a way of systematically reporting how. And for an understanding of mechanism one must have at least a rudimentary idea of what one is searching a mechanism for—in short, what is the *relationship* among emotion, motivation, decision, reinforcement, attention, cognitive learning, memory, and perception.

In a trivial way, the connection between alternate states of consciousness and the alternate conceptual and experimental frames of psychological inquiry is obvious. Each school of psychology is conscious mainly of its own body of evidence but only dimly aware that alternate schools exist. Such dim awareness can take the form of complete dissociation and denial or of a more or less mild "putdown" or of active conflict. Only rarely (e.g., Estes, 1970; Pribram, 1970a) is any effort made to examine the relationship of the alternate conceptual-evidential frames to one another.

The recent literature on alternate states of consciousness follows a somewhat similar pattern. Each state is more or less fully described; however, in contrast to scientific psychology, at least occasionally the route that leads from one state to another is also taken into account. It is this additional description that gives me the hope that by pursuing the problem of the organization of mind and brain in alternate states of consciousness I can discern in a nontrivial manner a way to come to grips with the tower of Babel that now is scientific psychology.

Definitions

The definition of the assigned topic presupposes that consciousness is organized into states—that psychological processes operate within one or another frame or state that by definition excludes for the time being other states. There is evidence, some of which will presently be reviewed here, to the effect that a good deal of behavior, behavior modification (learning), verbal communication, and verbal report of awareness and feeling is state dependent. This presentation will therefore accept the definition that consciousness is organized into alternate states, with the provision that considerable supportive evidence for this initial acceptance will follow.

In diverse literature on consciousness (see reviews by Ornstein, 1972, 1973; Tart, 1971) a surprisingly long list of states exists. The most commonly agreed to are: (1) states of ordinary perceptual awareness;

(2) states of self-consciousness; (3) dream states; (4) hypnagogic states; (5) ecstatic states, such as are experienced orgastically; (6) socially induced trance or trancelike states; (7) drug-induced states; (8) social-role states; (9) linguistic states, as when a multilingual person thinks in one rather than another language; (10) translational states, as when one linguistic universe is being recorded (e.g., in stenotyping) or communicated in another; (11) ordinary transcendental states, such as those experienced by an author in the throes of creative composition; (12) extraordinary transcendental states, which are achieved by special techniques; (13) other extraordinary states, such as those that allow "extrasensory" awareness; (14) meditational states; (15) dissociated states, as in cases of pathological multiple personality; and (16) psychomotor states manifest in temporal lobe epilepsies.

Most of us have personal experience with close to a dozen of these alternate states and so know at first hand the mutual exclusiveness of at least some of them, not only in the moment but also in memory. Let us therefore consider this aspect of the problem in more detail to see whether a clue to the organization of mind and brain can be provided by the analysis.

Consciousness as Control

Characteristic of the separateness of the various states listed is that their distinctive quality depends on overall organization, not on elements of content. Thus, the same elements can be identified in a dream as in an ensuing hypnogogic period and in ordinary awareness. A bilingual person (see Kolers, 1966, 1968) refers to the same content in both languages, but not at the same time or according to the same rules of reference (or perhaps even grammar). What is created during transcendental authorship is recognized later in ordinary perception—it only seems strange that authorship should have occurred at all. Even extraordinary states share considerable content with ordinary ones (see Barron, 1965).

At least three sources can be identified as giving rise to the events operated upon in consciousness: sensory stimuli, physiological "drive" stimuli arising within the body, to which the central nervous system is directly sensitive, and mnemic stimuli stored within the brain tissue. The fact that diverse conscious states share to some considerable extent the content given by these sources suggests that the separateness of these states cannot be attributed to sensory processes, to mechanisms arising in body physiology, or to the way in which memory storage occurs. This does not mean that such stimuli cannot serve as triggers that initiate one or another of the conscious states—in fact, there is good evidence (Ornstein, 1972, 1973; Tart, 1971) that triggering stimuli of all three sorts abound. However, the organization of a particular conscious state cannot be coordinate with stimulus content but must reflect some particular brain state.

What, then, characterizes a particular brain organization in one or another conscious state? We have already ruled out the structure of the memory store as critical. Accordingly, there must be involved some organizational process akin to that responsible for retrieval. Such processes usually are referred to as *programs* or as *control functions* (Miller, Galanter, & Pribram, 1960). These map the array of anatomical receptor-brain connectivities into ambiences that process invariances in the stimulus into more or less coherent and identifiable structures. In short, the conclusion to be drawn is that alternate states of consciousness are due to alternate control processes exercised by the brain on sensory and physiological stimulus invariants and on the memory store.

The Regulation of Input

Even before the heyday of classical behaviorism, it was considered a truism that the brain controlled motor function as expressed in behavior. This control was conceived to take place by way of abstractive and associative mechanisms that progressively recoded the input into adaptive motor organizations. Today there is a considerable body of evidence in support of the conception that neural systems provide "feature analyses" and that an "association by contiguity" takes place in the brain. However, additional insights into feature organization and the meaning of the term *contiguity* have been achieved (see Pribram, 1971, chap. 14, for a review).

The best known of these insights is that everywhere in the central nervous system closed loops are formed by neural connections. These closed-loop circuits feed part of the output signal back to their input source. Thus, subsequent input is influenced by its own previous output. When this feedback is inhibitory it regulates the circuit. A good number of the neurophysiological studies of the 1950s and the early 1960s, some in my own laboratory, were addressed to discerning the feedback characteristics of such circuits (see Pribram, 1974; Pribram & McGuinness, 1975).

Neural control circuits have long been well known. Walter Cannon's laboratory (Cannon, 1929) established the concept of homeostasis to describe the finding that physiological stimulation from an organism's body was under feedback control. More recent is the discovery that feedback control exists everywhere in the central nervous system and regulates sensory as well as physiological input to the brain (for a detailed example see Dowling, 1967).

The ubiquity of feedback control made it necessary to alter our conception of what constitutes association (Pribram, 1971, chap. 14). Contiguity no longer refers just to an accidental coincidence in time and place but also to a controlled influence of temporally and spatially connected feedback units. Homeostats were found (Ashby, 1960; Pribram, 1969) to be multilinked to produce stable systems that could be perturbed only by gradually establishing new and independent input circuits (habituation). Such systems have the characteristic of matching input to the stable, current organization—perturbations indicate novelty; their absence, familiarity. The stable system provides the context in which the input or content is processed. Association by contiguity therefore turns out to refer to a context-content matching procedure not just to a simple, haphazard, conjoint happening.

In addition, it was possible to establish which parts of the brain accounted for the maintenance of a stable context and which were directly involved in habituation to novelty. A feedback model of the associative functions of the brain thus emerged from a variety of neurophysiological and neurobehavioral studies (see Pribram & McGuinness, 1975, for a review).

Cognitive Processes

Meanwhile, theorists, neurophysiologists, and psychologists independently became interested in another aspect of the organization of mind and brain (e.g., Miller, Galanter, & Pribram, 1960). Beginning in the mid-1960s, concerted effort was directed to the study of cognitive processes and of information processing by the brain. A new theoretical distinction was achieved when it was realized that open-loop, helical organizations characterized certain brain organizations, making voluntary and other forms of preprogrammed behavior possible (e.g., MacKay, 1969; McFarland, 1971; Mittelstaedt, 1968; Pribram, 1971; Teuber, 1960). Such behavior runs its course, insensitive to the effects it is producing. Of course, most behavioral processes combine feedback and feedforward operations, but there is a sufficient number of relatively pure cases of each to make the analysis possible.

The classical example of feedforward behavior is eye movement. Once initiated, an eye movement is insensitive to feedback from that movement. Corrective influence must await its completion (see discussion by McFarland, 1971; Pribram, 1976). The problem of control is limited to initiation and cessation, although of course a program must have been constituted either through the genes or through previous learning for the behavior to be carried to completion. Thus, feedforward control is programmed control; it shows considerable similarity to the operations performed in today's serial computers.

The distinction between closed-loop, associative, feedback control and open-loop, helical, feedforward control is not a new one in science. Feedback control is error-sensitive control. It is sensitive to the situation, the context in which the operation takes place. In contrast, feedforward control operates by virtue of preconstituted programs that process signals essentially free from interference from the situation in which the program is running. Interference can only stop the program. As already noted, homeostatic mechanisms are error-processing mechanisms: Every action begets an equal and opposite reaction when the feedback is inhibitory, leaving the system essentially unchanged. Feedforward control, on the other hand, proceeds to change the basic operating characteristics of the system. This change can be quantitatively represented as a change in efficiency of operation.

These concepts were initially embodied in the first and second laws of thermodynamics. The first law deals with the inertia or stability of systems, their resistance to change. The second law provides a measure—entropy—of the efficiency of operation of the system: the amount of work—i.e., organization—that the system can accomplish per unit time. More recently, the second law has been shown to apply not only to engines but also to communications systems, where the term *information* is used to indicate the reciprocal of entropy. Feedforward systems that exercise control through programs are therefore properly called information-processing systems (Brillouin, 1962).

Primary and Secondary Processes

The distinction between error-processing feedback organizations and programmed information-processing feedforward control is a useful one. Elsewhere (Pribram & Gill, 1975) I have detailed the suggestion that this distinction brings into sharp focus an earlier one made by Freud. Psycho-analytic metapsychology, which concerns the mechanisms that underlie psychological processes, distinguishes between primary and secondary processes. Primary processes are composed of homeostatic, feedback, associative mechanisms; secondary processes are cognitive, volitional, and programmed, under the control of an executive (the ego) much as in today's time-sharing, information-processing computer systems. The terminology *primary* and *secondary processes,* however, is not unique to psychoanalysis. Other biologically oriented disciplines have expressed similar insights. Thus, at a recent meeting of experimentalists working on hypothalamic function, it was proposed and agreed to that primary, diencephalic, homeostatic regulations were influenced by secondary, higher order programs originating in the forebrain.

The distinction between primary and secondary processes, which was based originally on clinical observation, has thus been given a more sub-stantive theoretical foundation, based on a variety of experimental and analytical techniques. Often, clinically based concepts by necessity are plagued by considerable vagueness, which gives rise to unresolvable con-flict of opinion. The sharpening that occurs when data from other disci-plines become available to support and clarify a distinction is therefore a necessary preliminary if the conceptions are to become more generally useful in scientific explanation.

Psychology Today

This caveat holds not only for clinically derived definitions and con-cepts but also for any that are based on a single discipline or technique alone. As indicated previously, theoretical psychology is today made up of narrowly based concepts, rigorous in definition and rich in detail but poorly understood in relationship to one another. Let us therefore con-sider these relationships in the light of some of the issues discussed in this presentation.

First we discerned that the organization of the memory store could be distinguished from the organization of alternate states of conscious-ness. Memory psychologists and biologists conceptualize a distinction be-tween long-term and short-term memory. This often, though not al-ways, corresponds to the distinction made here. In order to correspond, the data must deal with the organization of the memory store, not with the recognition or recall of remote experience. Recognition and recall obviously involve retrievals and control operations that are therefore as well the domain of decision and attention theory. Decisions may be arrived at consciously or unconsciously; attention is usually defined as involving awareness.

But controls are often exercised by programs, as we have seen. And these programs also demand storage. Thus, the memory store must be composed in part of items representing events and in part of programs that organize the items into information. Programs come hierarchically arranged—some simply act as assemblers, others constitute executive controls that determine priorities. Ordinary language and philosophy speak of such programs as constituting the intentions of the organism.

We do not as yet know the nature of the anatomical distinction between item storage and program storage in the brain. Nor do we know how programs act to assemble items. Still, some initial experimental analyses have been accomplished (Pribram, 1971). The important point learned so far, however, is that the two types of neural storage can be distinguished.

Another point must be added. Not all storage occurs in the brain. Environmental storage in repeatedly experienced situations also is acted upon by control programs. Thus, we may make internal searches of our brain's memory or externally search a library for the same items of information.

The actualization of the operation of a control program on stored items is the decision process. We can distinguish conscious decisions from unconscious ones. Conscious decisions involve attention, defined as the *holding* (Latin *tendere,* to hold) to one rather than to another program at any moment.

It must, of course, be kept clearly in mind that the initiation and cessation of the operation of a program may be determined reflexly—i.e., by homeostatic processes. The neural substrates of these "go" and "stop" mechanisms have been thoroughly investigated (for reviews see Pribram, 1971; Pribram & McGuinness, 1975). The "stop" signals appear to be the more primitive and homeostatic; whereas "go" involves the entire intentional system of neural programs.

The identification of stop and go mechanisms also has eased problems of definition that have beset the concepts emotion and motivation (Pribram, 1971, chaps. 9, 10, 11). The difficulties disappear in part by initially correlating emotion with stop mechanisms and motivations with go mechanisms. More complete resolution comes when the more subtle distinction is made between feeling and expression (Pribram, 1970a, 1970b). Feelings, both emotional and motivational, are found to be homeostatically controlled. Thus, the stop mechanisms (which process input from both physiological drive and sensory stimuli and are located in hypothalamic and other core brain structures) sense equilibrium and match, which corresponds to the emotional feelings of stability and satiety, or they sense perturbation and mismatch, which corresponds to the motivational feelings of appetite and affect. Expression or intended expression, on the other hand, involves the (basal ganglia-centered) go mechanisms of the brain. It is interesting to note that the legal definition of guilt respects this formulation. A person is declared guilty of a crime on the basis of his intentions, not his emotional or motivational feelings, though these may be taken into account in sentencing. Thus, a crime may be committed for love or for need, both eminently respectable motives in our society. It is the intended or actual expression of these motives in behavior that is judged (Miller, Galanter, & Pribram, 1960).

Alternate States of Consciousness

On concluding this essay I return to the definition of attention as "holding" to one rather than another program that has been initiated by some homeostatically based emotional or motivational feeling and actualized by a decisional mechanism to organize mnemic or sensory invariants into an information process. Holding implies span, competency, and effort, all topics of considerable interest and the focus of much experimental activity in contemporary attention theory (Kahneman, 1973; Pribram & McGuinness, 1975). Holding implies also that certain consistency over time which characterizes a state. Therefore, different conscious states are due to the maintenance in operation of different neural programs that structure mnemic events and sensory invariants in different ways. Memory theorists investigate the organization of the storage of mnemic events and the programs that are used to process these items. In like manner, students of perception investigate the organization of sensory invariants and the programs that are used to process these invariants. Decision theorists are concerned with the emotional and motivational mechanisms that result in one rather than another stored program's becoming actualized. Attention theorists take over from decision theorists at this point and attempt to characterize the limitations on competency that determine whether the operation of one or another (or perhaps several) program(s)—cognitive processes—can be maintained over a sufficient reach of space and time to be recognizable as a state of consciousness. Investigators of consciousness are interested in the decisional steps that lead from one such state to another and in describing the content of these alternate states. Contemporary experimental psychology now makes sense to me: Obviously, the tower of Babel results from alternate emotional, motivational, decisional, attentional, and cognitive processes—in short, alternate states of consciousness.

9

The Missing Center

Arthur Deikman

THE CENTRAL PROBLEM OF UNDERSTANDING states of consciousness is understanding who or what experiences the state. Our theories evolve with the center missing; namely, the "I" of consciousness, the Witnesser. We need a science of the self with which to explore that center. With our present procedures and methods we cannot touch it and so we turn away to pay attention to everything else, the things that we can grasp. We are fascinated by unusual forms of consciousness. Yet the question remains: Considering the thousands of states of consciousness that we may have, what makes them "ours"? Perhaps the first step toward understanding is to examine the basic assumption that we are separate selves, objects in an object world.

Learning the Idea of Self

Imagine the infant's world: shifting fields of sensations within shifting levels of sleep and waking; swirling mists of warm sleep giving way to bright colors and simple patterns, mixed with gnawing feelings, persistent and demanding; then muscle tensing and crying sounds; then the warmth and pleasure and the smell of mother, liquid warmth and mouth tensions; then dissolution into darkness—and then the light and color—discomforts—relief, and on and on. Memoryless, the flow holds all

230

attention. Gradually the patterns form: mother's smell and comfort, eyes and mouth, muscle grasping, mother's sounds.

Sensations separate: those that disappear and those that persist, becoming "inside" and "outside" much later on. Now, they come and go. Pain, hunger, touch, and smell are the teachers. Pain draws a line around the edges of fingers, and vision tidies up the clutter. Together they teach the body as the baby's will begins to command. Grab the bottle—grab the nose—pat fire—grab the food—stuff the mouth—drop the glass— move the fingers for the eyes to see. Pain, loss, and intention separate the world. Mother leaves, but pain remains; the arm can be moved, but the crib stays still (Freud, 1957, p. 232).

Yet the separation is not so clear. Crying can summon others' presence, and the baby may not be able to move from the holding arms. What is cause and what effect comes later. For the moment, patterns rule the day and may continue, if the culture wills it, without an automatic road of Time (Lee, 1950). At first, related only in the total moment, the world just happens.

The Human Object

We objectify our world and others in it. "Others," indeed!

[They] mostly treat contemporaries as physical objects or disregard them completely. Five in one room may each disregard one of the others. If two were together near an object, one may just push the other out of the way impersonally, as though he were an object . . . one as [he] climbs, pushes a second, who falls on a third. All ignore this. Or two may try to climb up in exactly the same place. Both struggle with each other, but merely for the space, not aggressively, as later. Child wanting to sit on chair filled by other child may either sit *on* other child or may spill him out. May walk around or just bump into other child. (Ames, 1952, p. 199)

So much skill has been acquired, so many lessons learned. Yet, still no Other. No Self like you in all your world because you know no Self— you, the person, are not there—although your memory, thoughts, sensations make up all the world.

At first your will is in the service of acquiring. It is possessive and slow to emerge. At twelve months of life, about to talk, with words to say and understand, "even the sense of personal possession is practically absent, and [the child] makes very meager distinctions between himself and others" (Gesell, 1940, p. 32). Possession comes late and precedes

Self; possessive pronouns are used first. "Child grabbed from may hang onto object; and may let it go and cry; may just let it go; may shout 'mine'" (Ames, 1952, p. 199). At twenty-four months of age, "pronouns, *mine, me, you,* and *I* are coming into use approximately in the order just given" (Gesell, 1940, p. 37). "Mine" leads to "me" (the object) and "you" (the object) and finally to "I"—an "I" whose shape and meaning are ruled by the possessive mode.

Growth of the Action Mode

When we see and when we think and walk and eat and breathe we serve ourselves, our purpose. The purpose guides the rest. In the beginning, floating in the maternal ocean, we allow the environment in and are nourished. Indeed, I should not say "allow." Allowing is an adult decision. In the womb we just exist in a state of permeation, perfused with the blood and vibrations of our world. Then, during the cataclysm of birth, we struggle for the first time. What had been only comfort is now pain, and we contract to shut it out, to gain control, to act and so to change the turbulence back into peace. With the first breath, and the first breast, peace does return. And then the infant body loosens, relaxing as the warmth flows in, allowing what is needed to enter once again, receptive to the world. In the early weeks all is intake, relaxation, sleep, and food. Briefly, however, between feeding and sleep, eyes focus on the world; they are active, following, reaching out in interest rather than in pain (Wolff, 1960). Now the motive differs, but the function is the same—to act upon the world. A mode of living has begun: life as doing—doing to all the objects of the object world, bringing about possession and relief from pain.

The lessons: bottle, ball, mother, nose—are lessons in possession, in reaching for what is shiny, bright, warm, and safe. Name what's good and squeeze it with fingers, draw it to the mouth and take it in. The baby reaches for the bottle, eyes focused, brain intent, arms extended and waving with excitement. Into the mouth pops the nipple—and what a change! The body softens, eyes cross, lids droop, arms relax. And then— sleep. All functions are eased—immersed back into a resting world. Action mode, receptive mode, phasing back and forth. Reception is the beginning and dominates the infant life.

School continues. More and more the action mode rules the day. With practice and reward it grows in scope until, with symbols, it creates thought. Abstraction is born. Words seem real. Memory and imagery establish Time. Mine, me, you, I: in that order we learn. Possession shapes the Self and the world.

As our bodies teach our minds, so our minds instruct our bodies. The desire for the ball will focus eyes. The broad, impressionistic world narrows to a central stage whose sharp details and clear edges separate the ball from all the the rest, which now recedes, vanishing into background. Muscles tense and capillaries shunt the blood from gut to muscles; adrenalin executes the change. Breathing hastens; chest expands. Eyes and neck and body synchronize, directed to the target. Watching the ball roll, learning what it does, teaches object logic: A is not B. Object thought is born with the rolling ball. The ball, an object; the ball, a thought. They are linked together, welded tight, until our thought blankets our perception.

Thinking is for action, for acquisition and control. Thinking guides effort until thought itself is effortful. The knitted brow, the intent look, the tensing of the eyes—all partners to a single purpose, a mode of being in the world. "Me" and "you" and "I" are sharpened, suitable for object games. "Mine" is the favorite, and clear boundaries are the rule. Day by day, body and mind coordinate, learning control, learning to manipulate the world. The action mode becomes the norm. Reception, where we started, is set aside for sleep and food and comforting.

As conscious doing is the essence of the action mode, allowing is the key to the receptive. With the action mode we divide and conquer our environment. With the receptive, we take in, receive and unify. It is the difference between breathing out and breathing in. Try it now. Take a full breath; breathe in and then breathe out. Notice the difference in your state of mind during those two phases. On inhaling, the world flows in, mental contents become diffuse, thinking tends to stop. On exhaling, energy flows out, the vision sharpens, boundaries are more clear, and thinking comes to life.

When manifesting in the action mode, when striving in the world, the electrical currents on the surface of the brain are fast and short. In the receptive mode, alpha waves appear: slow, irregular, and higher waves, they indicate a change in attitude, something subtle, beyond words (Deikman, 1975).

And words themselves, where do they belong? Our words are from the object world—the world we made by separation. Words are the tools of that mode: With them we discriminate and divide reality into pieces—objects and things—that we can grab with our minds or bodies. The Eskimo has many words for snow, the skier several, the average man just one—according to snow's importance in the action mode.

Objects have many names, sensations very few. We can discriminate a thousand hues of color but not name them. How many forms of love have we to match against the one word? The action mode has forms, boundaries, words, logic, and the Road of Time. The receptive mode is sensory, diffuse, and unifies; its Time is instantaneous and synchronous. The self merges into Now. What do you call relationships where A is B? I-Thou, Buber (1958) named it; relating in receptivity. I-It, the Other as object, occurs in the action mode.

The function, the goal we set, controls the mode. What's the goal? Is it combat, control, capture; or receive, synthesize, allow? It is not activity versus passivity. "Allowing" is an action but of a different kind. We say "I-It" and fire the bullet so that it intersects the racing deer. We say "I-Thou" and receive our love's embrace. We need both modes; each has its place and function. Merge with the infinite and you lose the deer. Calculate your "making love" and it becomes another task, depriving you of re-creation. Yet they can blend together. You can work in your garden, uprooting the weeds one by one, but still be receptive to the breeze and the soft earth.

Infants and children must perform their biologic task: survival in a biologic world. That primary need begins in the womb and pervades the childhood years; it has trained us all too well in the action mode. The receptive comes occasionally, hardly at command, as if it were an alien being. That which should be familiar we come to perceive as strange. Years later, as adults, we may go to special schools to learn receiving, to regain the mode with which our life began. Until then, the receptive mode lies dormant, receding from the repertoire but not forgotten.

> There was a time when meadow, grove and stream
> The earth, and every common sight,
> To me did seem
> Apparelled in celestial light,
> The glory and the freshness of a dream.

(Wordsworth, 1904, p. 353)

Glory? Not likely in the child. But when adults recover their receptive mode and grow to a new wholeness, recruiting to the soft, wide span of childhood vision the complex meanings of creative thought—then glory, then a dream transcending the dreams of one-eyed man.

Self, Time, and Anxiety

The action mode creates a world. The world has dimensions of its own, distinctive features, normally unquestioned in their status as elemental facts. Who does not assume a separate Self and the flow of Time? They are the pillars that uphold the world, but they were not given, they were grown.

The self grew, for the organism has its plan. Our starting self was pure happening; we were what was occurring in the womb. With the birth process, intention formed; fear and desire took their roots in that elemental chaos, then grew in strength like other parts. With intention, the body-self takes form. The body is the agent of intention and executes the biologic plan: possession. (Mine, me, you, I—in that order.) The body is the source of pain and pleasure, qualities that dominate our sensory world. Qualities so powerful that they define what is "personal."

Memory and symbol engage sensation: Objects and their laws emerge. Others see your body as an object, helping you to do so, too (Mead, 1934). "What a pretty smile you have! Come here!" "Wave your hand!" "Here is your bottle." "Give me the ball. Want the doll?" The body possesses and possession is the game. What the body hugs belongs to Self; what it does not touch may disappear.

First the ball, then the reaching arm, then the body of the arm, and then the reaching wish—"me"—all objectified into the landscape of the object world, seen from a window. The window frames the world, and in the space behind the window an invisible object forms—"I." Gradually, the solitary self is born.

Memory creates time and orders objects in the Past. Images and words create a Future, ordering the objects yet to come. Between the past and future, laws are found, connecting both in a smooth path on which walks the form of Self. Like a cage of tigers, the trained objects stiffen to the whip of logic and take their places in an even line, arrayed in a demonstration of predictive power. Wild applause greets success, but when the noise subsides, another character appears—anxiety. What if the tigers all jump down and in disordered rage make a bloody meal of the maestro? These shadows of the future, cast by the past, can overwhelm the bright display. The scene of gaiety and pride may give way to troubled dreams.

The action mode has welded past and future into an arrow. As it flies there can be no rest, for Now has disappeared. Xeno's paradox is lived by us. By the action mode we acquire Self, gain power, and survive. But Past and Future, joined by anxiety, has no room for Now. Scurrying in memory, images, and thought, there is no time to stop and be nourished by the world.

The Receptive Mode

Now change the goal, shift to Being. Receive the world. The gaze will soften, vision diffuse, maximizing entry of the sensate world (Allison, 1963). Time dissolves and Now emerges, accompanied by satisfaction. The Self subsides and the world enters. Muscle tension eases; breathing slows; judgments fall away. Beyond fear, beyond pleasure, Now is. All questions are answered—for the questions have disappeared; they are the product of another mode, another world. The mode of Being, the receptive mode, serves a different function—our nourishment, perhaps. It is not "higher," not more "spiritual," just breathing in instead of breathing out. Half a breath cycle is not enough. We need both halves to live. We need both modes.

But the action mode prevails—it has the school—and a hunger grows: dissatisfaction. Forgetting how to eat, we have begun to starve at the banquet. Believing what we're taught, we cannot fit the world.

More school, defining Self: boy, girl, good, bad, fast, slow, happy, sad, strong, weak, pretty, ugly, smart, dumb. The Self stands like a naked armature, and the others fire away, heaving globs of clay to spatter, stick, and lump together as the self-shape grows. "Tommy is a good boy with blonde hair, a nice smile, smart and fast. Jennie is a pretty girl, delicate and sweet, with brown hair, a merry laugh, and very understanding. Jim is a roughneck, not too bright. Helen has black hair and big feet, homely but kind." Animated sculptures taking shape, sitting in rows in school. Eyes peering out of the hardening clay.

Adolescence, we are told, is the time of identity. Teenagers intimately converse, "Who are you and who am I?" No wonder the question is asked. Awkwardly, the clay figures stagger around the room, trying to walk after a very different birth.

"You tell me and I'll tell you." (Maybe we'll find out that way.) "You are really very sensitive!" (Not much help, just more clay.) Rough places smoothed and a hole or two filled in. Adult statues serve as guides, and they so stiff they have forgotten what the young ones still can feel—that something doesn't fit. "It looks just fine!" (But it doesn't feel right.) The clay binds and cramps in all the wrong places. Still, a memory of freedom haunts the room.

When you reach adulthood, you look around and find that the strangest part of this strange world is yourself. There are so many varieties of you, moment by moment, state by state, that only a very selective memory allows the illusion of a constant, continuous self to be maintained.

Think about all the various conditions that constitute your moment-by-moment life. Sometimes you are in a state of remembering and 90 percent of you is—at that moment—memories. Sometimes you are emotional, sometimes angry or ecstatic or sad, and 90 percent of what is you is then emotion. At other times you may be what you see, or what you fantasize. Sometimes it's a mixture, 50–50 or 20–20–60; it really doesn't matter.

Through all these variations, all these changes, you assume you are there. Indeed, sometimes "I am" may be your only feeling, very powerful, very "spacy." Most of the time you're busy, so it's 90 percent something else.

There are so many selves: the thought-self, the body-self, the I am-self, the I want-self, the emotion-self; and now the left-brain self, the right-brain self, the limbic-self, the midbrain self. So many, so changing, not continuous at all. Each self appears and disappears, fades from view while another takes its place. So where in all this is you? If you are your experience and that experience always changes, what makes you think you have a self at all?

And what of the times when the "I" is zero: engrossed in a movie or performing some action too quickly to permit thought? Yet you assume, nevertheless, that you have been there all along. Your "I" is discontinuous, but your memory fills in the gaps, just as your eyes, creating an optical illusion, fill in the "correct" line.

"What's the difference?" you may ask. "Other people are witness that I don't disappear." You are right. But the "I" they see and the "I" you mean may not be the same.

When you began, age zero, you did not assume that "you" were there or that anyone else was there when they had passed from sight. "Out of sight, out of mind" and out of thought, as well. Maturation meant you could find the pea under the shell of memory. Once you remembered you could predict, and soon existence needed no proof—because existence itself had changed. Where once it had been all sensation, now thought and memory had become real, most real of all.

"Mine, me, you, and I" in that order. In that order we create ourselves. Emotions become "mine." Thoughts are "mine"—whose else could they be? Desires are mine—what is more me than my wants? And fear is "mine," for who else will die? "Mine" becomes "me," the social object, collector of labels, possessor of things. "Me" encounters "you," the object, the Other, who tells us we are objects, too, and tricks us into categories that enclose us like snug beds: man, woman, Indian chief.

What do you color the object-you? Color it with thinking, with emotion, with desires, and with fear. Use all the "inside" colors to make it bright and clear.

There is no end to object making. Go to India, climb the highest mountain, and sit cross-legged observing all the other objects, all the inside colors, until you become, finally, the Witness—the finest object of them all. Most of us are content with the usual "I's": old, handsome, dumb, and on and on. What a collection! Look at all we think we are: joy, anger, calculations, desires, objects, labels, fear, and "soul." Look at that merry-go-round, the way it spins, and then, watching it go 'round, perhaps suddenly you'll ask, "How do I know it's me?"

The question seems absurd and never does get asked aloud. The "I" of awareness is the last to join, but join it does—and so we enter Object-land. We become a Thing and reap a rich reward: identity with all the Others, the reassurance of our kind, something made necessary by Objecthood!

Possessing gives life to the Thing. "I want" almost everything (the energy of possession); "I have," the locus of possession, of substance and mortality; "I will," the energy of intention, put to work collecting; and, then, there is "me," the social object, staggering forward with all my attributes in a huge bundle on my back, like a peddler.

Possession creates suffering. Pain hurts because it's "mine." Pain, old buddy, what happens when I step a pace away, look you squarely in the eye, inspect you head to toe like a new recruit? "What's your shape, mister? What color are you? Hot or cold? Thick or thin?" Pain—old buddy—you seem to change, learn manners, drop your eyes, turn in your badge of power.

Behind pain, in a line, stand all the others: vision, hearing, joy, and grief—a whole company of pseudo-selves presented for inspection, more obedient, now, to my command.

Unlearning the Self

Eastern science takes a different route to knowledge, bypassing the intellect, to learn by being. Where we have journeyed outward, Eastern disciplines have gone within, hunting the true self among the decoys. Academies of Eastern science, called spiritual schools, teach the unlearning of the decoy self as preparation for discovery. All the selves you thought you were must go. The self of thought, the self of emotion, the self of desire, the self of sensation—all must be unlearned. These conditioned selves cling to you as shells and vegetation cling to a tide-washed rock. But the schools know what to do; they have many ways to clean the rock. Meditation is a velvet crowbar that pries thought-mussels loose, leaving the bare surface to be bathed again by the sea. The crowbar slides beneath emotions, too, those clumps of feeling, those subtle forms of memory, that open and close like the carnivorous flowers they are, all mouth and color—now separate from the rock, afloat in the wash of the tide. In school, in meditation, sitting like a rock, just sitting, sensations spatter like the spray and drip away, polishing the rock until it reflects the sun.

Desires are the last to loosen. They are lodged in the heart of the rock and must dissolve. Many things are tried: the ascetic life, koan dynamite, the hypnotic energy of dance, and the deep chant, resonating in the center, the teaching story, holding a mirror to the form of desire, and—finally—the Teacher, whose radiant vibration shakes the atoms of the rock into harmony and peace and praise in the rhythm of the sea.

The mirror of the school shows you many selves, shifting, changing: the I of intention, the I of I Am, the I of emotions, the I of possession, the I of the body, and the I made by Others. The selves come and go, and the mirror-school reflects them all. But it cannot show them all until they all are there. Our Western culture, like an obsessive tailor, has spent so much time on the intellectual jacket that it has yet to get around to the emotion-shirt and the body-pants. No wonder we are spectacles, displaying our new clothes, annoyed at yet haughty in the face of the laughter of children. Not long ago, some other tailors set up shops in California, where East meets West. There are so many tailors now they don't know whose needle they are using. Back then, the Esalen shop opened a new frontier, featuring the shirt and pants. The emotion-self and the body-self were taught in class. Encounter by the sea, nude bodies, massage and sex, here-and-now orgasms for "intimate strangers." How ridiculous! The New York tailors almost died of laughter but were saved by their indignation at the sight of so many customers discarding jackets in California. The colors of the shirts were often weird and the pants let it all hang out, but at least it was a suit of clothes for the whole person, giving warmth to the heart and covering all that land below the neck. Although Wilhelm Reich, a tailor of the body-self, died in prison (he opened up his shop too soon), times have changed; the body has returned, although it still is seen as an appendage of the head.

Esalen is more than laughs—how strange to find one's state of mind sparkle like a fresh-rinsed glass when it receives a body bath. The emotion-self emerging from a weekend smiles with delight to see the sky again. Strange how the wrinkles disappear and the face is young—how the thinking slows and senses sharpen when the rediscovery is made. Catharsis and the body—old-fashioned clothes indeed, to be selling so briskly—but that's the frontier West, you know, unsophisticated, no culture, no tradition.

Yes, the body has returned, bringing with it sensual life and feeling. Just in time. The spiritual schools teach letting go of self—but not to babies or retarded children or psychic cripples, deformed beyond belief. The Western student knocking at the door presents a gigantic inflated head, spindly legs, and a sunken chest, announcing with intellectual fervor, "I surrender!" What a prize! How can there be a harvest before the crop is grown? Before the self is ripe, what can you give away?

No wonder the schools have strange routines, depending on the students who stumble to the door. Weird diets, heavy work, incense, singing, meditation, dancing, breathing, postures, flowers, swords, or sex may be prescribed. Five or seven centers, say the texts, form the path and source of energy that needs to flow without constriction. You learn to open all the chakras. Until you are fully there, in all your strength, you do not have the power to surrender.

The many routines work, but for whom are they correct? The druggist lines his shelves with little bottles; a doctor must prescribe. Which meditation is right for you? Maybe none. Go to a doctor, if you can find one. The diagnosis should be made before the treatment starts, and you've been ill a long time. Leave the drugstore, you don't know what the labels mean, and it isn't candy on the shelves, despite the bright colors. Go find a doctor. Now.

"Where?"
"Try the Yellow Pages: If you are really sincere, you will find a doctor. The door is always open. You are already in the doctor's hands."

Not much help to a Western mind. The Yellow Pages show only religious listings. Perhaps it is time we broke that "spiritual" monopoly, remembering that our mandate to understand has no restrictive clauses—we gave no franchise to the monks.

Conclusion

"Who—or what—am I?" seems to concern every inquiring mind in its own way. It is the question I most want answered and am least equipped by training to understand; the science I have learned has been of objects, and no object is the self. The Eastern schools, employing traditional means, may not meet contemporary needs. New tools and a new curriculum would seem to be required, a form that suits a television world.

What must we do and how should we proceed? Perhaps we can construct a calculus of the subjective. Should we even try? Do language and logic have a place or will they interfere?

What do you suggest?

10

Subjective and Objective
Observation in Psychiatry:
A Note Toward Discussion

Joel Elkes

Author's Note

FOR REASONS EXPLAINED TO DR. ZINBERG, the author was unable to contribute a paper to the Conference. His only excuse for submitting the paper reproduced below is that, time notwithstanding, the problems touched upon therein appear still to be with us. However, recent discoveries on interhemispheric relations make one a little more hopeful with regard to the latter part of the paper.

I HAVE GIVEN much thought to the choice of subject for this lecture and was sorely tempted, at one stage, to examine some aspects of the physiology and pharmacology of the brain, inasmuch as they relate to behavior. I would have been much more comfortable in such a course; for at least, it would have given me the benefit of familiarity, arising out of personal experience over some years. Yet, central to any statement concerning a pharmacology of behavior, there is a description of behavior. Behavior is not an epiphenomenon, but the major phenomenon; not only

Reprinted, with permission of the publishers and author, from *The Harvey Lectures,* Series 57, Copyright 1963 by Academic Press, Inc. Lecture delivered February 15, 1962.

a phenomenon, but an instrument. In the strange no-man's land now extending between somatic chemical process and symbolic transaction, familiar rules and assumptions are strained, and new rules still in the making. For not only does neurobiology demand precision from a description of behavior, but the elaborateness of behavior makes demands on neurobiology, which, so far, it cannot even remotely meet. This interaction, and this deficiency, are rendered peculiarly poignant in the clinical field, where intracerebral chemical process can be guessed only inferentially, and where the varieties and subtleties of behavior challenge established techniques. If, therefore, I have chosen to dwell on the assessment of clinical phenomena in psychiatry, and have selected such phenomena from among the drug-induced states, this is done for a double reason. I happen to think that in the foreseeable future patients will still be seen by physicians: whatever the reliance on test procedures, and electronic data reduction techniques, the interpersonal clinical transaction will still be the cornerstone of treatment. I also happen to believe that psychopharmacology (as the subject has been sanguinely called) is forcing many issues which have lain dormant in psychiatry since its inception, and which are relevant to its aspirations as a clinical science. I have therefore intentionally omitted reference to the wealth of material that is pertinent in psychometrics. Nor do I wish to refer, except in passing, to some so-called psychophysiological equivalents. These have been amply reviewed (Lacey, 1956). My twin themes are thus an examination of the value of subjective and objective observation as sources of information in clinical psychiatry; and the ways and means by which we communicate this information to one another.

Subjective and Objective Observation: Some Trends in Nineteenth Century Psychiatry

On the day after Christmas, in 1799, young Humphry Davy (1800), twenty years old, made the following note following a self-experiment with nitrous oxide which he had carried out in his laboratory in the company of one Dr. Kinglake: "I felt a sense of tangible extension, highly pleasurable in every limb; my visible impressions were dazzling, and apparently magnified. I heard distinctly every sound in the room, and was perfectly aware of my situation. I lost all connection with external things; trains of vivid images rapidly passed through my mind, and even connected with words in such a manner, as to produce perceptions perfectly novel. I existed in a world of newly connected and newly modified ideas. I theorified; I imagined that I made discoveries. When I was awakened from the semidelirious trance by Dr. Kinglake who took the [gas] bag from my mouth, indignation and pride was the first feelings produced by the sight of persons about me. My emotions were enthusiastic and sublime; and for a minute I walked about the room perfectly regardless of what was said to me. As I recovered my former state of mind, I felt an inclination to communicate the discoveries I had made during the experiment. I endeavored to recall the ideas, they were feeble and indistinct; one collection of terms, however, presented itself: and, with the most intense belief and prophetic manner, I explained to Dr. Kinglake—'Nothing exists but thoughts!—the universe is composed of impressions, ideas, pleasures and pains.' "

In one bold empirical step, thus, young Davy had revealed the power of an anesthetic not only to obtund, but to enhance sensations, and to manifest aspects of mental life only sparingly used in normal waking existence: The features he described are common enough in such states. The intensity of personal feeling, the heightened perception, the connectedness among things normally disconnected, the synesthesia (i.e., the evocation of one sensory modality by another), the fusion, the feeling of devotion, of identity, the sense of insight and truth: and, above all, the inability to communicate the experience except in metaphor and allusion. A number of drugs have shared this power to evoke and to transcend: it is no accident that, throughout their long history, mescaline (Klüver, 1928) and the mushroom poisons (Wasson & Wasson, 1957) were used in complex religious rites in remote and inaccessible regions. In Europe, for reasons which have been examined elsewhere (Elkes, 1961a), things happened more slowly. De Quincey's confessions on the effects of opium were published in 1822. In 1845, Moreau wrote in his monograph on marihuana (hashish): "By its mode of action on the mental faculties, hashish gives him who submits himself to its strange influence the power of studying on himself the moral disorders which characterize mental illness, or, at least, the principal intellectual modifications which are the points of origin of all kinds of mental disturbances."

Some thirty years later, in 1874, Benjamin Blood, stimulated possibly by his predecessors, described "anaesthetic revelations" brought about in himself and his friends by the inhalation of ether. Lewin rediscovered mescaline (Klüver, 1928) in the Mexican hills; Kraepelin (1883) was experimenting with drugs in his newly founded laboratory, a trend continued by Weir Mitchell (1896) in England, and by the Heidelberg School of Beringer (1932) and Mayer-Gross (Mayer-Gross & Stein,

1926) in Germany. The chemical divining rod was thus found useful; it brought forth riches wherever it touched. In 1943, there occurred in the laboratory of Hofmann, in Basel, the accidental discovery of lysergic acid diethylamide (Stoll, 1947), a drug which in the infinitesimal amount of 50 μg. by mouth will produce marked mental changes in man. There followed the rediscovery of psychoactive mushroom poisons, the identification of psilocybin (Hofmann et al., 1958) and a host of synthetic derivatives, including other tryptamine derivatives (Szara, 1956), the *N*-substituted piperidyl benzilates (Abood et al., 1959) and 1-(1-phenylcyclohexyl) piperidine (Luby et al., 1959), to mention but a few. We who have learned to live with psychopharmacology know that we are still witnessing a mere beginning.

I mention this chemical path, trodden by many, to draw attention to a quieter way which, at any rate in medicine, was sought by relatively few until the turn of the century. For coincident in time with the above observations, there were others centering on subjective phenomena experienced without chemical aids, and sharing with drug-induced states their intensely personal, private, averbal, and incommunicable nature. Mentioned here may be the early observations of Johannes Müller (1848) on the so-called hypnagogic phenomena—experiences any of us know in the brief twilight states between wakefulness and sleep; or the analysis, at the hands of Frederick Galton, the father of medical genetics, of what he called "Visions of Sane Persons" (1881) and the "Statistics of Mental Imagery" (1880). In 1896 Weir Mitchell published his account of mescaline intoxication, observed in himself; and it is of interest to compare this account with Ladd's (1892) account on so-called "Visual Dreams" published four years earlier. Hovering over the field, but still very much at the periphery of medicine, there was the concept of unconscious or preconscious mental activity. Thus, there is Carus, writing, in 1846, on the "Developmental History of the Soul"; von Hartmann (1869/1931), in 1869, on the *Philosophy of the Unconscious;* Fechner (1860), Helmholtz (1863/1954), and Wundt (1862) speculating and experimenting on perception and threshold states of consciousness: and Carpenter laying down his *Principles of Mental Physiology* in 1874. Towering over others are the figures of Titchener (1909) and William James (1912), who regarded Benjamin Blood's "Ether Dreams" (1874) as a stepping stone in his own thinking. Indeed, much that went before culminates in James, and the titles of his essays. *The Varieties of Religious Experience* (1902/1929), "A Pluristic Mystic" (James, 1912), and "The Stream of Thought" (James, 1890/1950), tell their own tale. In his preoccupations with subjective phenomena (while incidentally building the first Experimental Psychology Laboratory at Harvard), he significantly deviated from the principal paths of nineteenth century science. As he says in this well-known quotation: "What must be admitted is that the definite images of traditional psychology form but the smallest part of our minds as they actually live. The traditional psychology talks like one who should say a river consists of nothing but pailsful, spoonsful, quartpotsful, barrelsful and other moulded forms of water. Even were the pails and pots all actually standing in the stream, still between them the free water would continue to flow. It is just this free water of consciousness that psychologists resolutely overlook. Every definite image in the mind is steeped and dyed in the free water that flows round it. With it goes the sense of its relations, near and remote, the dying echo whence it came to us, and the dawning sense whither it is to lead" (James, 1890/1950, p. 255).

These "echoes," and this "dawning sense" of knowing, are, as we saw in Davy's description, not unfamiliar in the drug-induced experience; and it is these private, subjective, personal, and incommunicable elements which rendered chemical devices so useful for purposes of religious rites. Somehow, then, it appeared, even in the nineteenth century, as though certain functional modalities which are part and parcel of the repertoire of human experience, but normally used only transitorily and sparingly in the waking state, could be chemically locked by drugs into more persistent manifestations. One would hesitate to claim identity among these various processes; there is, however, a family resemblance. The changes observed more recently in hypnosis, in sensory isolation (Solomon et al., 1961), in the dream process (Kleitman, 1961), attest to this affinity to this day.

In parallel with these developments, and complementary to them, there took place in psychiatry another development of great consequence. We know Philippe Pinel as the spirited Director of the Salpêtrière who, under the impetus of the French Revolution, unshackled patients in his native France and thus presaged the era of humane care of the mentally ill. Yet, it was he, also, who said, right at the beginning of his *Treatise on Insanity* published in English translation in 1806: "Nothing has more contributed to the rapid improvement of modern natural history than the spirit of minute and accurate observation. . . . [With this in view] . . . I therefore resolved to adopt that method of investigation which has invariably succeeded in all departments of natural history, viz. to notice successively every fact without any other object than that of collecting material for further use; and to endeavor as far as possible, to divest myself of the influence, both of my own prepossessions and the authority of others" (Pinel, 1860).

Pinel's work forms the first major descriptive treatise of the forms of insanity. Across the Atlantic, Benjamin Rush (1812), Professor of Chemistry at the Medical School in Philadelphia, guiding spirit of the Revolution, Treasurer of the Mint, published his *Observations on Disease of the Mind,* a volume which for decades remained the major available textbook of psychiatry in the United States. Pinel's pupil Esquirol (1772–1840) coupled the reform of mental hospitals with a major descriptive work on mental illness (Esquirol, 1838). The English school flourished under Tuke, Haslam, Prichard, Conolly, and, later, Maudsley; but it was not until Kraepelin (1856–1926) that a definitive nosology of psychiatric disorder was developed (Kraepelin, 1906). The exploration of subjective experience, and the classification and taxonomy of mental disorder thus proceeded in parallel within roughly the same century. There was overlap between the two approaches and a searching out of subjective elements in objective presentation and vice versa; there were shifts in emphasis; yet, with certain exceptions, the two lines exemplified attitudes—attitudes which are with us to this day.

There is, however, a third trend running through our field, the outlines of which can, in retrospect, be clearly distinguished. The implicit recognition of unconscious process at the hands of Carus (1846), von Hartmann (1869/1931), and Carpenter (1874) has already been mentioned. Yet it was not until Charcot's (1892) studies on hypnosis and hysteria that the clinical implications of this process were given their full due. Charcot's "lessons" were attended by many: Babinsky, Binet, Janet, Marie, and, of course, Freud. In 1893, Breuer and Freud published their preliminary communication on hysteria stating, quite simply, that "hysterics suffer mainly from reminiscences." The repressed, affectively laden memory trace thus emerged not only as a subjective phenomenon welling up randomly in dreams or in drug-induced states, but as a clinical entity, capable of affecting sensorimotor or visceromotor function. The exteriorization of the subjective memory into overt behavior (coupled, at a later date, with the concept of "acting-out" in a transference situation), assumed therapeutic as well as theoretical implications. Psychoanalysis and psychosomatics were thus cast in the same mold, psychoanalytic theory attempting to provide a conceptual link between subjective experience and overt behavior. We are not here concerned with the validation of the theory. What we would rather note are the many modifications at the hands of its originator which it underwent, emphasizing its tentative and empirical nature; and the minute serial observations of subjective states of mind over time, on which it was based.

Physics, and the Function of Language in Science

Discoveries such as these, however, fitted ill the brash innocence of a young emergent materialist science. An age set firmly in the framework of classical physics, wedded to the meter rule, the clock, and the kilogram, secure in its concept of space, time, matter, and causality, and propelled by the idea of evolution; such an age did not readily accept introspection as a source of evidence, or behavior as a phenomenon in its own right. Matter was the primary reality; and the studies of its properties—living or dead, silent or articulate—were judged the proper objectives of science. Physiology, though recognizing homeostasis and the self-regulatory properties of living systems, was wedded to chemistry and physics; and the inventiveness of the Russian schools of neurophysiology, leading to the evolution of the Pavlovian method, while providing penetrating techniques for the analysis of behavior, did not have the backing of present day neurobiology and mathematics to enable it to realize its full yield. Yet, as is well known in retrospect, forces of quite another kind were at work in that same age. The concept of the electromagnetic field—so new to a period preoccupied with the mechanical motion of matter—was consequent upon Michael Faraday's experiments. In 1856 Clerk Maxwell published his equations on Faraday's lines of force. It was the same Maxwell (1874/1890) who, in his paper on "Atoms" for the *Encyclopaedia Britannica* wrote: "There are thus two modes of thinking about the constitution of bodies which have had their adherents both in ancient and modern times. They correspond to two methods of regarding quantity—the arithmetical and the geometrical. To the Atomist the true method of estimating the quantity of matter in a body is to count the atoms in it. To those who identify matter with extension, the volume of space occupied by a body is the only measure of quantity in it."

Clerk Maxwell's ideas were followed by Ernst Mach's (1897) *Die Mechanik,* in which Mach questioned Newton's definition of space and the concept of absolute rest. (It is, incidentally, the same Ernst Mach who in 1886 published his *Analysis of Sensations, and the Relation of the Physical to the Psychical* and who, by implication, influenced the development of gestalt psychology.) What followed is well told by the men who partook of the change (Bohr, 1958; Einstein, 1934; Heisenberg, 1958). Within three decades, the theory of relativity was established and quantum mechanics was in being. Probability and chance had entered into the definition of the state of physical systems; and the concepts of "complementarity" of mutually exclusive states (such as particle vis-à-vis wave, position of particle vis-à-vis velocity and momentum) (Heisenberg, 1958, p. 49) were found to be a productive and substantially workable model in the description of the fine structure of matter. As Heisenberg (1958) dryly observed, "the possibility of playing with different complementary pictures has its analogy in the different transformation of the mathematical scheme; it does not lead to any difficulties" (p. 50). There is a profound truth in this fit of phenomena, and statement about the phenomena.

I have dwelt briefly on these developments in turn of the century physics because, in a way which, at least to me, is far from clear, they may well bear upon the evolutionary forces now at work in neurobiology, and the biology of behavior. I do not mean here the mere cracking of a crust of certainty by the expanding root of doubt. The dialectics of the process go deeper. What appears significant is that while denying subjective observation of fluid, multiple phenomena as a source of valid data, and forcing overt behavior into a materialistic frame which fitted it ill, that same frame—rigid, formidable, buttressed by the enormity of its industrial product—underwent a loosening and expansion which, within a few brief decades, presaged a new age. Concepts, strangely familiar, yet never rigorously applied to behavior, were being quietly incorporated into mathematical statements concerning the structure of matter. What had been regarded as universal statements (such as Newtonian mechanics and Euclidian geometry) were reduced to special instances of statements of even greater validity. States regarded as mutually exclusive were assumed, in Weizsäcker's timely phrase, to coexist (Heisenberg, 1958, p. 185). The mathematical scheme of quantum theory expanded the tenets of classical logic, the concepts of "either/or" giving way to the "also" and the "and," making classical logic a province of quantum logic. The deliberately open, probabilistic, mathematical statements were found, in the light of experiment, to provide a more precise description of reality than older and more circumscribed rules. Above all—and from the point of view which we are considering most important—a mathematical language for mechanics which had to serve the varied needs of the theoretician, the experimental physicist, the technician, and the engineer was treated more discretely, new symbolic inventions serving the needs of fine structure of matter and older devices remaining in use to run trains and to heat buildings. As with Berzelius' (1779–

1848) invention of a formal shorthand for chemistry, it is the evolution of a new, appropriate language which made modern physics what it is.

I suppose that whether we like it or not, we have now arrived at a crucial point in our discussion. For if behavior is to be described in a way accurate enough to predict its attributes, either in the individual or the group; if subjective experience is to be conveyed even to oneself, in terms which clearly and strongly apprehend its significance and meaning, languages are required to model and symbolize the processes with which they are concerned. I hope, as we proceed, to give some instances of such devices in current usage, if only to point to the pain which goes into their making and the limitations from which they suffer at present. A thorough exploration of the limits of language is presented in Susanne K. Langer's (1942/1958, 1957) writings; and the problem of communication and validation of subjective clinical data has been examined by Henry K. Beecher (1959a) in his recent monograph. I have learned a great deal from reading these sources and gladly acknowledge my debt to them.

There can be little dispute of the attributes of language, even if there be discussion as to its function. Language is "our most faithful and indispensable picture of human experience" (Langer, 1942/1958, p. 76), a heuristic symbolic instrument shaping modes of observation and interpretation, and interpenetrating deeply with experience. Phonemes and morphemes condense meaning into words, and the relation between word-symbols is regulated by rules of syntax and grammar. Such rules— rules of astonishing logic and economy—go, as Whorf (1956) showed, into the fabric of even the most primitive language. They make for the smooth use of language as an instrument of social adaptation and communication. They order the relation of the fact-symbols to each other, and to the world which they represent. To serve such adaptive functions, the rules imposed by syntax must be strictly followed, and the symbols presented in a certain order. It is evident that "Tom followed Harry" does not mean the same as "Tom follow Harry" or "Harry followed Tom." Conventional logic imposes a linear, sequential quality, which has come to be known as "discursiveness" (Langer, 1942/1958, p. 77), and it is in this sense that the laws of reasoning and logic are sometimes known as "the laws of discursive thought" (Langer, 1942/1958, p. 77).

There is, however, another quality in words implicit in the one just discussed. For, while carrying certain meanings in one context, words carry a totally different meaning in another; and even standing alone they may—as anyone who has traced the origin of a word in a dictionary—carry on accretion of different meanings in a sort of strange algebra and calculus of their own. This economy, this logic, this dependence on context is characteristic even of the most primitive language (Whorf, 1956). Words are thus not mere labels, cards, stacked for reference in one of Broca's areas; they are states, sets, depending on relation, and context; they carry multiple meanings. Carnap (1937/1959), in *The Logical Syntax of Language*, has examined the capacity for expression of any given linguistic system. What is remarkable in that analysis is how little our ordinary means of communication measures up to the standard of meaning which a serious philosophy of language, and hence a logic of discursive thought, demands.

It would thus seem that there are large areas in communication and in self-communication (i.e., the symbol making not exteriorized in overt behavior) which are not represented by ordinary language. For whereas grammar and speech are essentially sequential, linear, discursive, the characteristic of these other subjective states is the multiple simultaneous presentation of internalized objects and relations. The form of the "unspeakable" is as different from the "speakable" as the structure of a dream, or even a day dream, is from the structure of deliberate action. In such symbolic forms totality is apprehended simultaneously at different levels; mutually occlusive elements coexist; time is of no consequence; and serial ordering in time, that backbone of causal reasoning, gives way to simultaneously perceived relationships. The philosophy of language tends to dismiss this type of presentational activity as falling into the sphere of subjective experience, emotion, and feeling. As Russell (1927) put it: Our confidence in language is due to the fact that it shares . . . the structure of the physical world. Perhaps that is why we know so much physics and so little of anything else."

I would submit that we know so little of that large "anything else" because, all too often, we have tried to force discursive language and method on phenomena in which they have no business. Nor is a relegation of such matters to the mystique of intuition at all helpful. There is nothing mystical, for example about recent developments in sensory physiology. Here the data suggest a unique capacity of the brain to build up a central representational system through the juxtaposition of simultaneously coded transforms of multiple sensory inputs, modulated and gated by an interplay between central and peripheral, specific and nonspecific systems (Livingston, 1958). Sense experience is thus a fundamental way of creating form; and a mind working with meaning must have organs that supply it with forms (Langer, 1942/1958, p. 84).

Having said as much, I now want to consider some empirical approaches to the problem of measurement in clinical psychiatry with special reference to the effects of drugs on human behavior. Time allows only a few examples, a mere listing, in fact. The various approaches have been ably reviewed (Uhr & Miller, 1960).

Subjective and Objective Observation in the Single Subject

Take, for example, the sensation of pain and its relief by analgesics. Like other subjective experience, pain can manifest in motor behavior; however, it need not. It is a sensation difficult to define operationally; one "known to us by experience, and described by illustration" (Lewis, 1942). There are other puzzling features about pain. In the single individual it can be estimated by a variety of experimental procedures, registering the so-called pain threshold (Beecher, 1959a, p. 92). Yet a careful review of the field leads Beecher (1959b) to the surprising conclusion that "some 15 groups of investigators have utterly failed to demonstrate any effectiveness of morphine on experimental pain threshold" (p. 102). This sounds odd, in view of the patent usefulness of the drug in the clinical situation, a usefulness which is confirmed when the drug is tried in a carefully controlled clinical setting. Here there is remarkable agreement between data from Lasagna and Beecher's (Beecher, 1959b, pp. 104–105; Lasagna & Beecher, 1954) laboratory and from the group of Houde and Wallenstein (1953) concerning the effectiveness of 10 mg. morphine in pain of different origin (postoperative vis-à-vis metastatic cancer), and agreement concerning the reproducibility of data in successive experiments extending over three years by different groups of investigators in the same laboratory (Beecher, 1959b, pp. 104–105). In reviewing the effect of morphia on wound pain Beecher (1959a, p. 164) quotes evidence how attitudes to a wound determine the need for the drug. Thus, soldiers, to whom a wound can be the symbol of survival (rather than evidence of injury), require less morphine than civilian postoperative patients, to whom (despite far less tissue damage), the operation may signify severe disability. The subjective reaction to the injury, the "psychic processing" (Beecher, 1959a, p. 158) in a total behavior situation modifies not only the original sensation, but evidently its reaction to pharmacological intervention. Mood and attitude are thus all pervasive; and the measurement of change of mood is an all pervasive problem in psychiatry.

There are a number of scales to quantify mood; anxiety and depression, being common symptoms, have been particularly studied in this respect. Taylor (1953) and Cattell (1960) have developed instruments for the measurement of anxiety; Cattell isolated a "universal index" and a number of more discrete factors. A number of scales have been elaborated for estimating depression (Grinker et al., 1961; Hamilton, 1960). Such scales although still in the process of trial appear to be reliable (Hamburg et al., 1958), there being good agreement among raters, and also between subjective self-assessment and objective observation.

Another method, founded on the work of Nowlis and Nowlis (1956) has recently been developed by Clyde (1960). It makes use of a list of adjectives describing various mood states in simple, nontechnical terms, found empirically to be least ambiguous. Each term is printed on an IBM punch card; the subject is asked to sort these cards in four piles to describe the degree to which they describe his feelings, ranging from "not at all" to "extremely." Patients like this card sorting task, and prefer it to a check list. After sorting, the cards are fed directly into an electronic computer, for scoring and analysis. Specific categories of mood and behavior (such as "friendly," "aggressive," etc.) can be arrived at according to the grouping of words which describe them. Above all, subjective self-ratings can be compared with observer's ratings. By having a central clearing house for the cross validation of this and other scales (such as is available at the Psychopharmacology Service Center of the National Institute of Mental Health under Dr. Jonathan Cole's very able leadership), confidence levels for various instruments can be determined and clinical reaction forms (as manifested by clustering of items) agreed upon. These scales have a further advantage. Being self-administered, they make possible the careful study of fluctuation over time in a single case; and particularly of diurnal variation and variation on successive days. These variations can be quite marked and can vitiate baseline readings (Knight, 1963). It is also possible to use these scales to gauge interaction between personality structure and the effect of a particular medication. Time does not permit a consideration of this most important area. It has been recently reviewed (Lindemann & von Felsinger, 1961). In any event, pain, anxiety, anger, and depression, all common enough clinical symptoms, can at present be approached in quantitative terms.

It is much more difficult to quantify other symptoms, such as the disorders of perception or of cognitive function manifested, for example, in the states induced by dysleptic ("psychosomimetic") drugs. For here, as we saw, the flux, the speed, the intensity, the variety, the strangeness, the multiplicity of phenomena strain language and instruments built with ordinary language. Silence can be more eloquent than words, and the small guttural noise can carry the quintessence of meaning. The experience can be projected in a drawing, or in a poetical condensation.

It can also be item analyzed, in a self-rating questionnaire. Some 47 items have been listed by Abramson, Jarvik, et al., (1955); some 300 in a card sort test used by Ditman (1960). Yet here a difficulty arises. Answering a questionnaire requires attention; attention breaks continuity; the very act of attending, or of speaking, may alter the phenomena; the answers, even if they are informative are only partial answers; and the more trained the subject and observer, the more familiar with the inner space which he is exploring, the more informative the answers. Such item analysis, however, has great merit. It gives rank order and pattern to individual responses and maps the distribution of symptoms over time. A shorthand can be devised to describe various categories and their fluctuation over time, and such categorization can be reinforced by retrospective self-description and the playing back of tape-recorded responses. The symptoms can also be related to striking alteration in the sense of time, noted in these states (Boardman et al., 1957). One other advantage of this longitudinal approach is that symptom intensity can be correlated with metabolic findings. Thus, in our laboratory Dr. Szara has attempted to correlate symptom intensity produced by diethyltryptamine, a powerful dysleptic, with the pattern of excretion of its metabolite, 6-hydroxydiethyltryptamine. There are some, admittedly slender, indications of a possible correlation between symptom intensity and the excretion of 6-OH-diethyltryptamine in man (Szara & Rockland, 1962).

What is the objective counterpart to this kind of subjective observation in the single subject? The sensory or social isolation experiments demand such observation (Solomon et al., 1961). There, the throat microphone, the periscope, the closed-circuit television camera are useful technical devices. However we may briefly note one situation in which the behavioral output of an isolated individual is continuously monitored in a controlled situation. This approach, known as the operant conditioning approach, is based upon Skinner's (1938) classical studies. It allows a piece of behavior to "operate" upon the environment in the light of past occurrence, so as to "obtain" a "reward" or "avoid" "punishment": The behavior thus determines the consequences of behavior. The "reward" and "punishment" can be presented at regular ("fixed") or irregular ("variable") intervals, altering the levels of expectancy. Moreover the reward can be actual (Lindsley & Skinner, 1954) (candy, visual displays) or symbolic (points, won or lost, as in a game). Dr. Weiner, in our laboratory, favors the latter course; he is also exploring the relatively unknown area of the influence of "cost" in human operant behavior (Weiner, 1962). By suitable automatic programming, the "cost" of each response intended to procure a reward can be altered (i.e., the apparatus set so as to ensure that points are *lost* every time the subject seeks his reward); the economy with which a subject uses resources at his disposal can thus be assessed. The task is essentially a vigilance task— the detection of a light on a frosted glass panel, for which the subject is allowed to look by pressing a lever. Gain of points is signified by a bell. The responses are recorded on a cumulative recorder. The behavior under "cost" and "no cost" conditions is strikingly different; and already individual differences between subjects in terms of handling "cost" and "no cost" contingencies are apparent. This approach may, in time, give one an insight into the way individuals of different personality structure (or, for that matter, psychopathology) handle the very rapid transitional states (i.e., changes in anticipatory set) which some of the procedures demand. They also may teach one something of the individual variation in the experience of time; of the individual meaning of "gain," "loss," "reward," and "punishment." It has been of great interest and encouragement to Dr. Weiner, Dr. Waldrop, and their colleagues that patients respond to "symbolic" incentives more readily than to actual minor material rewards; and that performance remains remarkably stable in certain contingencies. With the equipment now available at the Behavioral and Clinical Studies Center of Saint Elizabeth's Hospital a number of patients can be tested simultaneously on different schedules. Printed circuit computer components make for an economy and flexibility of gear which would have been difficult to achieve with older devices. Moreover, a careful clinical study of the same patient and an enquiry into subjective states of mind during actual performance can proceed in parallel with the operant experiment. The data both warrant and are amenable to mathematical analysis.

Nonverbal and Verbal Behavior in the Dyadic Transaction— Cue and Expectation in Relation Response

There are thus some clinical responses in the single subject which, though unsatisfactorily, can be expressed in quantitative terms. It is significantly more difficult to measure a piece of behavior in an interpersonal field. The psychiatric interview or the analytical session are the prototypes of this situation. Much has been written on the nature and analysis of this transaction (Hilgard et al., 1952; Masserman, 1958); and it has, correctly in my view, been described as a system of expectations as well as of communication (Lennard & Bernstein, 1960). The interaction is here created by a continuum of individual signals—gestures, nonverbal sounds, words, sentences—each of which carries symbolic meaning. These are subjectively perceived and put out behaviorally, there being a constant interplay between subjective and manifest elements. The moment-to-moment input into this system is thus enormous; and the devices developed to reduce randomness and sources of variance can, to date, but mark a well-intentioned beginning. The traditionally "neutral" attitude of the psychoanalyst is such a device. The study of nonverbal cues in a transaction is another.

Gestures have been viewed by some as the most economical way of communication (Critchley, 1939), and have been examined with a view to disturbances in communication (Ruesch, 1957; Ruesch & Kees, 1959). A notation system for analysis of body motion and gestures known as "kinesics" has been developed (Birdwhistell, 1952). Separate silent and sound film analysis of a transaction presents another approach. A method has recently been introduced for the analysis of motion picture records by accurate geometrical fixation in successive planes (Dierssen et al., 1961). These techniques—because of the specialization and also the expense they involve—have so far been used only sparingly in psychiatry. Nevertheless, they may quantify cues which are among the oldest in the body of clinical medicine.

There are similar and more varied attempts to quantify aspects of verbal behavior; analysis of the nominative, connotative quality of words is but one of such analyses. There is suggestive evidence (through the use of appropriate filters) that the frequency spectrum alone—robbed of any connotative quality—can convey the affective quality of a speech sample (Hargreaves & Starkweather, 1963). Respiratory function during speech is another index (Goldman-Eisler, 1955) giving evidence of striking regularities in the relation of patterns to speech production, and particularly in regard to verbal output (syllables) per expiration. An extension of this time analysis of speech production is provided by the interaction chronograph (Chapple, 1940, 1949). Used in a standard, nondirective interview situation, this has already yielded valuable results. In essence, this instrument is an automatically controlled electronic stopwatch, measuring total speech time (irrespective of words) designated as action, pauses, silences, tempo, and other variables in both subject and observer. The coupling of the apparatus to data reduction devices increases the yield and makes possible the derivation of further measures, such as initiative and dominance. These measures have proved reasonably reliable (Matarazzo et al., 1956; Tuason et al., 1962), and there are indications that they may be sensitive to change, including drug-induced change (Tuason & Guze, 1961). *Time* of action thus emerges as an important element in communication, providing, with pitch, the matrix in which the detail of connotative meaning is embedded. Another feature may be noted at this point; as in operant conditioning behavior, time analysis forms an important element in verbal behavior. Verbal behavior is, in fact, operant behavior, a probabilistic symbolic game in which a piece of behavior operates on one's environment and determines outcome of behavior: Verbal conditioning (Luria, 1961) makes it possible to examine these contingencies experimentally. In this reciprocal feedback system of an interpersonal transaction it is not easy to separate patient behavior from therapist behavior; both therapist and patient are, in a sense, participant observers of each other, and the total transaction is the behavior of a two-group, or dyad (Lennard & Bernstein, 1960). It is in these contextual terms that the detail of verbal symbolic behavior must be viewed.

Some analysis of the naturalistic therapeutic transaction has been proceeding for some time and is beginning to bear fruit (Leary & Gill, 1959). The microscopic analysis of samples of speech with regard to word type, grammatical and syntactic structure, the themes referred to, and the context of such themes suggests that the technique is sensitive to drug effects (Gottschalk et al., 1956). Moreover, it is possible to assess, in a preliminary way the relationship between the specificity of a therapist's remarks and the expansion or constriction of the patient's statement which follows (Lennard & Bernstein, 1960). Patients talk more in response to verbalization of low structure. The more directive and constrictive the quality of activity, the more likely the negative reaction.

Buried in this obvious statement, there is another aspect of the same phenomenon. If linguistic transaction is in fact a system of mutual expectations, then expectation should influence subjective experience, as manifested in language. These expectations can be experimentally altered. There is, for example, some evidence (in need of much detailed study) that the mere presence of an observer in an experimental analytical situation significantly influences the imagery in psychoanalytic free association (Colby, 1960). In a more direct way expectation, manipulated either by direct instruction or by implied association, can markedly influence the subjective effect of a drug. This is most obvious in the old, old remedy of the placebo (Beecher, 1959a, p. 65). Moreover, when a drug (e.g., pentobarbitone) effect is compared with *both* placebo and untreated control, diametrically opposite results have been reported leading to the conclusion that "because of the several varieties of placebo reaction, as well as their potential for interaction with pharmacodynamic effects of drugs, this dynamic quality, which is inseparable from the act of drug administration in man, must be taken into account, and controls must be used which identify the direction as well as magnitude of the placebo effect. For this it may be necessary to use the *unblinded 'no-drug-at-all control'* to complement the usual identical dummies in the double blind setting" (Modell & Garrett, 1960, p. 539). A cognate approach is to examine the interaction between paradoxical instructive set and effect of a drug (for example, the administration of amphetamine with instructions appropriate to a barbiturate or vice versa). Such experiments are in progress (Fisher, 1962).

Group Interaction, Ward Setting, and the Clinical Trial

It is obvious from the foregoing that forces which powerfully influence a dyadic social field are bound to be manifest in an amplified degree in larger groups. The subject of small group interaction has been thoroughly reviewed (Hare et al., 1955; Nowlis, 1960), and classified for such factors as group size, the communication network, the personal and social characteristics of members, role differentiation, initial expectancy of members with respect to each other, and setting as important input variables. Various methods have been used to approach the subject. For example, the communication network can be controlled by varying the sequence of communication between subjects (Christie et al., 1952). A topographical system of notation (chain, wheel, star, circle) (Christie et al., 1952) has been introduced, and quantification is possible by means of devices such as the transmittance matrix (Roby & Lanzetta, 1958), linear graph analysis (Cartright & Harary, 1956) or measure of centrality (Leavit, 1951) or independence. The mathematical problems in the analysis of small group behavior have also been recently considered (Solomon, 1960). A physical task (e.g., getting a ball up a spiral plane) can be arranged to depend upon the collective skills and cohesion within a small group. In one such instance, such a task was found to be sensitive to sleep deprivation and medication (Laties, 1961). Even in the absence of a definitive task there are striking changes in the interpersonal field following medication. Thus one study (Rinkel et al., 1955) on the effects of LSD-25 reported a significant increase in avoidance, withdrawal, hostile, punitive, competitive behavior, while friendly reciprocal, equalitarian behavior was clearly reduced. The effect of a drug on behavior must thus be considered in a social field. The same drug, in the same dose, in the same subject will produce different effects according to the interpersonal and motivational situation in which it is given. This, particularly, applies to moderate doses of drugs.

It is much more difficult to study interaction in a large group, such as a ward population. Here both overt observation and observation by a participant observer assuming a patient role (Caudill et al., 1952) have been practiced. In our own laboratory, and arising out of the need of the clinical trial, a method known as the Social Interaction Matrix was developed by Kellam (1961). This device makes use of a suitably marked grid to record the amount and kind of social contact between patients on the basis of regular and frequent observations on the ward during the day. It is a scale deliberately designed to measure the amount of social mobility among patients, and one of the several instruments available to quantitate behavior on a psychiatric ward.

There are many such devices, and around them center some of the liveliest controversies in psychiatry. Should rating scales be used or should one rely on clinical observation only? If rating scales are to be used, who is to use them, how often, and why? Is the physician's rating based on a half-hour interview once a week more reliable than that of the Nursing Assistant, potentially having access to the patient for 8 hours? How should raters be selected, and how trained? Upon whose vocabulary is the rating scale to be built? What are minimal criteria for scale validity in terms of content and construct? When do criteria become predictive? These and many other questions continue to be asked, and have been authoritatively reviewed (Lorr, 1960). One can draw comfort from such opinions. It is possible, for example, to record serially, and adequately, behavior in a metabolic unit (Beauregard et al., 1961). The reliability of some scales is high, so much so that by careful selection of items of high information content, a reliability of 0.9 can be achieved with as few as 12 items (Lorr, 1960). Moreover, when such scales are used in a formal, controlled clinical trial of several phenothiazines (Casey et al., 1960; Kurland et al., 1961), the conclusions regarding rank order of the various compounds compare not at all badly with an open, nonblind, clinical assessment (Freyhan, 1959).

The native clinical experience evidently is still a match for artificial intelligence, and the computer we carry in our skull is at least equal to its metal counterpart. Somehow the experienced, sensitive, and skeptical clinician collates data for internal consistency and error simultaneously at many levels, arriving at a formulation which represents a creative act of very high order. It is humbling that, despite its limitations, ordinary language should be able to convey its message so clearly in such a formulation. Rating scales thus have their place, but should be used only where there is clinical judgment. It is, in fact, when rigid assessment precludes continuous observation of clinical process over time; when observation of the outer shell of behavior presumes either to ignore or to infer subjective states of mind, that it is well to send one's young colleague back to the ward to write a long anecdotal history. Refined statistical manipulation will not mask poor case selection, or coarse rating scales, or poor inter-rater agreement. Sooner or later truth will out. In this age of restless manipulation it is well to learn to stare at phenomena in the ward; to take up the fragment, and the detail, only after having had a sense of the subtlety of the whole.

On the Need for New Symbolic Systems in Psychobiology and Psychiatry

In 1854, George Boole, a man who, self-taught, had risen to a Royal Society Medal and a Chair in Mathematics at Queens College, Cork, published his *Investigation of the Laws of Thought*. In this work, as in an earlier one—*The Mathematical Analysis of Logic* (1847)—he examined the ability of symbols to express logical prepositions, "the laws of whose combination should be founded upon the laws of mental processes which they represent." In searching for such outward representation, he invented the theory of classes and sets and the nonassociative relation between them, devising a symbolic algebraic shorthand for the expression of these relations in which concepts such as product, complement, inclusion, and a number of others are clearly represented.

Boole's path-breaking contributions led by way of Frege (1879), Jevons (1864), Peirce (1880) to Whitehead and Russell's *Principia* (1910–1913) in our day. One may note, in passing, the titles of some of these earlier works. Jevons named his work *Pure Logic, or the Logic of Quality apart from Quantity*. Frege called his study a *Begriffschrift*— a "formula language" (Formelsprache) of pure thought. Somehow the inexpressible, the suggestive qualities which in other circumstances we would call intuitive grew into communicable notations and symbols of great propulsive power; and opened a world of relations hitherto considered closed. It is outside my competence to examine the influence of Boolean algebra on modern experimental physics. However, the relation of a theory of sets and classes to communication and information transfer is nearer at hand. For the very word "communication" (from "communicare") implies sharing—i.e., the sharing of properties; and any encoding process depends upon the apprehension of such shared properties among sets and classes. It is by this sharing, too, that redundancy, far from being wasteful, serves in the transfer of information; redundancy provides context and thus minimizes error; it is a safety device—a reserve—in the flow of information (MacKay, 1961); a reserve, incidentally, amply encountered in biological systems.

Yet how interdependent are the demands of a subject, and the demands of a language for a subject? When chemistry, or electrical engineering needed appropriate symbolic forms of notation, such systems were duly invented: and when turn of the century physics felt constrained by Newtonian mechanics, it was modified according to need. However, so young is biology as a science, and so much younger still is the biology of mental phenomena (which we will call psychobiology) that its great discoveries were made using a linguistic apparatus leased from chemistry and physics, and from the language of everyday use. This hybrid arrangement has served for a time: no one will deny the many advances made so far. Nevertheless, it is clear that demands of quite a different order are pressing on the biology of our day. Interaction in macromolecular systems, and the control mechanisms inherent in such systems, are evidently of a different order from reactions between simple inorganic compounds; any accounting for the flow of information in such systems (as, for example, in the obvious instances of the gene or the immunological specificity of proteins) demands a language in which mere chemical or descriptive language is no longer sufficient. Woodger (1952) has indeed attempted to define the elements of a concise formal language for some aspects of genetics and evolutionary theory: a difficult but enormously worthwhile task.

It is the fortunate, if embarrassing, feature of the phenomena of behavior and of mental life that by their very nature they brook less compromise in such matters than any other branch of biology. The purely physical and chemical analogies do not hold; and the psychochemical correlates demand, as we have seen, a much more detailed specification and description of behavior, and of concomitant chemical change, than is currently available. For behavior implies multiple simultaneous change of a system in time, and *form* in behavior is really a topology in time. Discursive, linear, metric language does not apprehend such patterns. Presentational, experiential language suggests intricate simultaneous relationships, but does not define them. Yet it is the characteristic of every culture that it has invented symbols for such subjectively experienced relationships; it is significant, too, that in its own evolution, physics (and the branch of mathematics known as topology) has developed a shorthand for the apprehension of cognate simultaneous relations in the so-called outside physical world.

Could it, thus, be that in behavior and subjective experience we could see—if we wished to look—most clearly and cogently the "laws of thought" of which Boole spoke and which govern our understanding of the physical world? And could it be that the two uses of language which we distinguished represent two mutually complementary ways— one multiple, simultaneous, and another serial, successive by, which the brain constructs its models of reality? I have elsewhere (Elkes, 1961b) tentatively examined the possible relation of schizophrenic thought dis- order to information processing, or misprocessing, by the brain. In this scheme I suggested that transformations proceeded simultaneously at different yet closely interrelated neural levels, and distinguished between an ability to organize information serially in time—to structure in time—(in terms of the immediate adaptive demands of the "Here" and "Now") and a much more pervasive function of nervous tissue which depended upon its ability to organize simultaneously changing multiple inputs into a temporal topology of high information content. In this context the distinction between "serial" and "parallel" programming of computers concerned with pattern recognition is of special, if topical, interest (Selfridge & Neisser, 1960). Essentially, the distinction is one between asking questions serially one at a time, i.e., letting each answer determine the next question by successive elimination; or asking, as Neisser (1963) put it, all the questions at once. It is found, for example, that in the recognition of patterns of letters of different calligraphic quality the multiple, parallel method is more economical and effective. The mental intelligence thus turns up with a familiar linguistic problem; and there is at least inferential evidence that, at one level of its organiza- tion, the nervous system has the capacity of asking many questions all at once. The multiply connected reticular mixing pool may provide a sub- strate for precisely such transactions. The illogical thought process of intense subjective experience, of the dream, and so-called primary process (Freud, 1900) may thus have its parallel in presentational language, in the "geometric" thinking of Clerk Maxwell, the principles of comple- mentarity and coexistence of physics, and the multiple (or "parallel") approach of the modern computer; the logical, structured, sequential pattern of conscious deliberate action (sometimes called "secondary pro- cess") may be mirrored more closely in discursive language, the arith- metical approach, the scale, the serial analysis. Counting and pattern, rating and correlation, are thus at opposite ends. One feeds into the other, and science draws on them both. This process is well illustrated in Harvey's famous passage in Chapter VIII of *De motu cordis* (1628), where, following the minute sequential observation described in the preceding parts, the "movement, as it were, in a circle" is first conceived. "Movement in a circle" implies an intuitive seeing of a relation in time. Indeed, time would appear to be the main axis around which we build our models of reality; and nowhere is this more apparent than in the models we construct to represent behavior, including human behavior.

It would seem advisable, in view of the foregoing, to give early thought to the development of adequate new symbolic systems in the study of interpersonal processes, and to relate such attempts, whenever possible, to existing instruments in the natural sciences. The creation of such new systems would require long-term planning within small groups. It would require highly trained observers and highly trained subjects, capable of self-observation, to whom unfamiliar phenomena have become familiar through practice, as foreign territories are to seasoned travelers, and who are capable of developing operational definitions of states experienced and observed. Such an endeavor would require close cooperation between psychiatrist, psychologist, mathematician, and communication engineer; it may require training of one discipline in the skills of the other, to ensure a most direct personal contact with the phenomena. It will require much debate, and much crude trial and error. Yet, the history of science suggests that once such a beginning is made, progress can be quite rapid. It may be not too much to hope that concepts only partly or inadequately covered by present day language may, before very long, find a more adequate expression in new symbolic systems of greater precision and power. The usefulness of such systems may—and I would venture to say, will—not be confined to the study of behavior. For the phenomena of behavior pose, in a most poignant way, some fundamental issues in biology, particularly in regard to the storage and transfer of information in living systems. Indeed, the chief merit of behavior may perhaps lie in its intolerance of facile analogies borrowed from other branches of science, and its compelling need for rules in its own right. The Behavioral Sciences, and that vast body of experience known as Clinical Psychiatry, thus need not look apprehensively over their shoulder; having been nourished by the natural sciences, they may well be in a position to repay a longstanding debt. It is one's hope—and, if pressed, would be one's contention—that a science of Clinical Psychiatry is in the making in our day; and that in its growth it will enlarge the realm of the very sciences on which, quite properly it still depends.

Bibliography

ABOOD, L. G., BIEL, H. J., & OSTFELD, A. M. In P. B. Bradley, P. Deniker, & C. Radouco-Thomas (Eds.), *Neuropsychopharmacology: Proceedings of First International Congress.* Amsterdam: Elsevier, 1959.

ABRAMSON, H. A., JARVIK, M. E., KAUFMAN, M. R., KORNETSKY, C., LEVINE, A., & WAGNER, M. *Journal of Psychology,* 1955, *39,* 3–60.

ADOVASIO, J. M., & FRY, G. Prehistoric psychotropic drug use in northeastern Mexico and trans-Pecos Texas *Economic Botany,* 1976, *30,* 94–96.

ALLISON, J. Cognitive structure and receptivity to low intensity stimulation. *Journal of Abnormal and Social Psychology,* 1963, *67,* 132–138.

AMES, L. B., The sense of self of nursery school children as manifested by their verbal behavior. *Journal of Genetic Psychology,* 1952, *81,* 193–232.

ANASTASI, A., & SCHAEFER, C. E. Biographical correlates of artistic and literary creativity in adolescent girls. *Journal of Applied Psychology,* 1969, *53,* 267–273.

ANGYAL, A. Disturbances of thinking in schizophrenia. In J. S. Kasanin (Ed.), *Language and thought in schizophrenia.* Berkeley: University of California Press, 1944.

ANTROBUS, J. S., COLEMAN, R., & SINGER, J. L. Signal-detection performance by subjects differing in predisposition to daydreaming. *Journal of Consulting Psychology,* 1967, *31,* 487–491.

ANTROBUS, J. S., & SINGER, J. L. Visual signal detection as a function of sequential variability of simultaneous speech. *Journal of Experimental Psychology,* 1964, *68,* 603–610.

ANTROBUS, J. S., SINGER, J. L., GOLDSTEIN, S., & FORTGANG, M. Mindwandering and cognitive structure. *Transactions of the New York Academy of Sciences,* 1970, *32,* 242–252.

ANTROBUS, J. S., SINGER, J. L., & GREENBERG, S. Studies in the stream of consciousness: Experimental enhancement and suppression of spontaneous cognitive processes. *Perceptual and Motor Skills*, 1966, *23*(2), 399–517.

ASHBY, W. R. Design for a brain: *The Origin of adaptive behavior* (2nd ed.). New York: Wiley, 1960.

AX, A. F. The physiological differentiation between fear and anger in humans. *Psychosomatic Medicine*, 1953, *15*, 433–442.

BABB, L. A. *Walking on flowers in Singapore: a Hindu festival cycle*. Working Paper No. 27 of the Department of Sociology, University of Singapore, 1974. Unpublished manuscript.

BARBER, T. X. *LSD, marihuana, Yoga, and hypnosis*. Chicago: Aldine, 1970.

BARBER, T. X. Suggested ("hypnotic") behavior: The trance paradigm versus an alternative paradigm. In E. Fromm & R. Shor (Eds.), *Hypnosis: research developments and perspectives*. Chicago: Aldine, 1972.

BARRON, F. The psychology of creativity. In *New directions in psychology* (Vol. 11). New York: Holt, 1965.

BARTLETT, J. C. *The coding of naturalistic sounds*. Unpublished doctoral dissertation, Yale University, 1975.

BATESON, G. *Steps to an ecology of the mind*. New York: Ballantine, 1972.

BEAN, L. J., & SAUBEL, K. S. *Temalpakh: Cahuilla Indian knowledge and usage of plants*. Mrongo Indian Reservation, Calif.: Malki Museum Press, 1972.

BEATTY, J. Similar effects of feedback signals and instructional information on EEG activity. *Physiology and Behavior*, 1972, *9*, 151–154.

BEAUREGARD, R. M., WADESON, R. W., & WALSH, L. *Journal of Chronic Diseases*, 1961, *14*, 609–628.

BEECHER, H. K. *Measurement of subjective responses*. London and New York: Oxford University Press, 1959. (a)

BEECHER, H. K. In D. R. Laurence (Ed.), *Quantitative methods in human pharmacology and therapeutics*. New York: Pergamon, 1959. (b)

BERGSON, H. *L'Evolution creatrice*. Paris: Presses Universitaires de France, 1946, (Originally published, 1907).

BERINGER, K. *Nervenarzt*, 1932, *5*, 346–357.

BIRDWHISTELL, R. L. *Introduction to kinesics*. Louisville, Ky.: University of Louisville Press, 1952.

BLATT, S. J. Levels of object representation in anaclitic and introspective depression. *Psychoanalytic Study of the Child*, 1974, *29*, 107–157.

BLOOD, B. P. *The anaesthetic revelation and the gist of philosophy*. Amsterdam, New York: 1874.

BOARDMAN, W. K., GOLDSTONE, S., & LHAMON, W. T. *A.M.A. Archives of Neurol. Psychiatry*, 1957, *78*, 321–327.

BOHR, N. *Atomic physics and human knowledge*. New York: Wiley, 1958.

BOOLE, G. *The mathematical analysis of logic*. Cambridge: 1847.

BOOLE, G. *An investigation of the laws of thought*. London: Walton & Maberly, 1854.

BORING, E. G. *The physical dimensions of consciousness*. New York: Dover, 1963. (Originally published, 1933.)

BOURNE, L. E., EKSTRAND, B. R., & DUMINOWSKI, R. L. *The psychology of thinking*. Englewood Cliffs, N. J.: Prentice-Hall, 1971.

BREGER, L., HUNTER, I., & LANE, R. W. *The effect of stress on dreams*. New York: International Universities Press, 1971.

BRENER, J. A general model of voluntary control applied to the phenomena of learned cardiovascular change. In P. A. Obrist, A. H. Black, J. Brener, & L. V. DiCara (Eds.), *Cardiovascular psychophysiology*. Chicago: Aldine, 1974.

BREUER, J., & FREUD, S. *Neurologisches Zenir*, 1893, *12*, 4–10.

BRILLOUIN, L. *Science and information theory* (2nd ed.). New York: Academic Press, 1962.

BROADBENT, D. E. *Perception and communication*. New York: Pergamon, 1958.

BROADBENT, D. E. *Decision and stress*. London: Academic Press, 1971.

BROWN, B. B. Awareness of EEG-subjective activity relationships detected within a closed feedback system. *Psychophysiology*, 1970, *7*, 451–464. (a)

BROWN, B. B. Recognition of aspects of consciousness through association with EEG alpha activity represented by a light signal. *Psychophysiology*, 1970, *6*, 442–452. (b)

BUBER, M. *I and thou*. New York: Scribner's, 1958.

BUDZYNSKI, T. H. Biofeedback procedures in the clinic. *Seminars in Psychiatry*, 1973, *5*, 537–547. (a)

BUDZYNSKI, T. H. Some applications of biofeedback produced twilight states. In D. Shapiro, T. X. Barber, L. V. DiCara, J. Kamiya, N. E. Miller, & J. Stoyva (Eds.), *Biofeedback and self-control 1972: An Aldine Annual on the regulation of bodily processes and consciousness*. Chicago: Aldine, 1973. (b)

BURT, C. L. Consciousness. In *Encyclopaedia Britannica*. Chicago: Encyclopaedia Britannica, 1972.

CANNON, W. B. *Bodily changes in pain, hunger, fear and rage*. New York: Appleton, 1929.

CARNAP, R. The logical syntax of language. Paterson, N.J.: Littlefield, Adams, 1959. (Originally published in English, 1937, Routledge, Kegan, and Paul, London).

CARPENTER, W. B. *Principles of mental physiology*. London: King, 1874.

CARRIGAN, P. M. Extraversion-introversion as a dimension of personality: A reappraisal. *Psychological Bulletin*, 1960, *57*, 329–360.

CARTRIGHT, D., & HARARY, F. *Psychological Review*, 1956, 63, 277–293.

CARUS, C. G. *Psyche. Zur Entwickelungsgeschichte der Seele.* Pforzheim, Ger.: Flammer & Hoffman, 1846.

CASEY, J. F., LASKY, J. J., KLETT, C. J., & HOLLISTER, L. E. *American Journal of Psychiatry*, 1960, 117, 97–105.

CASTANEDA, C. *The teachings of don Juan: A Yaqui way of knowledge.* Berkeley: University of California Press, 1968.

CASTANEDA, C. *A separate reality: Further conversations with don Juan.* New York: Simon & Schuster, 1971.

CASTANEDA, C. *Journey to Ixtlan: The lessons of don Juan.* New York: Simon & Schuster, 1972.

CATTELL, R. B. In L. Uhr & J. G. Miller (Eds.), *Drugs and behavior*, New York: Wiley, 1960.

CAUDILL, W., REDLICH, F. C., BRODY, E. B., & GILMORE, H. R. *American Journal of Orthopsychiatry*, 1952, 22, 314–334.

CHAPPLE, E. D. *Genetic Psychology Monographs*, No. 22, 1940, 1–247.

CHAPPLE, E. D. *Personnel*, 1949, 25, 295–307.

CHARCOT, J. M. *Leçons du Mardi a la Salpêtrière.* Paris: Battaille, 1892.

CHRISTIE, L. S., LUCE, D. R., & MACY, J., JR. *Communication and learning in task oriented groups.* (Tech. Rep. 321). Cambridge: Massachusetts Institute of Technology, Research Laboratory of Electronics, 1952.

CLYDE, D. J. In L. Uhr & J. G. Miller (Eds.), *Drugs and behavior.* New York: Wiley, 1960.

COLBY, K. M. *Behavioral Science*, 1960, 5, 216–232.

CRITCHLEY, M. *The language of gesture.* London: Arnold, 1939.

CSIKSZENTMIHALYI, M. *Flow: Studies of enjoyment* (Report No. RO1HM22-883-02). Washington, D.C.: U.S. Public Health Service, 1974.

DAVIS, B. B. *Science, objectivity, and moral values* (Newsletter 2). Cambridge: Harvard University, Program in Public Conceptions of Science, 1975.

DAVY, H. *Researches. Chemical and philosophical; Chiefly concerning nitrous oxide of dephlogisticated nitrous air, and its respiration.* Bristol, Eng.: Biggs & Cottle, 1800.

DEIKMAN, A. J. De-automatization and the mystic experience. *Psychiatry*, 1966, 29, 329–343.

DEIKMAN, A. J. Bimodal consciousness. *Archives of General Psychiatry*, 1971, 25, 481–489.

DEIKMAN, A. J. *The relationship between EEG, EMG and meditation.* Paper at the Conference on Altered States of Consciousness and Suggestology, Pepperdine University, Los Angeles, May 1975.

DELONG, J. V. The drugs and their effects. In Drug Abuse Council, *Dealing with drug abuse: A report to the Ford Foundation.* New York: Praeger, 1972.

DEMENT, W. C. An essay on dreams: The role of physiology in understanding their nature. In F. Barron, W. C. Dement, et al., *New directions in psychology*, (Vol. 2). New York: Holt, 1965.

DE QUINCEY, T. *Confessions of an English opium eater*. London: Oxford University Press, 1822.

DIERSSEN, G., LORENC, M., & SPITALERI, R. M. *Neurology*, 1961, *11*, 610–618.

DITMAN, K. S. In H. A. Abramson (Ed.), *The use of LSD in psychotherapy*. New York: Josiah Macy, Jr., Foundation, 1960.

DONALDSON, T. *The George Catlin Indian gallery* (Report for 1885, Pt. II). Washington, D.C.: Smithsonian Institution, 1886.

DOWLING, J. E. The site of visual adaption. *Science*, 1967, *155* (3760).

DOYLE, J. C., ORNSTEIN, R., & GALIN, D. Lateral specialization of cognitive mode: II. EEG frequency analysis. *Psychophysiology*, 1974, *11*, 567–578.

DRUG ABUSE COUNCIL. *Altered states of consciousness: Current views and research problems*. Washington, D.C.: Drug Abuse Council, 1975.

DURÁN, FRAY D. [*Book of the gods and rites and the ancient calendar*] Fernando Horcasitas & Doris Heyden (Trans.). Norman: University of Oklahoma Press, 1971.

ECCLES, J. C. *The understanding of the brain*. New York: McGraw-Hill, 1973.

ECCLES, J. C. Personal communication, 1974.

EFRON, D. H. (Ed.). *Ethnopharmacologic search for psychoactive drugs*. (U.S. Public Health Service Publication No. 1645). Washington, D.C.: U.S. Government Printing Office, 1967.

EINSTEIN, A. *Essays in science*. New York: Philosophical Library, 1934.

EISENSTEIN, S. *The film sense*. New York: Harcourt, 1942.

ELIADE, M. *Shamanism: Archaic techniques of ecstasy*. New York; Pantheon, 1964.

ELIADE, M. *Yoga: Immortality and freedom*. Princeton, N.J.: Princeton University Press, 1969.

ELIOT, T. S. Hamlet and his problems. In *Selected essays*. New York: Harcourt, 1950. (Originally published, 1919).

ELKES, J. In J. Folch-Pi (Ed.), *Chemical pathology of the nervous system*. Oxford: Pergamon, 1961. (a)

ELKES, J. Psychotropic drugs: Observations on current views and future problems. In H. Brosin (Ed.), *Lectures on experimental psychiatry*. Pittsburgh: University of Pittsburgh Press, 1961. (b)

ELLIS, H. Mescal: A study of a divine plant. *Popular Science Monthly*, 1902, *41*, 52–71.

EMSHWILLER, E. *Dialogue on film*. Beverly Hills, Calif.: American Film Institute, Center for Advanced Film Studies, January 1973.

ENGSTROM, D. R. Hypnotic susceptibility and the EEG. In G. E. Schwartz &

D. Shapiro (Eds.), *Consciousness and self-regulation: Advances in research* (Vol. 1). New York: Plenum, 1976.

ESQUIROL, E. *Des maladies mentales. Considerées sous les rapports médical hygienique et médico-légal.* Paris: Ballière, 1838.

ESTES, W. K. Theoretical trends and points of controversy. In *Proceedings of the International Conference on Psychology of Human Learning* (Vol. 2). Prague: Czechoslovak Academy of Sciences, 1970.

EVANS, F. J. Hypnosis and sleep: Techniques for exploring cognitive activity during sleep. In E. Fromm & R. E. Shor (Eds.), *Hypnosis*. Chicago: Aldine, 1972.

FECHNER, G. T. *Elemente der Psychophysik.* Leipzig: Brietkopf & Hartel, 1860.

FISHER, SEYMOUR. Personal communication, 1962.

FISKE, D. W., & MADDI, S. R. *Functions of varied experience.* Homewood, Ill.: Dorsey, 1961.

FREGE, G. *Begriffschrift, eine der Arithmetischen Nachgebildete Formelsprache des reinen Denkens.* Halle, Ger.: 1879.

FREUD, S. [The interpretation of dreams.] In *The basic writings of Sigmund Freud.* New York: Modern Library, 1938. (Originally published, 1900).

FREUD, S. [A metapsychological supplement to the theory of dreams.] In J. Strachey (Ed.), *The standard edition of the complete psychological works of Sigmund Freud* (Vol. 14). London: Hogarth, 1957. (Originally published, 1917.)

FREUD, S. [On narcissism: An introduction.] In *The standard edition of the complete psychological works of Sigmund Freud* (Vol. 14). London: Hogarth, 1957. (Originally published, 1914.)

FREUD, S. [The unconscious.] In E. Jones (Ed. and trans.), *The collected papers of Sigmund Freud.* New York: Basic Books, 1960. (Originally published, 1915).

FREYHAN, F. *American Journal of Psychiatry,* 1959, *115,* 577–585.

FUNK & WAGNALLS. *Standard college dictionary.* New York: Funk & Wagnalls, 1968.

FUNKENSTEIN, D. H. The physiology of fear and anger. *Scientific American,* 1955, *192,* 74–76.

FURST, J. L. Personal communication, 1975.

FURST, P. T. *Hallucinogens in Precolumbian art.* In M. E. King & I. R. Taylor, Jr. (Eds.), *Art and environment in native America.* (Special Publication No. 7.). Lubbock: Museum of Texas Tech University, 1974.

FURST, P. T. Fertility, vision quest and auto-sacrifice: Some thoughts on ritual blood-letting among the Maya. In M. G. Robertson (Ed.), *Iconography and dynastic history of Palenque, Segunda Mesa Redonda de Palenque.* Pebble Beach, Calif.: Robert Louis Stevenson School, 1976. (a)

FURST, P. T. *Hallucinogens and culture.* San Francisco: Chandler & Sharp, 1976. (b)

FUSELLA, V. *Blocking of an external signal through self-projected imagery: The role of inner-acceptant personality styles and categories of imagery.* Unpublished doctoral dissertation, City University of New York, 1972.

GALIN, D. Implications for psychiatry of left and right cerebral specialization: A neurophysiological context for unconscious processes. *Archives of General Psychiatry*, 1974, *31*, 572–583.

GALIN, D., & ORNSTEIN, R. Lateral specialization of cognitive mode: An EEG study. *Psychophysiology*, 1972, *9*, 412–418.

GALTON, F. *Mind*, 1880, *5*, 301–318.

GALTON, F. The visions of sane persons. *Popular Science Monthly*, 1881, *19*, 519–531.

GARNER, W. R. *The processing of information and structure.* Potomac, Md.: Erlbaum, 1974.

GAZZANIGA, M. S. The split brain in man. In *Altered states of awareness: Readings from Scientific American.* San Francisco: Freeman, 1972.

GESELL, A., et al. *The first five years of life: A guide to the study of the preschool child.* New York: Harper, 1940.

GIAMBRA, L. Daydreaming across the life span: Late adolescent to senior citizen. *Aging and Human Development*, 1974, *5*, 116–135.

GILL, M. Topography and systems in psychoanalytic theory. *Psychological Issues* (Monograph No. 10). New York: International Universities Press, 1963.

GILL, M., & BRENMAN, M. *Hypnosis and related states: Psychoanalytic studies in regression.* New York: International Universities Press, 1959.

GOLDMAN-EISLER, F. *British Journal of Psychology*, 1955, *46*, 53–63.

GOLEMAN, D. J. The Buddha on meditation and states of consciousness: Part 1. *Journal of Transpersonal Psychology*, 1972, *4*, 1–44.

GOLEMAN, D. J. *Meditation and stress reactivity.* Unpublished doctoral dissertation, Harvard University, 1974.

GOLEMAN, D. J. Meditation and consciousness: An Asian approach to mental health. *American Journal of Psychotherapy*, 1976, *30*, 41–54.

GOTTSCHALK, L. A., KAPP, F. T., ROSS, D. W., KAPLAN, S. M., SILVER, H., MACLEOD, J. A., KAHN, J. B., VAN MAANEN, E. F., & ACHESON, G. H. *Journal of the American Medical Association*, 1956, *161*, 1054–1058.

GREELEY, A. M., & MCCREADY, W. C. Are we a nation of mystics? *New York Times Magazine*, January 26, 1975, pp. 12–25.

GREEN, E. E., GREEN, A. M., & WALTERS, E. D. Voluntary control of internal states: Psychological and physiological. In T. X. Barber, L. V. DiCara, J. Kamiya, N. E. Miller, D. Shapiro, & J. Stoyva (Eds.), *Biofeedback and self-*

control 1970: An Aldine Annual on the regulation of bodily processes and consciousness. Chicago: Aldine, 1971.

GREENFIELD, N., & STERNBACH, R. (Eds.), *Handbook of psychophysiology.* New York: Holt, Rinehart & Winston, 1972.

GRINKER, R. R., MILLER, J., SABSHIN, M. A., NUNN, R., & NUNNALLY, J. C. *The phenomena of depressions.* New York: Hoeber/Harper, 1961.

GUILFORD, J. P. *Personality.* New York: McGraw-Hill, 1959.

HAMBURG, D. A., SABSHIN, M. A., BOARD, F. A., GRINKER, R. R., KORCHIN, S. J., BASOWITZ, H., HEATH, H., & PERSKY, H. *A.M.A. Archives of Neurol. Psychiatry,* 1958, *79,* 415–425.

HAMILTON, M. *Journal of Neurology, Neurosurgery, and Psychiatry,* 1960, *23,* 56–62.

HARDING, W. M., & ZINBERG, N. E. The effectiveness of the subculture in developing rituals and social sanctions for controlled drug use. In B. M. Du Toit (Ed.), *Drugs, rituals and altered states of consciousness.* Rotterdam, Neth.: A. A. Balkema Publishers, 1977.

HARE, P., BORGATTA, E. F., & BALES, R. F. (Eds.). *Small groups: Studies in social interaction.* New York: Knopf, 1955.

HARGREAVES, W. A., & STARKWEATHER, J. A. Personal communication, 1963.

HARTMANN, E. L. *The functions of sleep.* New Haven: Yale University Press, 1973.

HARVEY, W. *Exercitatio anatomica de motu cordis et sanguinis in animalibus.* Frankfurt: Fitzer, 1628.

HASSETT, J., & SCHWARTZ, G. E. Relationships between heart rate and occipital alpha: A biofeedback approach. *Psychophysiology,* 1975, *12,* 228. (Abstract)

HEBB, D. O. Drives and the central nervous system. *Psychological Review,* 1955, *62,* 243–253.

HEFFERLINE, R. F., & BRUNO, L. J. J. The psychophysiology of private events. In A. Jacobs & L. B. Sachs (Eds.), *The psychology of private events.* New York: Academic Press, 1971.

HEISENBERG, W. *Physics and philosophy.* New York: Harper, 1958.

HELMHOLTZ, H. VON. [*On the sensation of tone as a physiological basis for the theory of music*] (A. J. Ellis, Trans.). New York: Dover, 1954. (Originally published, 1863.)

HELSON, R. Childhood interest clusters related to creativity in women. *Journal of Consulting Psychology,* 1965, *29,* 352–361.

HILGARD, E. R. *Hypnotic susceptibility.* New York: Harcourt, 1965.

HILGARD, E. R. *The experience of hypnosis.* New York: Harcourt, 1968.

HILGARD, E. R. Levels of awareness. In R. B. MacLeod (Ed.), *William James:*

Unfinished business. Washington, D.C.: American Psychological Association, 1969.

HILGARD, E. R. A neodissociation interpretation of pain reduction in hypnosis. *Psychological Review,* 1973, *80,* 396–411.

HILGARD, E. R., KUBIE, L. S., & PUMPIAN-MINDLIN, E. (Eds.). *Psychoanalysis as science.* Stanford, Calif.: Stanford University Press, 1952.

HILGARD, E. R., MORGAN, A. H., & MACDONALD, H. Pain and dissociation in the cold pressor test: A study of hypnotic analgesia with "hidden reports" through automatic key pressing and automatic talking. *Journal of Abnormal Psychology,* 1975, *84,* 280–289.

HILGARD, J. *Personality and hypnosis: A study of imaginative involvement.* Chicago: University of Chicago Press, 1970.

HOFMANN, A., HEIM, R., BRACK, A., & KOBEL, H. *Experientia,* 1958, *14,* 107–109.

HOLT, R. Imagery: The return of the ostracized. *American Psychologist,* 1964, *19,* 254–264.

HOLTON, G. *Scientific optimism and societal concerns: A note on the psychology of scientists.* Cambridge: Harvard University, Jefferson Physical Laboratory, February 1975.

HOROWITZ, M. J. *Image formation and cognition.* New York: Appleton, 1970.

HOROWITZ, M. J. Hallucinations: An information-processing approach. In L. S. West & R. J. Segal (Eds.), *Hallucinations: Behavior and theory.* New York: Wiley, 1974.

HOROWITZ, M. J., & BECKER, S. The compulsion to repeat trauma. *Journal of Nervous and Mental Diseases.* 1971, *153,* 32–40.

HOUDE, R. W., & WALLENSTEIN, S. L. *Drug Addiction and Narcotics Bulletin.* Washington, D.C.: National Research Council, 1953.

HUBA, G., SEGAL, B., & SINGER, J. L. *Daydreaming, drinking, and drugs: A multivariate analysis.* Hillsdale, N.J.: Erlbaum, in preparation.

HULL, C. *Hypnosis and suggestibility: An experimental approach.* New York: Appleton, 1933.

HUMPHREY, G. *Thinking: An introduction to its experimental psychology.* New York: Wiley, 1963.

HUMPHREY, R. *Stream of consciousness in the modern novel.* Berkeley: University of California Press, 1954.

HUXLEY, A. D. *The doors of perception.* New York: Harper, 1952.

ISAACS, D. *Cognitive styles in daydreaming.* Unpublished doctoral dissertation, City University of New York, 1975.

IZARD, C. *The face of emotion.* New York: Appleton, 1971.

JAMES, W. A pluristic mystic. In *Memories and studies.* New York: Longmans, Green, 1912.

JAMES, W. *The varieties of religious experience.* New York: Modern Library, 1929. (Originally published, 1902.)

JAMES, W. *The principles of psychology.* New York: Dover, 1950. (Originally published, 1890.)

JESSOR, R., JESSOR, S., & FINNEY, A. Social psychology of marijuana use: Longitudinal studies of high school and college youth. *Journal of Personality and Social Psychology,* 1973, *26,* 1–15.

JEVONS, W. S. *Pure logic, or the logic of quality apart from quantity.* London: 1864.

JOHNSON, D. M. *The psychology of thought and judgment.* New York: Harper, 1955.

JOYCE, J. *Ulysses.* New York: Random House, Modern Library Edition, 1934.

KAGAN, J., & KAGAN, N. Individual variation in cognitive processes. In P. Mussen (Ed.), *Carmichael's manual of child psychology* (Vol. 1). New York: Wiley, 1970.

KAHNEMAN, D. *Attention and effort.* Englewood Cliffs, N.J.: Prentice-Hall, 1973.

KAMIYA, J. Operant control of the EEG alpha rhythm and some of its reported effects on consciousness. In C. Tart (Ed.), *Altered states of consciousness.* New York: Wiley, 1969.

KELLAM, S. G. *Journal of Nervous and Mental Disease,* 1961, *132,* 277–288.

KHANTZIAN, E. J., MACK, J. E., & SCHATZBERG, A. F. Heroin use as an attempt to cope: Clinical observations. *American Journal of Psychiatry,* 1974, *131,* 160–164.

KIMURA, D. The asymmetry of the human brain. *Scientific American,* 1973, *228,* 70–78.

KLEITMAN, N. In G. E. W. Wostenholme & M. O'Connor (Eds.), *The nature of sleep.* Boston: Little, Brown, 1961.

KLINGER, E. *Structure and functions of fantasy.* New York: Wiley, 1971.

KLINGER, E. *Consequences of commitment to a disengagement from incentives.* Book in preparation, 1976.

KLÜVER, H. *Mescal: The divine plant and its psychological effects.* London: Kegan Paul, Trench & Trubner, 1928.

KNAB, T. Personal communication, 1976.

KNIGHT, R. A. In M. Rinkel (Ed.), *Specific and non-specific factors in psychopharmacology.*

KOHLBERG, L. A cognitive-development approach to socialization, morality, and psychosexuality. Paper presented at the meeting of the Midwestern Society for Research in Child Development, Bowling Green State University, Bowl-

KOLERS, P. A. Reading and talking bilingually. *American Journal of Psychology*, 1966, *79*(3), 357–376.

KOLERS, P. A. Bilingualism and information processing. *Scientific American*, 1968, *218*(3), 78–86.

KRAEPELIN, E. *Philosophical Studies*, 1883, *1*, 573–603.

KRAEPELIN, E. *Lectures on clinical psychiatry*. London: Ballière, 1906.

KRIS, E. On preconscious mental processes. In D. Rapaport (Ed.), *Organization and pathology of thought*. New York: Columbia University Press, 1951.

KUHN, T. S. *The structure of scientific revolution*. Chicago: University of Chicago Press, 1962.

KURLAND, S. A., HANLON, T. E., TATOM, M. H., OTA, K. Y., & SIMOPOULOS, A. M. *Journal of Nervous and Mental Disease* 1961, *133*, 1–18.

LA BARRE, W. Old and New World narcotics: A statistical question and an ethnological reply. *Economic Botany*, 1970, *24*, 73–80.

LA BARRE, W. Hallucinogens and the shamanic origins of religion. In P. T. Furst (Ed.), *Flesh of the gods: The ritual use of hallucinogens*. New York: Praeger, 1972.

LA BARRE, W. The peyote cult (Rev. and enl. ed.). Hampden, Conn.: Shoestring Press, 1974. (Originally published, 1959).

LACEY, B. C., & LACEY, J. I. Studies of heart rate and other bodily processes in sensorimotor behavior. In P. A. Obrist, A. H. Black, J. Brener, & L. V. DiCara (Eds.), *Cardiovascular psychophysiology*. Chicago: Aldine, 1974.

LACEY, J. I. *Annals of the New York Academy of Sciences*, 1956, *67*, 123–163.

LADD, G. T. *Mind*, 1892, n.s. *1*, 299–304.

LAING, R. D. *The divided self: An existential study in sanity and madness*. Baltimore: Penguin, 1965.

LAING, R. D. *The politics of experience*. New York: Ballatine, 1968.

LANG, P. J. Learned control of human heart rate in a computer directed environment. In P. A. Obrist, A. H. Black, J. Brener, & L. V. DiCara (Eds.), *Cardiovascular psychophysiology*. Chicago: Aldine, 1974.

LANGER, S. K. *Philosophy in a new key* (Rev. ed.). New York: New American Library, 1958.

LANGER, S. I. *Problems of art*. New York: Scribner's, 1957.

LASAGNA, L., & BEECHER, H. K. *Journal of Pharmacology*, 1954, *112*, 306–311.

LATIES, V. G. *Journal of Psychiatric Research*, 1961, *1*, 12–25.

LEARY, T., & GILL, M. In E. A. Rubinstein & M. B. Parloff (Eds.), *Research in psychotherapy*. Washington, D.C.: American Psychological Association, 1959.

LEAVIT, H. J. *Journal of Abnormal and Social Psychology*, 1951, *16*, 38–50.

LEAVITT, R. P. To walk on fire you must first master yourself. *New York Times*, April 29, 1973, Section 10, p. 1.

LEE, D. Codifications of reality: Lineal and nonlineal. *Psychosomatic Medicine,* 1950, *12*(2), 89–97.

LENNARD, H. L., & BERNSTEIN, A. *The anatomy of psychotherapy.* New York: Columbia University Press, 1960.

LEWIS, T. *Pain.* New York: Macmillan, 1942.

LINDEMANN, E., & VON FELSINGER, J. J. *Psychopharmacologia,* 1961, *2,* 69–92.

LINDSLEY, O. R., & SKINNER, B. F. *American Psychologist,* 1954, *9,* 419–420.

LIVINGSTON, R. B. In J. Field, H. W. Magoun, & V. E. Hall (Eds.), *Handbook of physiology, Section 1: Neurophysiology.* Washington, D.C.: American Physiological Society, 1958.

LOCKE, J. *An essay concerning human understanding.* Vol. 1. New York: Dover, 1959. (Originally published, 1690.)

LORR, M. In L. Uhr & J. G. Miller (Eds.), *Drugs and behavior.* New York: Wiley, 1960.

LUBY, E. B., COHEN, B. D., ROSENBAUM, G., GOTTLIEB, J. S., & KELLY, R. *A.M.A. Archives of Neurol. Psychiatry,* 1959, *81,* 363–369.

LUDWIG, A. Altered states of consciousness. In C. Tart (Ed.), *Altered states of consciousness.* New York: Wiley, 1969.

LURIA, A. *The role of speech in the regulation of normal and abnormal behavior.* New York: Liveright, 1961.

LUTHE, W. Autogenic training: Method, research and application in medicine. *American Journal of Psychotherapy,* 1963, *17,* 174–195.

MACH, E. [*The analysis of sensations, and the relation of the physical to the psychical*] (C. M. Williams, Trans.). Chicago. Open Court, 1914.

MACH, E. *Die Mechanik in ihrer Entwicklung.* Leipsig: Brockhaus, 1897.

MACKAY, D. M. *The science of communication.* Inaugural lecture at University College of North Staffordshire, Keele, England, 1961.

MACKAY, D. M. *Information, mechanism and meaning.* Cambridge: MIT Press, 1969.

MARCUSE, H. *Eros and civilization.* New York: Vantage, 1955.

Marihuana-hashish epidemic and its impact on United States security. Hearings before the Subcommittee to Investigate the Administration of the Internal Security Act and Other Internal Security Laws of the Committee on the Judiciary, United States Senate. Washington, D.C.: U.S. Government Printing Office, 1974.

MASSERMAN, J. H. (Ed.). *Science and psychoanalysis.* New York: Grune & Stratton, 1958.

MATARAZZO, J. D., SASLOW, G., & GUZE, S. B. *Journal of Consulting and Clinical Psychology,* 1956, *20,* 267–274.

MAUPIN, E. W. Individual differences in response to Zen meditation exercise. *Journal of Consulting Psychology,* 1965, *29,* 139–145.

MAXWELL, J. C. Transactions of the Cambridge Philosophical Society [1856]. In W. D. Niven (Ed.), *Scientific papers of J. C. Maxwell* (Vol. 1), 155–229. Cambridge, Eng.: 1890.

MAXWELL, J. C. Atoms. In W. D. Niven (Ed.), *Scientific papers of J. C. Maxwell* (Vol. 2), 445–484. Cambridge, Eng.: 1890. (Originally published, 1874).

MAYER-GROSS, W., & STEIN, H. 1926, *101*, 354–361.

McFARLAND, D. J. *Feedback mechanisms in animal behavior.* London: Academic Press, 1971.

McKELLAR, P. *Imagination and thinking: A psychological analysis.* New York: Basic Books, 1957.

McKENDRICK, J. G. Sleep. In *Encyclopaedia Britannica* (11th ed.). New York: Encyclopaedia Britannica, 1911.

MEAD, G. *Mind, self and society.* Chicago: University of Chicago Press, 1934.

MEDEWAR, P. *The art of the soluble.* London: Methuen, 1967.

MERTON, T. *The way of Chiang Tzen.* New York: New Directions, 1969.

MESKIN, G., & SINGER, J. L. Daydreaming, reflective thought, and the laterality of eye-movements. *Journal of Personality and Social Psychology,* 1974, *30*(1), 64–71.

MILLER, G. A., GALANTER, E. H., & PRIBRAM, K. H. *Plans and the structure of behavior.* New York: Holt, 1960.

MILLER, N. E. Learning of visceral and glandular responses. *Science,* 1969, *163*, 434–445.

MILLER, N. E., et al. (Eds.). *Biofeedback and self-control.* Chicago: Aldine, 1973.

MISCHEL, W. *Personality and assessment.* New York: Wiley, 1968.

MISCHEL, W. *Introduction to personality.* New York: Holt, 1971.

MITCHELL, S. W. *British Medical Journal,* 1896, *2*, 1625–1629.

MITTELSTAEDT, H. Discussion. In D. P. Kimble (Ed.), *Experience and capacity.* New York: New York Academy of Sciences, Interdisciplinary Communications Program, 1968.

MODELL, W., & GARRETT, M. *Nature,* 1960, *185*, 539.

MOREAU, J. *Du hachisch et de l'aliénation mentale. Études psychologiques.* Paris: Masson, Fortin, 1845.

MORGAN, A. H., MACDONALD, H., & HILGARD, E. R. EEG alpha: Lateral asymmetry related to task and hypnotizability. *Psychophysiology,* 1974, *11*, 275–282.

MULHOLLAND, T. Feedback electroencephalography. *Activitas Nervosa Superior,* 1968, *10*, 410–438.

MULHOLLAND, T. Objective EEG methods for studying covert shifts of visual attention. In F. J. McGuigan & R. A. Schoonover (Eds.), *The psychophysiology of thinking*. New York: Academic Press, 1973.

MULLAHY, P. *Oedipus: Myth and complex*. New York: Hermitage, 1948.

MÜLLER, J. [*The physiology of the senses, voice, and muscular motion with mental facilities*] (Taylor, Trans.). London: Walton & Maberly, 1848.

MUSES, C., & YOUNG, A. M. (Eds.). *Consciousness and reality, the human pivot point*. New York: Dutton, 1974.

NAHAS, G. G. *Marihauna—deceptive weed*. New York: Raven, 1973.

National Commission on Marihuana and Drug Abuse. *Drug Use in America: Problem in perspective*. Washington, D.C.: U.S. Government Printing Office, 1973.

NEISSER, U. *Psychological Review*, 1963.

NEISSER, U. *Cognitive psychology*. New York: Appleton, 1967.

NORADA, T. *A manual of Adhidhamma*. Kandy, Sri Lanka: Buddhist Publication Society, 1968.

NOWLIS, D. P., & KAMIYA, J. The control of electroencephalographic alpha rhythms through auditory feedback and the associated mental activity. *Psychophysiology*, 1970, 6, 476–484.

NOWLIS, V. In L. Uhr & J. G. Miller (Eds.), *Drugs and behavior*. New York: Wiley, 1960.

NOWLIS, V., & NOWLIS, H. H. *Annals of the New York Academy of Sciences*, 1956, 65, 345–355.

OAKESHOTT, M. Lecture, London School of Economics, London, October 1968.

ORNE, M. T. On the social psychology of the psychological experiment, with particular reference to demand characteristics and their implications. *American Psychologist*, 1962, 118, 1097–1103.

ORNE, M. T. On the simulating subject as a quasi-control group in hypnosis research: What, why and how. In E. Fromm & R. E. Shor (Eds.), *Hypnosis*. Chicago: Aldine, 1972.

ORNSTEIN, R. E. *On the experience of time*. Baltimore: Penguin, 1969.

ORNSTEIN, R. E. *The psychology of consciousness*. San Francisco: Freeman, 1972.

ORNSTEIN, R. E. *The nature of human consciousness: A book of readings*. San Francisco: Freeman, 1973.

OTT, J. Psycho-mycological studies of Amanita: From ancient sacrament to modern phobia. *Journal of Psychedelic Drugs*, 1976, 8, 27–35.

PAIVIO, A. *Imagery and verbal processes*. New York: Holt, 1971.

PASKEWITZ, D. A., LYNCH, J. J., ORNE, M. T., & COSTELLO, J. The feedback control of alpha activity: Conditioning or disinhibition. *Psychophysiology*, 1970, 6, 637–638. (Abstract)

PASKEWITZ, D. A., & ORNE, M. T. Visual effects on alpha feedback training. *Science*, 1973, *181*, 360–363.

PEIRCE, C. S. *American Journal of Mathematics*, 1880, *3*, 15.

PEPER, E. Localized EEG alpha feedback training: A possible technique for mapping subjective, conscious, and behavioral experiences. *Kybernetik*, 1972, *11*, 166–169.

PERERA, V. Foreign notes: The firewalkers of Udappawa. *Harper's*, May 1971, 18–21.

PINEL, P. [*A treatise on insanity*]. London: Cadell & Davis, 1806.

PLATT, J. J. "Addiction proneness" and personality in heroin addicts. *Journal of Abnormal Psychology*, 1975, *84*, 303–306.

PLINER, P. L. Effects of cue salience on behavior of obese and normal subjects. *Journal of Abnormal Psychology*, 1973, *82*(2), 226–232.

PLINER, P. L. Effect of external cues on thinking behavior of obese and normal subjects. *Journal of Abnormal Psychology*, 1973, *82*(2), 233–238.

POLLOCK, S. H. The psilocybin mushroom pandemic. *Journal of Psychedelic Drugs*, 1975, *7*(1), 73–84.

PRIBRAM, K. H. The neurobehavioral analysis of limbic forebrain mechanisms: Revision and progress report. In D. S. Lehrman, R. A. Hinde, & E. Shaw (Eds.), *Advances in the study of behavior*. New York: Academic Press, 1969.

PRIBRAM, K. H. The biology of mind: Neurobehavioral foundations. In A. R. Gilgen (Ed.), *Scientific psychology: Some perspectives*. New York: Academic Press, 1970. (a)

PRIBRAM, K. H. Feelings as monitors. In M. Arnold (Ed.), *Feelings and emotions*. New York: Academic Press, 1970. (b)

PRIBRAM, K. H. The primate brain and human learning. In *Proceedings of the International Conference on Psychology of Human Learning* (Vol. 1), Prague: Czechoslovak Academy of Sciences, 1970. (c)

PRIBRAM, K. H. *Languages of the brain: Experimental paradoxes and principles in neuropsychology*. Englewood Cliffs, N.J.: Prentice-Hall, 1971.

PRIBRAM, K. H. How is it that sensing so much we can do so little? In F. O. Schmitt & F. G. Worden (Eds.), *The neurosciences study program* (Vol. 3). Cambridge: MIT Press, 1974.

PRIBRAM, K. H. Self-consciousness and intentionality: A model based on an experimental analysis of the brain mechanisms involved in the Jamesian theory of motivation and emotion. In G. E. Schwartz & E. Shapiro (Eds.), *Consciousness and self-regulation, advances in research* (Vol. 1). New York: Plenum, 1976.

PRIBRAM, K. H., & GILL, M. M. *Freud's project for a scientific psychology: Preface to contemporary cognitive theory and neuropsychology. New York: Basic Books, 1975.

PRIBRAM, K. H., & GILL, M. M. *Freud's "project" reassessed.* New York: Basic Books, 1976.

PRIBRAM, K. H., & McGUINNESS, D. Arousal, activation and effort in the control of attention. *Psychological Review,* 1975, *82,* 116–149.

PRIBRAM, K. H., NUWER, M., & BARON, R. The holographic hypothesis of memory structure in brain function and perception. In R. C. Atkinson, D. H. Krantz, R. C. Luce, & P. Suppes (Eds.), *Contemporary developments in mathematical psychology.* San Francisco: Freeman, 1974.

RADFORD, J. Reflections on introspection. *American Psychologist,* 1974, *29,* 245–250.

RAPAPORT, D. Consciousness: A psychopathological and psychodynamic view. In *Problems of consciousness.* New York: Josiah Macy, Jr., Foundation, 1951. (a)

RAPAPORT, D. *Organization and pathology of thought.* New York: Columbia University Press, 1951. (b)

RAPAPORT, D. The psychoanalytic theory of motivation. In M. R. Jones (Ed.), *Nebraska symposium on motivation.* Lincoln: University of Nebraska Press, 1960.

RECHTSCHAFFEN, A., & EAKINS, E. (Eds.), *Sleep and dream research: A bibliography.* Los Angeles: UCLA, Brain Information Service, n.d.

REICHEL-DOLMATOFF, G. The cultural context of an aboriginal hallucinogen: *Banisteriopsis caapi.* In P. T. Furst (Ed.), *Flesh of the gods: The ritual use of hallucinogens.* New York: Praeger, 1972.

REIK, T. *Listening with the third ear.* New York: Farrar, Straus, 1948.

RESCORLA, R. A., & WAGNER, A. R. A theory of Pavlovian conditioning: Variation in the effectiveness of reinforcement and non-reinforcement. In A. Black & W. F. Prokasy (Eds.), *Classical conditioning* (Vol. 2). New York: Appleton, 1972.

RINKEL, M., HYDE, R. W., SOLOMON, H. C., & HOAGLAND, H. *American Journal of Psychiatry,* 1955, *3,* 881–895.

ROBERTS, A. H., KEWMAN, D. G., & MACDONALD, H. Voluntary control of skin temperature: Unilateral changes using hypnosis and feedback. *Journal of Abnormal Psychology,* 1973, *82*(1), 163–168.

ROBERTSON, M. G. *The ritual bundles of Yaxchilán.* Paper presented at the Tulane University Symposium on the Art of Latin America, New Orleans, April 1972.

ROBY, T. B., & LANZETTA, J. T. *Psychological Bulletin,* 1958, *55,* 88–101.

RODIN, J., & SINGER, J. L. Laterality of eye-shift, reflective thought and obesity. *Journal of Personality,* 1977, in press.

Rose, S. *The conscious brain.* New York: Knopf, 1973.

Rosenthal, R. *Experimenter effects in behavioral research.* New York: Appleton, 1966.

Rosenthal, R. Body-talk and tone of voice: The language without words. *Psychology Today,* 1974, 64–71.

Roszak, T. *Where the wasteland ends.* New York: Doubleday, 1973.

Ruesch, J. *Disturbed communication.* New York: Norton, 1957.

Ruesch, J., & Kees, W. *Nonverbal communication.* Berkeley: University of California Press, 1956.

Ruíz de Alarcón, H. Tratado de las supersticiones y costumbres gentilicas que oy vieuen entre los Indios Naturales desta Nueua Espana. Mexico, D. F.: *Anales de Museo Nacional de Mexico,* 1892 (1900), 126–223.

Rush, B. *Medical inquiries and observations upon the diseases of the mind.* Philadelphia: Kimber & Richardson, 1812.

Russell, B. *Philosophy.* New York: Norton, 1927.

Rychlak, J. F. Time orientation in the positive and negative free phantasies of mildly abnormal vs. normal high school males. *Journal of Consulting and Clinical Psychology,* 1973, *41,* 175–180.

Sahagún, Fray B. de [*The Florentine Codex: General history of the things of New Spain*] (Vol. 11) (A. J. O. Anderson & C. E. Dibble, Trans.), 1963. Santa Fe, N.M.: School of American Research and the University of Utah, 1950–1963.

Sarbin, T. R. & Coe, W. C. *Hypnosis: A social psychological analysis of influence communication.* New York: Holt, 1972.

Scarf, M. Tuning down with TM. *New York Times Magazine,* February 9, 1975, 12, 52–55, 63.

Schachter, S. The interaction of cognitive and physiological determinants of emotional state. In P. H. Leiderman & D. Shapiro, *Psychobiological approaches to social behavior.* Stanford, Calif.: Stanford University Press, 1964.

Schacter, S., & Rodin, J. *Obese humans and rats.* Washington, D.C.: Erlbaum, 1974.

Schultes, R. E. *A contribution to our knowledge of Rivea corymbosa, the narcotic ololiuhqui of the Aztecs.* Cambridge: Harvard University, Botanical Museum, 1941.

Schultes, R. E. The place of ethobotany in the ethnopharmacologic search for psychotomimetic drugs. In D. H. Efron (Ed.), *Ethnopharmacologic search for psychoactive drugs.* Washington, D.C.: Public Health Service Publication No. 1645, 1967.

Schultes, R. E. An overview of hallucinogens in the Western Hemisphere. In

P. T. Furst (Ed.), *Flesh of the gods: The ritual use of hallucinogens.* New York: Praeger, 1972.

SCHWARTZ, G. E. Voluntary control of human cardiovascular integration and differentiation through feedback and reward. *Science,* 1972, *175,* 90–93.

SCHWARTZ, G. E. Biofeedback, self-regulation, and the patterning of physiological processes. *American Scientist,* 1975, *63,* 314–324.

SCHWARTZ, G. E., SHAPIRO, D., & TURSKY, B. Learned control of cardiovascular intergration in man through operant conditioning. *Psychosomatic Medicine,* 1971, *33,* 57–62.

SEAMAN, J. Imagery codes and human information retrieval. *Journal of Experimental Psychology,* 1972, *96,* 468–470.

SEGAL, B., & SINGER, J. L. Daydreaming, drug and alcohol use in college students: A factor analytic study. *Addictive Behavior: An International Journal,* 1976, *1,* 227–235.

SEGAL, S. J. *Imagery: Current cognitive approaches.* New York: Academic Press, 1971.

SEGAL, S. J., & FUSELLA, V. Influence of imaged pictures and sounds on detection of auditory and visual signals. *Journal of Experimental Psychology,* 1970, *83,* 458–464.

SEIDMAN, J. M. *The adolescent: A book of readings* (Rev. ed.). New York: Holt, 1960.

SELER, E. Die Lichtbringer bei den Indianern der Nordwestküste. In *Gesammelte Abhandlungen zur Amerikanischen Sprach und Altertumskunde* (Vol. 5.). Graz, Aust.: Akademische Druck- u. Verlagsanstalt, 1961. (Originally published, 1892.)

SELFRIDGE, O. G., & NEISSER, U. *Scientific American,* 1960, *203,* 60–68.

SELMAN, R. The development of social-cognitive understanding: A guide to educational and clinical practice. In T. Lickona (Ed.), *Morality: Theory, research, and social issues.* New York: Holt, 1975.

SHAPIRO, D., & SCHWARTZ, G. E. Biofeedback and visceral learning: Clinical applications. *Seminars in Psychiatry,* 1972, *4,* 171–184.

SHAPIRO, D., & SURWIT, R. S. Learned control of physiological function and disease. In H. Leitenberg (Ed.), *Handbook of behavior modification and behavior therapy.* Englewood Cliffs, N.J.: Prentice-Hall, 1976.

SHEEHAN, P. *The function and nature of imagery.* New York: Academic Press, 1972.

SHOR, R. E. Hypnosis and the concept of the generalized reality orientation. In C. Tart (Ed.), *Altered states of consciousness.* New York: Wiley, 1969. (Originally published, 1959.)

SINGER, J. L. The experience type: Some behavioral correlates and theoretical implication. In M. R. Rickers-Ovisiankina (Ed.), *Rorschach psychology*. New York: Wiley, 1960.

SINGER, J. L. *Daydreaming*. New York: Random House, 1966.

SINGER, J. L. Research applications of projective methods. In A. Rabin (Ed.), *Projective techniques in personality assessment*. New York: Springer, 1968.

SINGER, J. L. Some experimental studies of the stream of thought: In R. B. MacLeod (Ed.), *William James: Unfinished business*. Washington, D.C.: American Psychological Association, 1969.

SINGER, J. L. *The child's world of make-believe: Experimental studies of imaginative play*. New York: Academic Press, 1973.

SINGER, J. L. *Imagery and daydream methods in psychotherapy and behavior modification*. New York: Academic Press, 1974.

SINGER, J. L. *The inner world of daydreaming*. New York: Harper, 1975. (a)

SINGER, J. L. Navigating the stream of consciousness: Research in daydreaming and related inner experience. *American Psychologist*, 1975, 30, 727–738. (b)

SINGER, J. L., & ANTROBUS, J. S. A factor analysis of daydreaming and conceptually related cognitive and personality variables. *Perceptual and Motor Skills*, 1963, 17, Monograph Supp. No. 3, 187–209.

SINGER, J. L., & ANTROBUS, J. S. Daydreaming, imaginal processes and personality: A normative study. In P. Sheehan (Ed.), *The function and nature of imagery*. New York: Academic Press, 1972.

SIROTA, A. D., SCHWARTZ, G. E., & SHAPIRO, D. Voluntary control of human heart rate: Effect on reaction to aversive stimulation. *Journal of Abnormal Psychology*, 1974, 83, 261–267.

SKINNER, B. F. *The behavior of organisms*. New York: Appleton, 1938.

SNOW, C. P. *The two cultures and the scientific revolution*. New York: Cambridge University Press, 1959.

SNYDER, S. *Uses of marijuana*. New York: Oxford University Press, 1971.

SOKOLOV, YE N. *Perception and the conditioned reflex*. Oxford: Pergamon, 1963.

SOLOMON, H. (Ed.). *Mathematical thinking in the measurement of behavior*. New York: Free Press, 1960.

SOLOMON, P., KUBZANSKY, P. E., LEIDERMAN, P. H., MENDELSON, J. H., TRUMBULL, R., & WEXLER, D. (Eds.). *Sensory deprivation*. Cambridge: Harvard University Press, 1961.

SPERRY, R. W. The great cerebral commissure. In *Psychobiology: Scientific American reprints*. San Francisco: Freeman, 1966.

SPERRY, R. W. A modified concept of consciousness. *Psychological Review*, 1969, 76, 532–536.

STARKER, S. Daydreaming styles and nocturnal dreaming. *Journal of Abnormal Psychology*, 1974, 83, 52–55.

STOLL, W. A. *Schweizer Archiv fuer Neurologie, Neurochirugie und Psychiatrie*, 1947, *60*, 279–323.

STOYVA, J. Sleep onset imagery: A model for naturally-occuring hallucinatory experiences? In F. J. McGuigan & R. A. Schoonover (Eds.), *The psychophysiology of thinking*. New York: Academic Press, 1973.

STOYVA, J., & KAMIYA, J. Electrophysiological studies of dreaming as the prototype of a new strategy in the study of consciousness. *Psychological Review*, 1968, *75*, 192–205.

SZARA, S. *Experimentia*, 1956, *12*, 441.

SZARA, S., & ROCKLAND, L. H. *Proceedings of the Third World Congress of Psychiatry*, *1*. Toronto: University of Toronto Press, 1962.

TART, C. (Ed.). *Altered states of consciousness*. New York: Wiley, 1969. (a)

TART, C. Toward the experimental control of dreaming: A review of the literature. In C. Tart (Ed.), *Altered states of consciousness*. New York: Wiley, 1969. (b)

TART, C. Marijuana intoxication: Common experiences. *Nature*, 1970, *226*, 701–704.

TART, C. *On being stoned: A psychological study of marijuana intoxication*. Palo Alto, Calif.: Science & Behavior Books, 1971.

TART, C. (Ed.). *Altered states of consciousness: A book of readings* (2nd ed.). New York: Doubleday, 1972. (a)

TART, C. Measuring the depth of an altered state of consciousness, with particular reference to self-report scales of hypnotic depth. In E. Fromm & R. Shor (Eds.), *Hypnosis: Research developments and perspectives*. Chicago: Aldine, 1972. (b)

TART, C. Scientific foundations for the study of altered states of consciousness. *Journal of Transpersonal Psychology*, 1972, *3*, 93–124. (c)

TART, C. States of consciousness and state-specific sciences. *Science*, 1972, *176*, 1203–1210. (d)

TART, C. Samsara: A psychological view. In T. Tulku (Ed.), *Reflections of mind*. Emeryville, Calif.: Dharma Press, 1975. (a)

TART, C. *States of consciousness*. New York: Dutton, 1975. (b)

TART, C. (Ed.). *Transpersonal psychologies*. New York: Harper, 1975. (c)

TART, C., & FRIDGEN, J. *The transition from ordinary consciousness to being intoxicated with marijuana*. In progress.

TART, C., & KVETENSKY, E. Marijuana intoxication: Feasibility of experiential scaling of level. *Journal of Altered States of Consciousness*, 1973, *1*, 15–21.

TAYLOR, J. A. *Journal of Abnormal and Social Psychology*, 1953, *48*, 285–290.

TEDLOCK, B., & TEDLOCK, D. Personal communication, 1976.

TEUBER, H-L. Perception. In J. Field, H. W. Magoun, & V. E. Hall (Eds.),

Handbook of physiology (Vol. 3). Washington, D.C.: American Physiological Society, 1960.

TEYLER, T. J. Introductory remarks. In *Altered states of awareness: Readings from Scientific American*. San Francisco: Freeman, 1972.

THOMPSON, J. E. S. Sixteenth and seventeenth century reports on the Chol Mayas. *American Anthropologist*, 1938, 40, 584–604.

THURBER, J. The bear who let it alone. In *Fables for our time*. New York: Harper, 1952. (Originally published, 1940.)

THURBER, J. The secret life of Walter Mitty. In *My world and welcome to it*. New York: Harcourt, 1942.

TITCHENER, E. B. *Lectures on the experimental psychology of the thought process*. New York: Macmillan, 1909.

TOMKINS, S. *Affect, imagery, and consciousness* (2 Vols.). New York: Springer, 1962–1963.

TUASON, V., & GUZE, S. B. *Clinical Pharmacology and Therapeutics*, 1961, 2, 152–156.

TUASON, V., GUZE, S. B., McCLURE, J., & BENGUELIN, J. *American Journal of Psychiatry*, 1962, 118, 438–446.

TURNER, R. H. Role taking, role standpoint, and reference group behavior. *American Journal of Sociology*, 1956, 61, 316–328.

UHR, L., & MILLER, J. G. (Eds.) *Drugs and behavior*. New York: Wiley, 1960.

ULLMAN, M., & KRIPPNER, S. Dream studies and telepathy: An experimental approach. *Parapsychological Monograph* No. 12, 1970.

UNDERHILL, E. *Mysticism: A study in the nature and development of man's spiritual consciousness*. New York: Dutton, 1961. (Originally published, 1911.)

VAN DE CASTLE, R. L. *The psychology of dreaming*. New York: General Learning Press, 1971.

VAN EEDEN, F. A study of dreams. In C. Tart (Ed.), *Altered states of consciousness: A book of readings*. New York: Wiley, 1969. (Originally published, 1913.)

VERRINDER, F. Personal communication, 1975.

VOGEL, G., FOULKES, D., & TROSMAN, H. Ego functions and dreaming during sleep onset. In C. Tart (Ed.), *Altered states of consciousness: A book of readings*. New York: Wiley, 1969.

VON HARTMANN, E. *Philosophy of the unconscious*. New York: Harcourt, 1931. (Originally published, 1869.)

WALLACE, R. K., & BENSON, H. The physiology of meditation. In *Altered states of awareness: Readings from Scientific American*. San Francisco: Freeman, 1972.

WALLACE, R. K., BENSON, H., & WILSON, A. F. A wakeful hypometabolic physiologic state. *American Journal of Physiology,* 1971, *221,* 795–799.

WALSH, D. H. Interactive effects of alpha feedback and instructional set on subjective state. *Psychophysiology,* 1974, *11,* 428–435.

WASSON, R. G. *Soma, divine mushroom of immortality.* New York: Harcourt, 1968.

WASSON, R. G. What was the Soma of the Aryans? In P. T. Furst (Ed.), *Flesh of the gods: The ritual use of hallucinogens.* New York: Praeger, 1972.

WASSON, V. P., & WASSON, R. G. *Mushrooms, Russia and history.* New York: Pantheon, 1957.

WATSON, J. B. Psychology as the behaviorist views it. *Psychological Review,* 1913, *20,* 158.

Webster's New International Dictionary of the English Language (2nd ed.). Springfield, Mass.: Merriam, 1936.

WEIL, A. T. *The natural mind: A new way of looking at drugs and the higher consciousness.* Boston: Houghton Mifflin, 1972.

WEIL, A. T. When the sun dies. *Harper's,* November 1973, pp. 46–58.

WEIL, A. T. Mushroom hunting in Oregon. *Journal of Psychedelic Drugs,* Jan.– March 1975, *7,* 89–102.

WEIL, A. T. Personal communication, 1975.

WEINER, H. *Journal of Experimental Psychology: Animal Behavior Processes,* 1962, *5,* 201–208.

WEISMAN, A. D. *The existential core of psychoanalysis.* Boston: Little, Brown, 1965.

WHITEHEAD, A. N., & RUSSELL, B. A. W. *Principia mathematica* (3 vols.). London: Cambridge University Press, 1910–1913.

WHORF, B. L. *Language, thought, and reality: Selected writings 1927–1941.* New York: Wiley; and Cambridge: MIT Press, 1956.

WHYTE, L. L. *The unconscious before Freud.* New York: Basic Books, 1960.

WILBERT, J. Tobacco and shamanistic ecstasy among the Warao Indians of Venezuela. In P. T. Furst (Ed.), *Flesh of the gods: The ritual use of hallucinogens.* New York: Praeger, 1972.

WILSON, E. (Review of *Ulysses*). *New Republic,* 1922, *31,* 164.

WITKIN, H. A., & LEWIS, H. B. (Eds.). *Experimental studies of dreaming.* New York: Random House, 1967.

WOLFF, P. The causes, controls, and organization of behavior in the neonate. *Psychological Issues,* 1960, *5,* 41–43.

WOODGER, J. H. *Biology and language.* London and New York: Cambridge University Press, 1952.

WOODS, R. W. (Ed.). *The world of dreams.* New York: Random House, 1947.

WOOLF, V. Modern fiction. In *The common reader.* New York: Harcourt, 1953. (Originally published, 1925.)

WORDSWORTH, W. Intimations of immortality. In *Complete poetical works of William Wordsworth.* Boston and New York: Houghton Mifflin, 1904.

WUNDT, W. *Beiträge zur Theorie der Sinneswahrnehmung.* Leipzig: Winter, 1862.

YANKELOVICH, D. How students control their drug crises. *Psychology Today,* October 1975, 39–42.

ZINBERG, N. E. Psychoanalysis and the American scene: A reappraisal. *Diogenes,* 1965, *50,* 73–111.

ZINBERG, N. E. "*High states*": *A beginning study.* Washington, D.C.: Drug Abuse Council, 1974.

ZINBERG, N. E. Addiction and ego function. *Psychoanalytic Study of the Child,* 1975, *30,* 567–586.

ZINBERG, N. E., BORIS, H. N., & BORIS, M. *Teaching social change: A group approach.* Baltimore: Johns Hopkins University Press, 1976.

ZINBERG, N. E., & DeLONG, J. V. Research and the drug issue. *Contemporary Drug Problems,* Spring 1974, 71–100.

ZINBERG, N. E., HARDING, W. M., & WINKELLER, M. A study of social regulatory mechanisms in controlled illicit drug users. In K. Blum, S. J. Feinglass, & A. H. Briggs (Eds.), *Social meaning of drugs.* New York: Basic Books, 1976.

ZINBERG, N. E., & JACOBSON, R. C. The natural history of "chipping." *American Journal of Psychiatry,* 1976, *133,* 37–40.

ZINBERG, N. E., JACOBSON, R. C., & HARDING, W. M. Social sanctions and rituals as a basis for drug abuse prevention. *American Journal of Drug and Alcohol Abuse,* 1975, *2,* 165–182.

ZUCKERMAN, M., BONE, R., NEARY, R., MANGELSDORFF, D., & BRUSTMAN, B. What is the sensation-seeker? *Journal of Consulting and Clinical Psychology,* 1972, *39,* 308–321.

ZUCKERMAN, M., NEARY, R., & BRUSTMAN, B. Sensation-seeking correlates in experience (smoking, drugs, alcohol, "hallucinations," and sex) and preferences for complexity (designs). *Proceedings of the 78th Annual Convention of the American Psychological Association,* 1970, *4,* 317–318. (Summary)

Index